Companion Planting

Companion Planting

Margaret Roberts

BRIZA

Published by

BRIZA PUBLICATIONS
CK 1990/011690/23

PO Box 56569
Arcadia 0007
Pretoria
South Africa

www.briza.co.za

First edition, first impression, 2007
First edition, second impression, 2009

ISBN 978 1 875093 48 9

Disclaimer
Although care has been taken to be as accurate as possible, neither the author nor the publisher makes
any expressed or implied representation as to the accuracy of the information contained in this book
and cannot be held legally responsible or accept liability for any errors or omissions. This book contains
numerous quoted examples of medicinal or other uses of plants. Neither the author nor the publisher can
be held responsible for claims arising from the mistaken identity of plants or their inappropriate use. The
publisher and author do not assume responsibility for any sickness, death or other harmful effects resulting
from eating or using any plant in this book. Readers are strongly advised to consult professionals, and any
experimentation or prolonged usage is done entirely at your own risk.

Project manager: Reneé Ferreira
Design and layout: Alicia Arntzen, The Purple Turtle
Cover design: Sally Whines, The Departure Lounge
Printed and bound by Tien Wah Press (Pte.) Ltd, Singapore

Photo credits: Cover photograph and pages 2 and 8 by Connall Oosterbroek; photographs on pages 32, 37, 41,
51, 58, 60, 86 and 97 by Ben-Erik van Wyk. All other photographs by Gail Roberts and Sandy Roberts.

Contents

Acknowledgements

Of all the many books I have written, it is this book that has taken the longest to complete, and it was during the writing of this book that a new baby was born to Sandra, the youngest of my three children and my partner in the entire Herbal Centre business. Sandra's battle to regain her health with a tiny baby, and, at the same time, my mother's illness and subsequent death, filled many dark days, and I lost the ability to write – to even think. Little Skye now fills our days with such activity and is growing so fast and being a hands-on grandmother, finding time to write has been a feat in itself.

So it is with a grateful heart that I thank my sympathetic publishers so sincerely for extending the deadlines, and to my commissioning editor and project manager, Reneé Ferreira, who has walked long paths with me as editor to so many of my books for her support and understanding. I think I have tried each one beyond endurance – but how grateful I am that the Briza team is so kind and so considerate.

Writing is a lonely profession, and most of my writing is done in the small hours of the morning when worries drown me and sleep eludes me, and it's Annatjie van Wyk who deciphers and tames my erratic night writings and scattered pages. I have a huge thank you from my heart for you, Annatjie, for your efficiency and friendliness and for all the e-mails and order of pages you send off to my editors. It seems to have been going on forever!

For the first time, I have had Gail and Sandra, my two daughters, doing the photographs for one of my books. I am thrilled by their willing competency, their enthusiasm, and their interest in the plants. I have loved the rush and flurry of finding the plants, and watching buds open just in time, and that they so lovingly gave so much of their time to be there to photograph it! I have loved the fun and the laughter we had photographing the first strawberry and the sunflower on my birthday luncheon table, before we could begin the meal in mid-winter, and the excitement of finding these necessary plants to photograph.

Working with my two girls has filled me with such gratitude and delight, it has made the book extra special.

During all the time of writing the Herbal Centre buildings have been renovated, in some cases virtually rebuilt, and builders with every conceivable problem have brought us all to our knees! No wonder writing and thinking have been impossible! It is nothing short of miraculous that these pages are, at last, visible and completed!

There is one person who has steadfastly kept the Herbal Centre gardens together, the almost non-existent water supply going through drought and heat never before experienced, and often single-handed, through all the trials and tribulations that have made up these difficult times – and that is the Headman at the Herbal Centre for all the years, Johannes Mangwane. When I first began the Herbal Centre 22 years ago, it was he who helped me develop and lay out the gardens, it was he who set up the clever watering systems, and he who managed the garden staff, and it was he who began the compost heaps! He has two passions – the water and the compost!

I am able to keep the gardens going with Johannes, and his attention, his devotion to this bit of Africa, and to Sandra and me, fills me with awe and such gratitude and admiration for a man who neither reads nor writes, but who can think out and do and accomplish more than anyone I have ever known. From leaking roofs to faulty plumbing, from flat tyres to flat batteries, to everything else in between, he quietly gets on and does it, with ease, with laughter, and with a smile.

Out in the marketplace there is an array of *natural* insecticides, super chargers, fungicides, compost activators, and more under the Ball Straathofs Margaret Roberts label. Johan Gerber, who is an agricultural scientist and who knows both the chemical pesticide industry and the environmentally responsible pest solutions, developed, tested and registered my recipes, and together with Leonie Coulsen, the then marketing manager at Ball Straathofs, they accomplished this feat, in spite of the red tape and the registration nightmare, and the many and varied setbacks – they did it, and for this I am eternally grateful. Thanks to them, there is an alternative pest control range suitable for environmentally safe gardening and crop management.

I recommend Johan's book, *The Garden Guardian's Guide to Environmentally Responsible Garden Care.*

This book is like no other and the first for South African gardeners – addressing problems which have a safe and natural solution.

Finally, my gratitude goes to the many students who attended the companion planting classes I have given through the years, for their interest and our shared passion of making our fragile and threatened planet a better place – this book has come into being.

The Herbal Centre

De Wildt

North West Province

South Africa

February 2006

The insect war

It seems a hopeless battle,
With all insects running free,
With mealie bugs and waxy scale
And thrips on every tree!

With cutworms and those slimy snails,
And slugs and aphids here,
There's little hope of growing things –
In fact we shouldn't dare!

The beetle tribe is terrible,
With devouring, tearing jaws,
Those CMRs and chafers
In obliterating wars.

There's nothing left undamaged,
Caterpillars, borers, worms,
Black spot and codling moths and ants,
And flies with all their germs.

What happened to our paradise,
That Eden of our dreams?
All that's left is maggot rot,
And nothing's right, it seems.

Where are Nature's guardians
To help us fight and win –
Or will it all just end right there
Within the compost bin?

With every season there is hope,
And so we start again,
With watchful eye and guarded step
And armies to be slain.

Let's plant companions, pungent, strong,
Protection for the crop,
Side by side, watch pests soon flee,
At last, it's got to stop!

Pyrethrum, Tansy, Wormwood,
And Basil strong and true,
Alongside veggies, tender fruits,
And don't forget the Rue.

Help is here – we're not alone,
Protecting our urban plot.
Eden regained, it can be done,
And we'll have slain the lot!

Remember: Never reach for poisons,
It's a dangerous deadly game.
With contaminating chemicals,
Earth will NEVER be the same!

*Written by Margaret Roberts in
desperation one hot midsummer Sunday.*

Introduction

Companion planting. Two ordinary words with so much power and so much passion in them, so much to think about, so much to do about the concept and so much to gain from it. We should be using them every day to everyone, to make, without doubt, our little bit of world a better place! It's time for action. We cannot delay any longer.

Linked to these two words is another even more powerful word – organic. If you grow companion plants you will not need harmful sprays, dangerous chemical poisons or chemical fertilisers. With catch crops and green manure crops, you'll be growing and making your own natural composts and fertilisers that will be so inexpensive and fascinating to put in place, you'll be farming or gardening organically!

In my full and busy long life I have been passionate about a few things (besides my children and grandchildren!). Plants are one of my greatest interests, but my passion is growing plants that have a purpose, a use, to perfection. The second, all-absorbing passion is never to use chemicals or sprays that could harm my other passions – health and the environment. I have practised these enduring passions for my whole life. My dream is to make it all exciting enough, interesting enough and inspiring enough to have everyone growing organic vegetables, vines and even flowers, and never using harmful sprays.

I first learnt about companion planting from my grandmother and her sister, who lived at Gordon's Bay, when I was about seven years old. My sister and I spent several months of the year with them, as my father was in parliament for the session. Then we would return home to Pretoria for the rest of the year. We had "home schooling" for those months we spent in the Cape and I loved it!

Among the things we were taught in the afternoons was to make vegetable and flower gardens in the terraces overlooking the sea. The winter rain watered our plantings, and we made charts and notes and pressed flowers to remember what plant enjoyed the proximity of another, and how we could let nasturtiums trail over the rocky walls to "catch" the aphids so that they did not eat the new cabbages and broccoli. We learned that slugs will creep under the grapefruit skin shells that we saved from breakfast. The next morning we could lift the shells up and crush several slugs. We also learned that if you made a blanket of oak leaves, no snails or slugs would come near the lettuces. So we circled the lettuce plantings with a thick mulch of oak leaves. We rubbed handfuls of the leaves from our tomato plants on the windowsills to chase the flies, and we went for long walks into the mountain to collect pelargonium sprigs, those beautiful Cape scented geraniums, to plant in our gardens so that we could crush them and rub them on our blankets and pillows to chase mosquitoes. One very lemony-scented one which I grow so far from the sea, I still use today.

We planted radishes near cucumbers and around the peas, and ate radish sandwiches with homemade mayonnaise for tea every day – thick slices of homemade brown bread, so soft and moist we never got tired of that teatime break.

In the evenings my grandmother sat in front of the fire knitting us socks (in fine white crochet cotton on four needles – I was so impressed!). Outside the southeaster howled. My great aunt told us stories of the allotment garden she had worked in in England, and how people were able to rent little pieces of land in a large communal garden so they could grow their salads, vegetables and flowers for the house. She told us how they shared companion plants. She had a neighbour who loved roses, so my great aunt grew parsley in a long row at the edge of her allotment to accompany the roses that marked the border between her and her neighbour. On the other side, her neighbour grew three long rows of sweetcorn, so my great aunt grew pumpkins in their shade. No one was allowed to grow gladiolus, as strawberries hated the tall flowers and would die if there ever was a plant even at the opposite end of the allotment – and everyone grew strawberries! They planted pennyroyal under them to keep the worms and the beetles away.

I was enthralled. It was like plant warfare! Pennyroyal sounded such a grand word, but in those days there were very few herbs in our hot, sunny South Africa. Twenty-five years later I managed to import the first pennyroyal into South Africa – to grow under my own strawberries – and when the parcel finally arrived it was very pathetic and half dead, as it had been held in customs so long. Of those sad little black sprigs only about fifteen grew, and so pennyroyal began its life journey in a very different country far from its cool, moist and green native land. I like to think that the pennyroyal we buy today from nurseries everywhere are the little offspring from my fifteen brave little cuttings!

Our sea gardens at Gordon's Bay enthralled me. I was beside myself with joy pulling the first carrots, picking the first spinach and harvesting the Cape gooseberries creeping carefully under and between those smooth velvety stems, tiny basket in hand to reach the dry little lantern-like fruits, such golden globes, succulent and flavour-filled, for the gooseberry tart my grandmother baked. I loved the peeling of those papery husks and how the marble-sized fruit just popped in your mouth while grandmother was not looking, and I will always remember how we planted a row of yarrow near the gooseberry bushes "to give the gooseberries protection and to make many fruits".

The yarrow was used as a cut flower then, that lovely old-fashioned pink and white one, and it was good as a border around the vegetable garden, and it didn't mind

if you walked on it. Those were never-to-be-forgotten days, and the world revolved around plants, and the girls who helped in the house with the washing and the cleaning brought me a wild flower every day as they walked to the village from their home in the mountain. They were the first ones to teach me about pelargoniums and the other indigenous healing plants, and I kept the flowers on my dressing table in fish paste and Marmite jars, and learned all their common names.

My parents grew beautiful cottage garden flowers – my mother painted flowers in watercolours and pastels, and embroidered them. My father and I made compost and we had superb vegetable gardens. We grew rows of lettuce with radishes, and larkspur for my mother's flower arrangements in rows next to the spinach. We edged the beds with catnip and used sprigs of it to sweep onto the kitchen floor to chase ants, and spread it into the dogs' baskets to chase the fleas, with marigold leaves. We didn't think about it – we just did it. That was the way it was.

Catmint circled tomato plantings and thrived under the quince tree, and lemon verbena was planted in the corners of the vegetable garden because its leaves chased horseflies! And so it went on – all the time as I was growing up I was aware that you could interplant flowers and vegetables, and a trellis of peas with pansies at their feet looked beautiful. The peas were so tender you could cook them in their pods.

My grandmother sent me a letter full of fennel seeds. The fennel grew wild along the harbour road. (We picked the fennel leaves to cover the fresh fish we often bought from the fishing boats.) She reminded me to be careful where I planted it as quite a few plants didn't like fennel near them, like beans and tomatoes and even lemon verbena. So I planted it near the gem squashes and the spring onions, and it thrived and so did they. I added those notes to my little gardening notebook.

I grew up and left school and went to the university to study physiotherapy. I walked to lectures through the university gardens every day. I got to know an old Zulu gardener and he told me that nasturtiums should be planted near potatoes, and beetroot should be planted with spring onions. He had a patch of mealies near the kitchens, and I brought him tomato plants and mustard seed, pumpkin seed and spinach plants from our garden. He loved roses and showed me how to plant catnip under them to keep aphids away. He also taught me to look at the weeds. He ate purslane cooked with onion as he said it gave him energy, and it was a perfect compost maker with stinging nettles. So I then began to think about weeds and their importance. I sadly lost contact with my old gardening friend, but I never forget his wise teachings. I learned he had gone home to Zululand to retire and to make his own garden. His new young apprentice took lots of seeds back to him when he went home for Christmas, and in return the old man sent me a calabash. I've planted calabash seeds with yarrow wherever I have lived since then, and all came from that single calabash. He told me melons and cucumbers and calabashes have the strength to climb high and bear well, when planted with yarrow.

As a young bride on a remote farm I quickly realised I had no choice but to grow my own vegetables. I was given a small piece of land on the riverbanks deep in the bush. A small dam thick with bulrushes bordered it, and at the top end there was a narrow furrow that fed into the dam, which was my sole water source. The soil was black, heavy clay, and it was back breaking to dig – so compost heaps were a first priority.

I was alone. I had to make a life with only the birds for conversation. The heat, isolation and sense of helplessness engulfed me. The bleak whitewashed farm house nearby had no electricity and here I was, a city girl with a hospital career, people-filled and stimulating, and the comfort of a salary at the end of the month, now so utterly alone and having to find a way to make a new life. My husband left at five in the morning and came back long after dark. His farming activities were time-consuming and I had to get on with it and put a meal on the table. The distant town was too far to travel to for supplies – twice a month

The potager garden in front of the restaurant, everything is edible and thrives beside a good companion.

was all we could manage. But we had milk from the Friesland cows, and we had mealies from the huge tracts of land. The *Farmer's Weekly* magazine was sent in the postbag weekly and I studied every page. They even had a "planting by the moon" series. So I learned to plant carrots and beetroot at the right phase of the moon, and the above ground crops in the next phase. It was up to me. I had no one to turn to. I think I was one of South Africa's first real organic "farmers". My little beginnings expanded into flower-filled gardens, interplanted with spring onions, spinach and parsley. I partnered carnations, which I sold as cut flowers, and giant sprays of fine white Michaelmas daisies with tomatoes, marrows and garlic. I trailed gem squashes through rows of chillies and green peppers and lavender, and my sweetcorn became a marvellous support for Flying Saucers morning glory – those brilliant sky-blue, saucer-sized "morning glorious" flowers that inspired me to draw. My calabashes planted with marigolds provided succulent vine tips for stir-fries, and young delicious squash-like fruits, and the dried matured gourds sold well on the roadside stall, unstung and unblemished thanks to the marigolds.

These are the things that have formed my thinking, my planning and my planting – I lived off the land. I continued to make notes. I experimented, I ached with loneliness, and I had to make a path where no one had trodden before. To this day I really hate digging! But I learned to mulch, which keeps the soil friable, and I learned about the seasons and the summer bounty, and I still fight the good fight against the insects, the voracious birds, the destructive monkeys, and the neighbour's cows that trashed my ripening rows of vegetables in my first riverbank garden. An endless battle, but I know the satisfaction as I sit down to dinner of my own beans, my own broccoli, my own gem squashes, my own lettuce and tomatoes, and my own fabulous strawberries. It's truly worth it!

So here are my notes of the many years of organic growing with companion plants which began at seven years of age, now in grown-up form – a notebook that began in a school exercise book and which has grown bigger and bigger with all the fascinating growing facts I have gathered in my planting experiments through the years. I include in it my years of experiments with natural sprays and the beneficial weeds, and I hope to inspire you, the reader, to grow an edible garden. Would it not be wonderful if we all grew flowers with vegetables (like I did at seven – I noted that "egg plants look pretty with blue flax and you can eat the flax flowers"), and what a paradise that would be! We'd all be healthy, wealthy and wise, and fit from all the physical activity, and passionate from all the interest, and excited and filled with such satisfaction that we are doing something towards making this sad old polluted world of ours a better place.

Note to the reader

The plants in this book are arranged alphabetically according to their botanical name. For example, the first plant in this book is Yarrow, as its botanical Latin name is *Achillea millefolium*. A handy list of common names, in alphabetical order, and their page numbers, can be found on the front and back cover flaps.

Some botanical names have changed in recent years, for example the Latin name for Costmary is now *Chrysanthemum balsamita*. The former name of *Tanacetum balsamita* – and many other older botanical names – has been included in the alphabetical index at the back of the book for ease of reference.

Yarrow

ACHILLEA MILLEFOLIUM

CARPENTER'S WEED • SOLDIER'S WOUNDWORT

YARROW IS AN ANCIENT, REVERED AND RESPECTED PLANT. SO IMPORTANT WAS IT THAT IT WAS ONCE KNOWN AS "HERBA MILITARIS", AS ITS LEAVES WERE USED TO STAUNCH BATTLEGROUND WOUNDS, AND ACHILLES REPUTEDLY USED YARROW LEAVES TO HEAL THE WARRIORS DURING THE BATTLE OF TROY – HENCE ITS LATIN NAME *ACHILLEA*.

Beautiful and very easy to grow, yarrow was found in every cottage garden, every castle garden, every public place, and the leaves and flowers were pressed into precious books and folded into embroidered robes and even sewn into the hems of brocade curtains and cloaks to keep them free of moths, fish moths, weevils and fleas. Yarrow was used as a strewing herb in the courts and in meeting places, and the monks preserved it in vinegar to treat the sick and to heal the soldiers' wounds during the long snowbound winters.

Native to Europe and Western Asia, the original varieties were white, or pink flowered fading to white as they mature. The new colourful hybrids do not have those medicinal actions – so do not substitute. Yarrow – only that old-fashioned pink and white variety – has been used through the centuries to treat fevers, inflammation and bleeding. Just apply warmed crushed leaves – wash them in hot water first, then pat dry in a clean towel – to the affected area, and hold in place with a crêpe bandage. Warmed leaves held behind an ear ease earache. A cup of yarrow tea will help to lower high blood pressure, regulate menstrual flow and relieve premenstrual tension. Use ¼ cup fresh leaves and pour over this 1 cup of boiling water, stand 5 minutes, strain and sip slowly. Excellent for colds and flu, and it can be used as a mouthwash to clear infections in the mouth and throat. For chicken pox, measles, rheumatism and diabetes, yarrow is an age-old treatment, taken a cup a day for a week, then give it a break for 2 days and repeat.

But even more wonderful than its tried, tested and medically approved medicinal uses, is its tremendous tonic effect on all plants growing near it. Yarrow is beneficial to everything! All vegetables thrive near it, particularly cucumbers, calabashes, melons, mealies and tomatoes, and it increases the aromatic oils in origanums, winter savory and lemon verbena, and even roses have a stronger perfume near yarrow. So, in the herb garden yarrow is indispensable!

But here is where I am in awe of yarrow: its leaves help to break down compost and a strong tea made of yarrow leaves is a superb fertiliser. For organic growers yarrow is king, and a handful of fresh leaves dug into the compost heap will quickly activate it, and ferment even the toughest material in a matter of weeks. Yarrow is also a beneficial host to ladybirds and parasitic wasps that prey on garden pests like aphids, and yet it also repels many pests who cannot stand its pungent scent! It's quite a herb, not only for its styptic properties, but for its tonic effects on nearby plants, and as a natural fertiliser it is remarkable and simply invaluable.

Grow it abundantly in full sun, divide the clump yearly, rooted runners can be dug off the main clump any time, and it thrives in rich moist soil.

USES
Medicinal, compost maker, fertiliser, insect repellent

COMPANIONS
Calabashes, cucumbers, lemon verbena, marjoram, mealies, melons, oregano, roses, tomatoes, winter savory

Leek

PART OF THE GREAT ONION FAMILY, THE LEEK HAS BEEN AROUND FOR CENTURIES AND IS A MUCH LOVED WINTER ANNUAL. IT IS SO IMPORTANT IN THE VEGETABLE GARDEN IT NEEDS TO BE BROUGHT INTO THE LIMELIGHT AGAIN!

I am absolutely mad about leeks – I cook the most exciting and delicious dishes with them, and I can convert the most resistant anti-leek visitor to sublime submission with my leek and cheese sauce tarts!

Leeks are easy to grow and fascinating to watch as they develop from weak pencil-thin single blades planted 30 centimetres apart to a fan of succulent and luscious leaves, strong, robust and free from any pests, a thick white stalk of goodness and flavour, and a huge asset in the garden next to cabbages, lettuce, radishes, celery, celeriac and carrots, with leeks between each row.

Leeks are heavy feeders and have a mass of anchoring roots, so they need particularly rich soil – compost and manure. The soil needs to be deeply dug twice, as in this way the leek will grow tall and straight. The lower part can be blanched by drawing up the soil close around the base to exclude the light and to keep it white and succulent.

One year I experimented with sowing caraway seed between the leeks and both thrived in the cold in the full sun. In the hot spring that followed each shaded the other so that I was still pulling out tender juicy leeks well into the summer. The twice weekly watering leeks need in winter was increased in the warmer weather to three times a week, and I did add extra compost in spring. For commercial farmers this caraway companion could be beneficial. By the time the last leeks were pulled, the caraway had set seed ready for reaping. So that bonus crop was well worth it.

It is thought the leek originated in the Eastern Mediterranean region where wild leeks still grow today. Leeks were cultivated in the Middle East 3 000 years ago, and are still grown for both food and medicine in many parts of the world today. The Greeks and the Romans prized it as a delicacy cooked in goats' milk with caraway seeds. It featured in banquets and as strengthening food for soldiers going into combat. Traditional dishes in these areas often feature leeks in cheese and milk sauces, and served thinly sliced and fried with brinjals and peppers.

In the Middle Ages, the monks used leek medicine to ease sore throats, coughs, colds and chest ailments, and to improve the voice. It was the Romans who took the leek throughout Europe and introduced it to Britain around AD 600. When the Welsh went into battle against the Saxons in AD 640 the soldiers, well fed with leeks for strength and courage, made the leek their emblem and were the victors of that battle. So the leek became the national emblem of Wales.

Rich in potassium, calcium, folic acid and vitamins A, C and K, the leek is cleansing, a natural diuretic and eliminates uric acid. For gout sufferers and those with rheumatism, stiffness and aches and pains, start preparing your leek beds!

USES
Culinary, medicinal

COMPANIONS
Cabbages, caraway, carrots, celeriac, celery, lettuces, radishes

Onion

THE ONION FAMILY IS HUGE, EASY TO GROW, AND A STAPLE FOOD ALL OVER THE WORLD. IT IS SO RICH IN DIVERSITY AND VARIETY, IT HAS TO BE ONE OF THE MOST FASCINATING OF ALL CROPS TO GROW.

Rich in vitamins, particularly vitamin C, and minerals like calcium, magnesium, phosphorus, potassium, folic acid, beta carotene, sulphur and the rare quercetin, the onion has been a source of respected medication through the centuries. Along with leeks, shallots, spring onions, chives, garlic chives, garlic and Welsh onions, the huge variety in size from pickling onions to those saucer-sized flat onions, there is something for everyone and for every garden!

I have grown onions since childhood. My rows of neat, almost perennial spring onions were the best in town, and I learned early on how to pull up only portions of the little tuft – "make-more onions" my grandmother called them – so I was never without them. I planted them round roses and between the strawberry rows, and everything thrived!

Raw onions are rich in natural antibiotic substances, so they boost the immune system, cleanse the blood, flush the kidneys, fight infections, reduce spasms and tension in asthma, so are natural antispasmodic. They help to clear cholesterol and remove heavy metals from the blood, as well as parasites within the body.

More than just a health food, onions are a vital player in their other role – a valiant soldier in the garden. Not only as a superb companion plant for the cabbage family, beetroot, spinach, strawberries, carrots, green peppers, lettuces and tomatoes, but planted under apple trees, onions keep apple scab away. Under roses, fruit trees and vines spring onions and the bigger, taller giant spring onions will trap black aphids and whitefly, and everything will taste better!

giant spring onion

Interestingly, everything smells better too – even roses and lilies. One year I planted rows of the pretty mauve-flowered wild garlic (*Tulbaghia violaceae*) along a row of tall Madonna lilies – both thrived, looked spectacular and the lilies were more richly scented than I ever knew them before.

I plant spring onions in between cabbages and kale, and the wild garlic around pumpkins and next to carrots, and I dig in lots of compost. Leeks look marvellous with frilly red lettuces next to them and I find it's easier to make small rows of onions between peppers, brinjals and spinach. However, don't plant them near peas or beans – they will literally become stunted. Fork into the soil onion skins and roughly chopped-up onion leaves once you reaped them, and in spring plant chamomile in between the new little onion seedlings to keep them healthy. Make an onion spray of ¾ of a bucket of chopped up onion leaves, skins and onions. Cover with boiling water, mash and stir well. Leave overnight. Next morning strain, add ½ cup grated Sunlight soap and use to spray thrips and aphid infestation, and pour into ant holes. For scale on bay trees, add ½ to 1 cup of cooking oil and shake the spray bottle frequently.

USES
Culinary, medicinal, insect spray

COMPANIONS
Beetroot, cabbages, carrots, chamomile, fruit trees, kale, lettuces, peppers, roses, spinach, strawberries, tomatoes, vines

DISLIKES
Beans, peas

15

Garlic

GARLIC IS ONE OF THE WORLD'S MOST ANCIENT, MOST LOVED AND MOST RESPECTED HEALING PLANTS. IT HAS BEEN USED MEDICINALLY SINCE 15 BC, AND THE ANCIENT ROMANS, GREEKS AND EGYPTIANS RECORDED ITS MEDICINAL USES AND ITS REMARKABLE POWERS OVER THE CENTURIES.

If you think that the pyramid builders, the slaves who gave their lives to the incredible building of the pyramids, were given garlic daily to increase their strength and to maintain their health, you'll understand why garlic has been so respected and so frequently included in the diet. It has never lost its popularity and it has never been more used and more appreciated than it is now.

Rich in an amazing array of health-boosting components, garlic is a natural antibiotic, an antiseptic and a blood tonic, toner and cleanser. If taken regularly, it will remove toxic build-up, lower high cholesterol and ease high blood pressure, as well as acting as a general invigorating tonic to the whole system. This is not just for humans, but for birds and animals as well. Most importantly, garlic is an excellent tonic and health builder for the garden!

Garlic is a superb protector of insect invasion around orange and lemon trees as it helps to prevent leaf curl. Planted in a circle close together 5 centimetres apart, it forms a barrier against borers, caterpillars and often cutworms. It seems they too can't stand the smell! I have experimented all over the garden with it and my most successful plantings are in thick double or even treble rows circling specific plantings such as lettuce, beetroot, my favourite cherry tomatoes, and the huge and succulent Malawian spinach. Britelites chard and ordinary chard are magnificent with garlic around it – lush, juicy and prolific and even better tasting when garlic is near!

Grow garlic liberally and learn to love it! Plant extra parsley and sage to eat with it as a breath freshener –

both finely chopped and served with garlic will help the pong as both are excellent deodorisers!

Choose large, mature bulbs of garlic at the greengrocer that are showing little tips of green if possible. They will be dry and easy to peel away the flaky white skin, then press them, tip side up, into moist, well-dug and richly composted soil 5 centimetres apart. Keep them shaded and cool with a light sprinkling of leaves, and always keep the area moist. The thin, green tips will emerge gradually and elongate into long narrow, strap-like leaves. All the work is going on below the ground, and an Italian chef showed me how delicious garlic is in its infancy by pulling up the tender shoots when they are only 6 or 7 centimetres tall. Then, after washing the whole plant, roots and all well, mash and thinly slice it with olive oil, salt and lemon juice to use as a spread on hot buttered toast!

So get planting! Be careful, though, not to plant garlic near beans, cabbages, peas, broccoli or strawberries – they hate it – but the roses will love it!

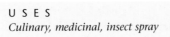

USES	COMPANIONS	DISLIKES
Culinary, medicinal, insect spray	*Beetroot, chard, lemon trees, lettuces, Malawian spinach, orange trees, roses, tomatoes*	*Beans, broccoli, cabbages, peas, strawberries*

Chives

CHIVES ARE PART OF THAT GREAT ONION FAMILY THAT IS SO IMPORTANT TO OUR HEALTH AND WELL-BEING. IT'S AN EASY-TO-GROW PERENNIAL THAT HAS WINTER DORMANCY AND IN SPRING OFFERS THE MOST BEAUTIFUL PINKY MAUVE FLOWERS AND MASSES OF DELICIOUS LEAVES.

Chives are never attacked by insects, fungus, or mildew or any disease. It has been used to plant around apple, peach and apricot trees. With cucumbers, squash and marrows it helps to clear powdery mildew, and the broader-leafed garlic chives have the same effect.

I grew circles of chives and garlic chives around my gem squash and patty pan, cucumber, melon and pumpkin plantings, about 3 metres in diameter, and had the best summer ever with bumper crops. I also sprayed heavily with a strong garlic spray (see recipe on page 121) literally every second day.

It seems that most insects really dislike the smell of anything to do with garlic or onion generally, and this is why if you plant rows of spring onions, garlic chives, onions, Welsh onions and chives in long, thick rows between melons and squash and pumpkins, you'll have a really good chance of reaping unstung and mildew-free fruits and vine tips and leaves.

One year it just so happened that I had planted cucumbers along a fence with a thick edging of garlic chives, not really aware of the power of garlic chives. I had the most beautifully crisp sweet cucumbers all summer and no mildewed leaves and hardly any stung fruits. I was amazed. Then I saw the garlic chives were thick with black aphids and no black aphids were anywhere else. So I sprayed them with a strong spray of khakibos and marigolds with soap (see recipe on page 106) two days running, and everything went back to normal. No aphids, no mildew, no stung fruit! I can only think that the garlic chives acted as a trap crop for the black aphids.

It's really worth experimenting. During the mild winter of 2005 I had black aphids on the garlic chives again – they were planted alongside calendula, celery and thyme. Once again I sprayed heavily with soapy water only, as it was winter and there was no khakibos or marigolds, and the aphids disappeared. Not one of the thin little dormant chive leaves was touched, right next to the garlic chives, but it did have a row of parsley beside it.

When I have planted chives next to lettuce, roses, beans, beetroot, spinach, green peppers and carrots, they have been untouched by insects or mildew, so now I plant chives every 4 to 5 rows and every plant seems robust, strong and uninfested with anything. It's worth making notes on your chive experiments. I've even edged paths with chives between the roses, and we grow a lot of red roses for our rose petal jams and syrups. With chives they taste better, and there's not an aphid or a whitefly in sight!

USES
Culinary, insect repellent

COMPANIONS
Beans, beetroot, carrots, cucumbers, fruit trees, green peppers, lettuces, marrows, melons, pumpkin, roses, spinach, squash

Lemon verbena

ALOYSIA TRIPHYLLA

THIS MUCH-LOVED, DEEPLY SCENTED SHRUB HAS BEEN PLANTED IN GARDENS THROUGH THE CENTURIES. ITS POWERFUL, REFRESHING SCENT ENVELOPES ONE, AND AS A CHILD I DAILY WALKED CLOSE TO IT, BRUSHING MY HANDS ALONG ITS ROUGH-FEELING LEAVES, AND TOOK GREAT BREATHS OF SUMMER INTO MY VERY SOUL.

Whenever I smell it, no matter the years between then and now, I can feel the hot stone pavers under my feet and I'm about six or seven years old, and I can hear my mother's voice calling me. It's called nostalgia, I think, because this is one of those memory-inducing herbs that everyone remembers.

We used the leaves, pressed in books, to mark the pages; we tucked branches behind the newly ironed sheets in the linen cupboard and made dried lavender and lemon verbena potpourris for the bathroom. We sewed the lemon-scented leaves with cloves and cinnamon and lemon peel into sachets to keep the pantry cupboards fresh, we added fresh bunches to our bathwater, and tied big bunches of fresh branches together with string and slapped them onto outdoor tables and chairs and over balustrades around the verandah to chase the flies and mosquitoes. Lemon verbena was the most useful plant we grew, and we've never stopped loving it.

I can close my eyes today and see my grandmother, my mother and father, my sister and my aunt and uncle sitting in a circle around the Sunday afternoon tea table under the cool pergola with a bunch or two of fresh lemon verbena leaves swinging gently, hanging behind their chairs, for the quick swatting of flies when needed. It was a way of life that seems to have gone forever. But flies still can't stand that fresh lemony smell, nor can whiteflies, aphids and midges. So plant a bush in full sun in a deep, compost-filled hole at the four corners of the vegetable garden, and notice how free from pests everything is!

The wonderful thing about lemon verbena is that it is prunable, clippable and trainable. It can be shaped and tamed, and it can be left wild to gracefully toss its fragrant branches and sprays of tiny white and mauve flowers in the breeze. It asks little, other than a deep weekly watering and a bucket or two of compost in late winter. In cold areas it will lose its leaves, and then in mid-winter can be tidied up and lightly pruned to await its spring-green tufts of fragrance.

Moths and fish moths hate it and if you lay sheets of tinfoil, shiny side up, over a shelf that has been lightly sprinkled with talc powder and tuck fresh lemon verbena sprigs behind it, your books, blankets and winter woollies will be safe from invading moths and fish moths. This is the only herb that can be tucked into a cupboard while still fresh and green without becoming mildewy.

A cup of lemon verbena tea will soothe tension, headaches, depression, nervous upsets, anxiety, palpitations and even heartache and hurt. Use ¼ cup fresh leaves to 1 cup of boiling water, stand 5 minutes, then strain and sip slowly. For cramp, bronchitis, colds, coughs, flu, nausea and aching muscles, this tea is superb. Isn't this enough reason to grow it?

USES
Medicinal, potpourri, insect repellent

COMPANIONS
All vegetables and fruit trees will benefit from lemon verbena's insect repelling qualities

18

Amaranth

THE MORE I USE AMARANTH, THE MORE EXCITED I AM ABOUT IT! IT IS A TOUGH, WASTE GROUND WEED THAT HAS ADAPTED TO MANY COUNTRIES ACROSS THE WORLD, A TRUE SURVIVOR.

The genus consists of sixty varieties of edible spinach annuals, some with long plumes of brilliant red flowers, the popular love-lies-bleeding amaranth, some with magenta leaves and some with valuable and nutritious seeds and leaves with so high a protein content with vitamins A and C (*Amaranthus hypochondriacus*) that it replaces meat and is often included in the daily diet, especially in Africa where it is known as "morogo".

Native to America, Mexico, India and China, these resilient plants reseed themselves everywhere, and come up in lush abundance in compost. If left to develop fully, they can reach a height of 2 metres!

Medicinally it is used to treat diarrhoea and to staunch bleeding – nosebleeds, wounds and excessive menstruation – and different countries have a variety of uses. Some use it as a wash for skin eruptions, for throat infections and ulcers in the mouth, as a gargle.

Young leaves can be eaten in salads and stir-fries, and the older leaves make excellent spinach with a high iron content.

What I find particularly amazing is its deep rooting abilities to literally aerate the soil, particularly heavy compacted soils, and by spreading so deeply into the soil it dredges up nutrients, which nourish its companions.

Traditional use of partnering amaranth with onions, mealies, sorghum, potatoes and beetroot crops has been in place for centuries, particularly in hot, dry countries where the shade amaranth offers results in rich growth of the vegetables and better flavour.

In America, organic farmers actually plant amaranth first in alternate rows before planting potatoes. The new potatoes are thus protected and shaded, and when they reach maturity, the amaranth has provided mineral-rich fibrous soil resulting in perfectly formed potatoes, and a nourishing mulch as it dies down to shade and cool the soil around the potatoes.

Farmers often let a field lie fallow for a season with a crop of wild amaranth, and once it has matured, it is ploughed into the soil, awaiting a new crop in spring. The nourishing minerals it puts back into the soil makes it a valuable "green manure" crop.

Ideal spacing is about 1 metre apart, and small, self-sown seedlings transplant well. The seed is a valuable grain, and formed an important part of the diet of people in the early centuries. The grain was cooked into a gruel or thin porridge or baked into a flat bread so rich in nutrients it is still today regarded as a health booster. Its red pigment is used in the food industry as a natural safe colouring.

USES
Culinary, medicinal, green manure

COMPANIONS
Beetroot, mealies, onions, potatoes, sorghum

Queen Anne's lace AMMI MAJUS

WE ARE ALL FAMILIAR WITH THE DAINTY, FROTHY, PRETTY QUEEN ANNE'S LACE FLOWER THAT IS SO MUCH A PART OF THE SUMMER ANNUAL SPREAD WE HAVE COME TO LOVE.

A much-planted cottage garden flower in the early centuries, our grandmothers planted it around beans, gem squashes and cucumbers to lure away whitefly and even mildew on the leaves of squashes. The added bonus is its marvellous long life in the vase as a cut flower – still popular today.

What is fascinating is that the dainty umbels of snowy-white flowers also act as a trap for beetles and flies who drink from their sweet nectar, and they perch peacefully on the flowers, sometimes all day.

Queen Anne's lace "grows lightly", as my grandmother used to say. It does not feed heavily on the soil, it has a small root system and so takes little from the soil, leaving the food for its companion crop.

I had the best crop of bush beans I have ever grown when I interplanted with Queen Anne's lace, and I had marvellously huge bouquets of it for the house. If it is left to mature,

it makes a superb dried arrangement – hang upside down to dry first.

It was once used as a condiment – the seeds can be ground with peppercorns. A rare and extraordinary use is as an external application in a cream base for vitiligo, which is the white patches of skin that give a piebald look of pigment loss. But these skin preparations are made into registered proprietary creams for use under a doctor's supervision only. In Southwest Asia and in Southern Europe, where it is indigenous, an active ingredient, psoralene, is extracted, which is said to stimulate pigment production in skin exposed to ultraviolet light. Astonishingly, it has a long history of use as a contraceptive in certain cultures.

Its close cousin, *Ammi visnaga* (sometimes known as *Daucus visnaga* or wild carrot) has been used in medical preparations to treat angina and asthma under a doctor's supervision – its properties include dilating of blood vessels without affecting the blood pressure. And here we thought it was just a pretty garden annual! In some countries it is subject to legal restrictions, so only be advised by your doctor, do not self-medicate.

Planted in rows with tomatoes, basil, beans of all sorts (my favourite Blue Peter does particularly well with it) and strawberries underneath it, you will be rewarded with a feast, both visually and culinary, and once it is over (it is a fairly short-lived annual) use it in layers on the compost heap to aerate the compost. Like yarrow, it will quickly break down the compost.

USES
Culinary, medicinal, cut flower, compost maker

COMPANIONS
Basil, beans, cucumbers, gem squash, strawberries, tomatoes

Dill

NATIVE TO SOUTHERN EUROPE AND CENTRAL AND WESTERN ASIA, DILL HAS BEEN A PRECIOUSLY PRESERVED HERB FOR CENTURIES. DILL SEEDS WERE FOUND IN EGYPTIAN TOMBS AND IN ROMAN AND ANCIENT GREEK BURIAL SITES OF OVER 500 YEARS AGO.

A soothing syrup for colic, gripe, heartburn and flatulence was made by the monks in the Middle Ages – a forerunner for the modern gripe water which has been on the chemists' shelves for many years and much loved and respected by many young mothers for their fretful babies.

The word dill comes from an ancient Norse word which means "to soothe" and that is exactly what dill does – it soothes. Chew a few seeds to sweeten the breath and refresh the mouth, to ease indigestion, colic, flatulence, hiccups, colds, coughs, whooping cough, tension, insomnia and menstrual cramps. A dill tea is quickly soothing for all the above ailments and will help a nursing mother increase her milk flow. Use ¼ cup fresh dill leaves and flowers in 1 cup of boiling water, stand for 5 minutes, strain and sip slowly.

A cool weather crop, dill just can't take the searing heat and dryness of summer, so sow the seeds in March for planting out in June in well-dug, well-composted, moist soil in full sun. Space the plants 30 centimetres apart and keep them moist and protected for their first month in the cold nights.

Partner dill with cabbages, cauliflower, broccoli and kale – I plant dill between them and they all thrive. For areas that don't have excessive heat, dill does well with tomatoes, which keep its roots cool. If planted on the eastern side of a row of mealies or a fence of cucumbers, the afternoon shade will keep it cool and happy. The rewards are masses of pretty yellow flowers which are delicious to eat in stir-fries, and those tasty

aniseed-like feathery leaves for salads, fish dishes and omelettes. And don't forget to add dill leaves, flowers and seeds to every pickle you ever make! I reap the seeds which I keep in a screw top jar next to the stove for adding to all sorts of dishes, and never tire of them.

Don't have dill flowering next to carrots – for some reason dill will reduce the carrots' yield. Growers often leave at least 20 metres between the dill and the bed of carrots. Remember also not to have dill too close to the more robust fennel – their flowers are so similar that they can cross fertilise, as bees and butterflies love them both and they cross fertilise easily.

Dill is sometimes sown as a cut flower. I once had the thrill of helping to cut the beautiful lime-green sprays of just ripened flowers. The new seeds were still firm and green. The plants grew up to my shoulders, and the bunches were almost a metre in length. The best variety to sow for cut flowers is *Anethum graveolens* var. *vierling*. The flowering heads are saucer-sized.

Dill is a delicate treasure to grow, but worth it!

USES
Culinary, medicinal, cut flower

COMPANIONS
Broccoli, cabbages, cauliflower, cucumbers, kale, mealies, tomatoes

Celery

LONG BEFORE I EVER KNEW THAT CELERY WAS SUCH AN IMPORTANT CROP, I HEARD MY GRANDMOTHER SAY OVER AND OVER EVERY YEAR, "REMEMBER TO PLANT A ROW OF CELERY NEXT TO THE CABBAGES." THEN, 30 YEARS LATER, I READ THAT IN 1951 A RESEARCH PROGRAMME IN GERMANY STATED THAT WHEN CABBAGES WERE GROWN IN THE VICINITY OF A ROW OF CELERY, THE CABBAGE WAS LESS AFFECTED BY MICRO-ORGANISMS. IN THOSE DAYS NO ONE REALLY THOUGHT ABOUT COMPANION PLANTING. YOU JUST DID IT!

Celery is a health food that has no equal! It is a detoxifier, a cleanser, an antiseptic, a diuretic, anti-spasmodic and a sedative. Celery eaten fresh, or its seed made into a tea, will ease gout, arthritis and rheumatism, lower high blood pressure, and it will dispose of the urates that cause the stiffness and pain associated with arthritis, as well as reducing acidity in the body. A word of warning: do not take celery or celery seeds if you are pregnant or if you suffer from a kidney disorder.

Organically grown celery is worth its weight in gold. The Chinese eat fresh celery with their food every single day, as it is so important as a cleanser and celery sticks are available at most eating houses. Why not serve celery sticks with drinks? Cut them into 12 centimetre lengths, sprinkle with a touch of herb salt and dredge them in lemon juice. It's delicious, and so much better for you than all those crisps and puffs and salted peanuts!

Growing celery often defeats the average gardener. It doesn't have to be blanched, so why not just grow a row and reap constantly the outer stalks and leaves and have these crisp and fresh in every stir-fry, with every sandwich, every snack and every salad?

Sow the seeds in trays and transplant into well-dug, well-composted moist soil in full sun when they are big enough to handle. Space them 30 centimetres apart, and partner them with beans, leeks, spring onions, tomatoes and African marigolds. A row of basil next to the tomatoes, then a row of celery, then a row of leeks, then climbing or bush beans, then a row of celery, then a row of spring onions, and finally a row of marigolds, is a garden made in heaven – nothing gets eaten, wilted or burned, and it all tastes magnificent.

In the flower garden I plant winter celery with pansies, violas and calendulas, and nothing touches them. Start the rows in March. Even if the winter is very cold, they all seem to thrive and shelter one another. Besides, it looks beautiful and the flowers are all edible. The celery will protect a row of butter lettuce too – so plant violas on either side of it. Celery rows between cabbage, kohlrabi and broccoli work particularly well in winter, and celery, parsley and land cress do well together as a border along a path.

Should you want longer stems, wrap a folded newspaper around the lower stem, leaves sticking out on top, and the newspaper tucked well into the soil. As the leaves stretch up to escape the paper, the stem will lengthen and whiten. Water deeply twice weekly and you'll have a reward that is so delicious you'll become addicted.

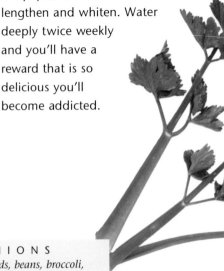

USES
Culinary, medicinal

COMPANIONS
African marigolds, beans, broccoli, cabbages, calendulas, kohlrabi, land cress, leeks, pansies, parsley, spring onions, tomatoes, violas

Horseradish

ARMORACIA RUSTICANA

DURING THE MIDDLE AGES, HORSERADISH WAS USED AS A PAINKILLER AS WELL AS A CONDIMENT, AND IN THEIR CLOISTER GARDENS THE MONKS USED IT TO TREAT CHEST AILMENTS, FEVERS, FLU AND CHILBLAINS. TO THIS DAY IT IS A LOVED AND RESPECTED HERB IN ITS NATIVE EUROPE AND WESTERN ASIA.

Hot and peppery, a single young leaf finely shredded is an exciting ingredient added to a stir-fry or to a potato salad, but it is those finely grated roots that are the most sought after for appetising sauces and salad dressings.

Easy to grow and undemanding, horseradish has been an important part of every cottage garden through the centuries, not only for its medicinal use and culinary assets, but also for its important role in the vegetable garden. Horseradish protects potatoes, peach trees, apricots, plums, mango and apple trees. It deters soil-borne diseases, and although it prefers a sunny position in richly composted, moist soil, it is tough and resilient and thrives in most areas, soils and circumstances, even under the dappled shade of the fruit trees. I am really very impressed with horseradish – once you have it, you will never be without it, as even the tiniest bit of root left behind after you have dug up the roots in autumn will grow again. By late spring you'll notice sturdy little plants emerging.

It is a pungent stimulant herb and perhaps its most important use is that it is a superb diuretic that also controls bacterial infection and lowers fevers by increasing perspiration. It literally irritates the tissues and so improves circulation. Today medical science proves what the ancient healers knew in those early centuries – horseradish actually eases arthritis, gout, urinary and respiratory infections. But a word of caution here: it should not be taken by those with stomach ulcers and thyroid problems.

For the cook, horseradish is simply delicious – the amazing fresh root can be grated and mixed with cream and grated apple for pasta, fish dishes and butter beans, or mixed with vinegar and cream or vinegar and brown sugar, served with roast beef, cold meats, cold chicken, hardboiled eggs, cooked cold chickpeas, lentils or kidney beans.

Every autumn for many years I would order a sack of horseradish roots from a nursery situated in a cool misty mountain area where it thrived, as we never seem to have enough of our own plants to use in our Herbal Centre restaurant. The sack would arrive moist and pungent, and the staff were filled with dread – horseradish is worse than onions to grate and chop, and we built a large concrete table outside the back door in order to process the roots without too much drama! Nevertheless, everyone was thankful when it was all safely bottled, and streaming eyes and noses could be given a chance to revive until the next year. Sadly, the nursery no longer exists and our incredible source has gone, much to the relief of the staff, but I still long for that experience every autumn as I tend our own horseradish beds in the heat of the African sun.

USES
Culinary, medicinal

COMPANIONS
Fruit trees, potatoes

23

The artemisias

THIS IS A GENUS OF OVER 300 SPECIES OF RICHLY FRAGRANT USUALLY PERENNIAL SHRUBS THAT GROW IN TEMPERATE REGIONS ACROSS THE WORLD. ALL HAVE THAT DISTINCTIVE RICHLY PUNGENT SCENT THAT CHASES INSECTS, AND BEAUTIFUL, OFTEN FINELY CUT FOLIAGE IN GREY-GREEN AND SILVER. HANDSOME IN THE GARDEN, THE ARTEMISIAS HAVE BEEN GARDENERS' AND LANDSCAPERS' FAVOURITES FOR CENTURIES, AND MANY HAVE MEDICINAL PROPERTIES TOO.

SOUTHERNWOOD (*Artemisia abrotanum*) is a familiar and aromatic hedge plant that was used by the early Romans as a hedge around their fields to protect food crops, in their gardens to repel insects, and as a strewing herb. Amazingly, the monks grew southernwood in their cloister gardens to spread onto the church floor at times when there was an outbreak of the plague, or during the winter to stop the spread of coughs and colds.

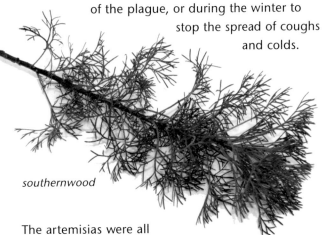

southernwood

The artemisias were all used in medieval times as strewing herbs. This means the plants were thrown on the floor to be walked on, thus releasing the pungent oils which would not only chase mosquitoes, flies, ants and fleas, but also clear germs and mask the smell of often unwashed visitors!

Southernwood contains disinfectant and antiseptic oils, and if it is planted near kennels, chicken runs and stables, it will deter ants, fleas, ticks and lice. Even dried southernwood will deter moths and ants, particularly fish moths in cupboards. An effective fish moth treatment for library shelves is to line the shelves with tin foil, shiny side up. Underneath sprinkle with talc powder – I use a baby powder – and give attention to the corners and all along the walls, spread it thicker there, then tuck fresh sprigs of southernwood on top of the tinfoil all along the back wall. Pack the books along and on top of the sprigs. You won't have a fish moth in sight!

Grow a row of southernwood around fruit trees to repel fruit flies, and around the roses to repel aphids. A row of southernwood in the vegetable garden will keep carrots, cabbages and beetroot aphid free.

The hedge needs a good clipping every now and then to keep it compact, neat and full. If left to its own, it quickly becomes straggly and untidy. Use every precious clipping in a wonderful spray for black and green aphids and whitefly. Fill a large bucket with fresh clippings, cover with boiling water and leave to cool and draw overnight. Next morning strain, discard the clippings and add half a cup of soap powder – this helps it to stick to the plants. Splash or spray onto the infected areas. Do this 2 or 3 days running to be sure the pests are gone. This spray will also deter moths and ants.

WORMWOOD (*Artemisia absinthium*) is another superb insect repellent and can be used in the same way as its cousin, southernwood. Wormwood tea will have an excellent tonic effect on the plants, and it is a well-respected spray for thrips, snails, slugs and red spider mites. It is worth growing wormwood as a

USES
Culinary (tarragon only!), insect repellent, antifungal garden spray

COMPANIONS
Beans, beetroot, brinjals, cabbages, carrots, fruit trees, gooseberries, green peppers, hollyhocks, nasturtiums, roses, strawberries

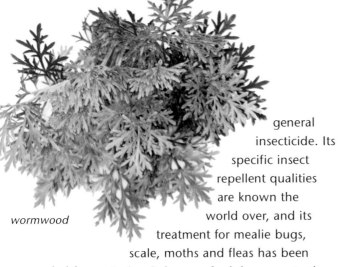
wormwood

general insecticide. Its specific insect repellent qualities are known the world over, and its treatment for mealie bugs, scale, moths and fleas has been recorded for centuries. Rub some fresh leaves onto the dog's fur, and have crushed wormwood in the rafters to repel mice, or around chicken runs to repel spiders, flies, stink bugs and even mice!

Many centuries ago, wormwood was used as a vermifuge to expel worms from the body, as it was considered to have such amazing worm-repelling qualities. In medieval times, the monks used it to treat the sick. It is best known as "absinthe", the flavouring for Vermouth & Absinthe. However, it caused such severe deterioration of the liver and digestive tract that it was later banned. One of its active ingredients, thujone, was also found to be addictive.

MUGWORT (*Artemisia vulgaris*), another of the amazing artemisias, is a spreading, sprawling, invasive herb, and it has been used to repel snails, slugs and ants. It was taken internally for thread worms and other parasites, and is used today as it was centuries ago as a wash for fungal infections. In the garden, mugwort tea is effective as a mildew treatment, but needs to be done several days in a row.

It's worth growing in the back bed where it can sprawl – it is so invasive I plant a collar of thick black plastic around it, 40 centimetres deep, which helps to restrain it, but it is

mugwort

so remarkable in a tea mixed with wildeals (see below) and southernwood for spraying aphids and scale and fungal areas that every organic gardener should be growing it.

In some old gardens, *Artemisia ludoviciana* ("Silver Queen") was grown as a snail repellent, and its attractive ground-covering silvery leaves make it a feature, especially on poor, rocky soil. Wormwood, mugwort and silver queen were dried, burned in metal buckets and taken through the house once a year much like a modern fumigant to clear fleas, bedbugs and white ants in the floorboards. The smoke would remain in the rooms – windows and doors sealed for a day and a night if possible – and fresh sprigs were crushed and laid on the floors (much like we use fresh khakibos). How much safer that would have been – no harsh and poisonous fumes could be inhaled.

WILDEALS
(*Artemisia afra*) is an indigenous artemisia, and great sprays are still used today in chicken runs, in kennels and in stables on the floors. My crop of strawberries with khakibos and wildeals sprays laid under the leaves and berries,

wildeals

produced an incredible crop of beautiful berries one year. As a mulch under green peppers and brinjals in the hot summer months, I had the best fruits ever in spite of the drought.

Wildeals will reach a height of over 1 metre, so give it space, and plant it along the back border of the garden.

Also a part of this great artemisia group is tarragon. There are two tarragons: **ESTRAGON** or **FRENCH TARRAGON** (*Artemisia dracunculus*) is the more flavour-filled one, and much loved by chefs and cooks throughout the world.

25

French tarragon

RUSSIAN TARRAGON

(*Artemisia dracunculoides*) is a finer-leafed, more spreading variety and is far easier to grow than its French cousin.

Both tarragons enhance the growth of brinjals, green peppers and gooseberries. If planted alongside beans, they will help the beans to remain insect free, even discouraging caterpillars, and they help the beans to thrive. A row of runner beans spaced over arches 3 metres apart with French tarragon growing in the partial shade under the arches, has quite an astonishing production of both beans and succulent French tarragon sprigs. There is enough sunlight to keep the tarragon happy, and the beans make the soil friable for good growth of the tarragon shoots. Old gardening journals state that the tarragons act as stimulators to plants around them, and the gardeners grew tarragon next to rare and precious medicinal plants with chamomile nearby, acting as a plant doctor!

There is a very pretty artemisia available for landscapers, *Artemisia powis castle*. It is a finely cut, grey, knee-high artemisia, softly sprawling and very attractive. If grown with hollyhocks and nasturtiums, it will keep them free of black aphids and whitefly.

An antifungal tea made of powis castle, mugwort, silver queen and wildeals is a very potent brew to spray onto mildew and fungus attacks. Pour 2 buckets of boiling water over 1 bucket of fresh sprigs of these four artemisias, and leave to stand overnight to cool. Strain the next morning, discard the herbs and add 1 bucket of water, 1 cup of Sunlight soap powder and ¾ cup of mustard powder mixed well into 1 cup of warm water. Mix well and use as a spray. Do this once a week for 3 weeks.

Artemisia powis castle

Moth-repelling sachet

Through the years I have made literally thousands of these wonderful sachets and grow a whole artemisia garden for this purpose. At one time it was quite a nice little money-spinner.

1 cup of cloves
1 cup of minced dried lemon peel
3 cups of lavender leaves and flowers (use Grandmother's lavender – *Lavandula latifolia*)
6 cups of dried southernwood, mugwort, wildeals and wormwood leaves
4 teaspoons lavender potpourri oil (not essential oil)

Add the lavender potpourri oil to the cloves and the lemon peel and store in a large glass jar with a good screw-on lid. Give it a daily shake. Add more oil if you want a stronger scent. Mix in the dried lavender and the artemisias. Add a little more oil if needed and store in a large tin or crock. Seal it well and give it a daily shake, every day, for 10 days. Then sew up sachets 15 to 20 cm square – choose a pretty cotton with a flowery design. (Do not choose a plain fabric as there may be a little oil that has not been fully absorbed into the leaves and it could mark the fabric.) Keep one side open and use a paper funnel to pour in the potpourri. Neatly sew it up and attach a loop of ribbon or a bow so that it can also hang in the cupboard. Keep it sealed in plastic so that no scent escapes until you want to tuck it in between the sheets or towels or behind the books or into the dog's bed, or hang it behind the bathroom door.

Asparagus

ASPARAGUS HAS BEEN AROUND SINCE 200 BC (AND WAS KNOWN AS "SPEARAGE" OR "SPARROW GRASS" IN ITS NATIVE EUROPE), AND HAS BEEN CULTIVATED AS A VEGETABLE AND A MEDICINE FOR OVER TWO THOUSAND YEARS!

Hardy, tough, resilient to drought, heat, cold, poor soil and neglect, it continues, a perennial that comes up year after year, with flavour-filled spears of huge medicinal value. No wonder it is still today an important crop worldwide. And it is fun to grow!

When my children were small, I would occasionally need to drive the long distance to Johannesburg to fetch supplies for my pottery business on the farm. I passed through a fertile valley of asparagus fields on the way. Rich, friable, compost-loaded soil, with a simple spraying system that was switched on three times a week in August, September and October, and twice a week thereafter, this crop really relied on summer rain, which was quite consistent in that valley. I would stop there on the way home to chat to the field workers who were harvesting in early August those fat, pale spears with sharp knives. It fascinated me. They taught me all I know today about asparagus, and I bought the fresh spears from the farmer whenever I could.

I began growing it in my garden from "crowns" that the farmer gave me. It is dead easy! All you do is ensure that your soil is well dug and richly composted. Then you add bone meal, two handfuls per square metre. Plant the crowns (which need to be renewed every 8 to 10 years) in full sun half to three quarters of a metre apart in rows one metre wide (leaving space for a secondary crop between them like tomatoes, carrots, beans, parsley, chervil and cabbages in the winter months).

Most amazing of all is that this crop – only really profitable for a mere month or so once a year – has never lost its popularity. It is one of nature's most loved and respected cleansing herbs. It acts directly on the liver, bowels and kidneys, flushing out toxins and giving that typical asparagin smell to the urine literally within an hour of eating it. Therefore, asparagus in the diet was considered to be beneficial to the whole system from the earliest centuries.

The water in which the asparagus was boiled was also used to treat cystitis, gout and rheumatism, and to build up the kidney function. Besides, it is a superb diuretic, so it is a popular beauty treatment as well.

Planted next to tomatoes, asparagus grows beautifully as tomatoes contain solanine, a substance that encourages growth in asparagus and protects them against insect attack. In return, the asparagus produces asparagin which kills nematodes in the soil – the way the African marigold does – and nematodes affect tomatoes. So a row of summer African marigolds grown on the other side of the tomatoes with asparagus and beans next, and parsley up against the asparagus and cabbage to replace the tomatoes in winter, there is quite a surprise about to happen – everything will grow beautifully, sturdily and strongly, and the asparagus field's yield will be well worth all the extra plantings!

USES
Culinary, medicinal

COMPANIONS
Beans, cabbages, carrots, chervil, parsley, tomatoes

Oats

NATIVE TO NORTHERN EUROPE AND ASIA, OATS HAVE BEEN GROWN AS A COMMERCIAL CROP ALL OVER THE WORLD FOR CENTURIES. A GENUS OF AROUND 15 SPECIES OF ANNUAL GRASSES, THE GRAMINEAE, THE ANCIENT WILD OATS, *AVENA FATUA*, IS A SOUTHERN EUROPEAN GRASS THAT REACHED NORTHERN EUROPE IN THE IRON AGE, AND BECAME THE MAIN FOOD CROP IN SCOTLAND.

From this wild beginning the oats we know today was developed, and it has never lost its popularity. But what we often don't think about, is that every garden really should have a row of oats in it frequently – for you can sow it literally at any time of the year, but best is in winter – as a luscious green manure crop and as a compost decomposer. Oats are brilliant as a quick soil-saving annual too. You dig them back in just as they are sending up tufts of their pretty seeds. First slash them, then dig in, or lay the green bounty as a mulch and the ripe yellow oats can be pulled up and placed under ripening strawberries, tomatoes, brinjals, green peppers or fruit salad plant (*Solanum muricatum*) that lie too close to the soil.

One of the most valuable tips I can give you is the combination of red clover and oats together – one row of oats on either side of a row of red clover – is incredibly rich in minerals and vitamins. These are the rows of oats you allow to mature for that superb oat straw tea for bone building and hot flushes in menopause, and as a tonic for heart, nerves, thymus gland, nervous exhaustion, shingles, herpes, and for depression.

Oats seeds are milled for porridge and muesli. They sop up cholesterol, and comfort and soothe rashes and eczema. Oats seeds sprouted for salads are valuable as an energy tonic.

There is literally no part of this ancient plant that is not useful and effective. A handful of oats tied in a face cloth and soaked in a hot bath, is the most extraordinary skin cleanser, exfoliator and rejuvenator you can ever buy, and leaves expensive cosmetics many miles behind. Just soak and wash and spread and massage in – it's the best facemask you've ever used!

But above all, it is the store of nitrates in the leaves and straw that fresh green oats will impart to the soil that will astonish you! I planted rows of oats interspersed with buckwheat over the poorest, most useless and pathetic soil you've ever seen. I let them grow to maturity and before they set seed I ploughed them in and let them lie. Two months later I reploughed – everything had broken down and the soil looked and smelled better. I resowed the oats and let them mature to golden and dry, and reaped the tops for teas. I slashed and ploughed in the rest and let the land lie fallow all winter. In spring I reploughed and made vegetable beds with only a little compost. Needless to say, I had the best vegetables ever and no one believed me it was only oats and a little buckwheat! Oats as a green manure is valuable and reliable!

USES
Culinary, medicinal, green manure, compost maker, fertiliser

COMPANIONS
Brinjals, fruit salad plant, green peppers, strawberries, tomatoes

Neem

WHEN YOU HEAR "ORGANIC INSECTICIDE", IT IS USUALLY THE NEEM THAT IS BEING SPOKEN ABOUT! THIS AMAZING TREE IS EXTRAORDINARY IN EVERY WAY, AND IS ONE OF MANKIND'S MOST USEFUL, MOST VERSATILE, MOST IMPORTANT TREES!

It has a myriad of traditional uses in its native India: it is grown for fuel, its workable timber, its medicinal properties, particularly in Ayurvedic medicine, and its seed-enriched oil, known as margosa oil which has insecticidal and antiseptic properties and is non-drying.

The Persian name Azaddhirakt means noble tree, and when you look at its impressive medicinal values, you'll understand it truly is a noble tree, and the source of much medicinal aid for the general population in India and Southeast Asia. It is a potent febrifuge used through the centuries to treat infections, fevers and malaria, and it also has antifungal, antiseptic, antiviral and anti-inflammatory properties.

The bark of the neem is utilised to make a tea traditionally used to treat jaundice and other liver disorders. The tender young branches and twigs are used as chewing sticks to treat mouth infections and to keep the gums and teeth healthy, and a tea made of crushed seeds is used to treat leprosy, bladder, kidney and prostate problems. A tea made of the leaves is used as a poultice and lotion to treat sprains, bruises, swollen glands, eczemas, rashes, boils, wounds and ulcers, and can be taken internally as a contraceptive, and to lower blood pressure. *Warning:* Do not give neem as a medicine for children under four years or for the elderly.

I have trialled the neem for the last ten years in the Herbal Centre gardens and have found it slow to get started. In those ten years it has only grown a couple of metres, but I have great heat, very little rainfall, a worrying scarcity of water and a high altitude. In more compatible circumstances it will grow fairly rapidly into a pretty shade tree that will grow to between 12 and 15 metres. It is quite hardy, but cannot take frost.

As an insecticide it will protect any plant that grows near it, and strong teas made from leaves and twigs in boiling water are excellent for chasing aphids, flies and mosquitoes. Watered into the ground round vegetables, the tea will repel cutworms and beetles. The wood resists insect attacks, so important papers and documents are stored in neem wood boxes, and grain and seeds are also stored in neem wood containers. As it resists insect attack, the wood is frequently used for building.

The leaves are added to spinach dishes with olive oil and onions and curry, and the small oval, still green fruit is added to stir-fries and soups and stews.

Note: Do not confuse neem with its close relative, the poisonous and invasive seringa tree or Persian lilac (*Melia azedarach*), which is a serious problem in South Africa as its berries seed everywhere.

USES
Culinary, medicinal, insect repellent, fuel

COMPANIONS
All vegetables and fruit trees will benefit from the neem's insect repelling qualities

Swiss Chard

BETA VULGARIS VAR. CICLA

WE TEND TO CALL THE WHITE-RIBBED AND STEMMED SWISS CHARD SPINACH, AND ALTHOUGH BOTANICALLY INCORRECT, THIS IS WHAT MOST PEOPLE KNOW AS SPINACH. THE REAL SPINACH (*SPINACEA OLERACEA*) IS A FAR MORE DIFFICULT PLANT TO GROW, AND FAR SMALLER AND MORE TENDER THAN ITS GIANT COUSIN. BOTH ARE EXCELLENT SOURCES OF VITAMINS AND MINERALS AND FILL THE ROLE OF HEALTH-GIVING, GREEN, LEAFY VEGETABLES ADMIRABLY.

What fascinates me about the Swiss chard is that it was known to the ancient Greeks who cooked the thick white midribs cut free of the green leafy part as a banqueting dish, served with butter and vinegar. It was also chopped up and cooked in soups, and the green part of the leaves was mixed with sorrel and cooked and eaten with hard-boiled eggs.

Ordinary spinach – the one Popeye popularised – is full of iron, but almost impossible for the body to fully utilise as it is not easy to assimilate. Nevertheless, eating your greens is very important as they are rich in beta carotene, folic acid, calcium, potassium, vitamins B6 and C and magnesium.

All the spinaches, even the New Zealand spinach (*Tetragonia tetragonioides*) help to boost the immune system, have anti-cancer properties, and help to build healthy bones and blood, and to regulate blood pressure. So that's why Popeye loved spinach so much!

In the vegetable garden, spinach is powerful as a good companion, and the bright red and yellow stems of the new Swiss chard, 'Bright Lights', looks so pretty in the garden, you'll be wanting to grow it everywhere. Any plant next to spinach will do well – it literally protects, tones and shelters plants next to it.

All the spinach varieties take heat and drought and bitter winter winds, but in very hot weather they can run to seed. So watch out for that seed spire emerging and cut it off. They need full sun, deeply dug, well-composted soil, and don't do well in the shade of taller plants. They love and protect strawberries and thrive with onions, beetroot, peas, celery, cabbages and green peppers. However, keep all spinaches away from grapes – they do not like to be near each other. Lately I have found spinach does not like sage – one or the other will die. So keep both sage and grapes away from spinach.

On the compost heap the tougher, older leaves are a great asset, and break down quickly if they are dug into the top layer of the compost immediately. The succulent spreading, creeping stems of New Zealand spinach are even quicker in breaking down the compost and act very compatibly with comfrey leaves. I grow them near each other in wet summers. The tender New Zealand spinach seeks comfrey's shade. Keep experimenting with spinach – it's worth it!

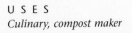

New Zealand spinach

Swiss chard

USES
Culinary, compost maker

COMPANIONS
Beetroot, cabbages, celery, green peppers, onions, peas, strawberries

DISLIKES
Grapes, sage

Beetroot

BEETROOT IS A VALUABLE CROP NEVER TO BE UNDERESTIMATED. IT CAN BE GROWN ALL THROUGH THE YEAR, OFFERING NOT ONLY ITS SUCCULENT UNDERGROUND ROOT, BUT A DELICIOUS DELICACY OF RED-VEINED LEAVES THAT CAN BE A SUPERB SPINACH.

Interestingly, the beetroot we know today was developed in the Middle Ages from a sprawling dune plant that grew on the shoreline of the Caspian Sea, known as sea-beet (*Beta vulgaris* var. *maritima*). In those days only the leaves were eaten as the root was underdeveloped. An improved beet was recorded in Roman literature in AD 200. By 300 BC, there were more varieties, yet only in the 16th century was the Roman beet recorded as a delectable food served with vinegar and onions!

The beautiful red colour of beetroot is due to the combination of a purple pigment, beta cyanin, and a yellow pigment, beta xanthin. These pigments are stable and have been used as natural food colourings.

Sugar beet (*Beta vulgaris* var. *vulgaris*) is another variety of beetroot, and it is farmed commercially in Europe as an economical source of sugar. This sugar is far more easily used by the body than cane sugar. Sugar beet grows well in the cooler, moist fields of Europe.

Beetroot is rich in beta carotene, calcium, magnesium, iron, phosphorus, folic acid, silica, vitamin B5, manganese and high in fibre. This means it acts as a natural laxative and it will break down kidney stones. As an antioxidant it will fight free radicals and boost the immune system. It helps to build the blood, and it clears rubbish, toxins and wrong eating debris from the kidneys and liver, and boosts energy. Raw beetroot in the juice extractor or grated finely, raw, with apple, is an important health builder.

Beetroot tonic

2 organically grown beetroots with 6 beetroot
  leaves, unpeeled and washed well
3 carrots and 1 carrot leaf
3 sticks celery and leaves
1 cup of fresh parsley
1 peeled apple, quartered

Push everything through the juice extractor for a superb energy drink that literally has you moving! The secret is to stand there with the glass and catch up the precious juice and drink it down immediately. If the apple is organically grown, there is no need to peel it.

Beetroot is a crop one literally has to grow. It's easy, it's a pretty plant in the garden and can be interplanted with flowers as well. It loves bush beans, cabbage, cauliflower, onions, leeks, kohlrabi and lettuce. One of my most fascinating plantings was my alternate beetroot and kohlrabi planted in a square. The pale green and dark red with 15 centimetres spacing between each plant made a beautiful pattern all winter long.

Another successful planting is one row lettuce, one row beetroot, one row leeks, one row beetroot, one row kohlrabi, one row onions, one row bronze lettuce, one row beetroot, etc. In summer, African marigolds, bush beans and onions are beetroot's companions, and with parsley as an edging, it is pretty enough for a show garden.

In the flower garden, plant beetroot with winter-flowering larkspurs on one side and calendula on the other side edged with parsley – the larkspur keeps the aphids away, and calendula is protective and edible, so you'll have a valuable show garden!

USES
Culinary

COMPANIONS
African marigolds, bush beans, cabbages, calendulas, cauliflower, kohlrabi, larkspur, leeks, lettuces, onions, parsley

Silver Birch

HAVE YOU EVER CONSIDERED THE BIRCH TREE TO BE A COMPANION PLANT? WELL, IT IS AN EXCEPTIONAL TREE TO NOURISH AND REVITALISE OLD SOIL, AND IF PLANTED ON THE OUTER EDGES OF THE COMPOST HEAP, IT WILL ENCOURAGE ACTIVE FERMENTATION OF THE HEAP.

Supposing you have had a poor crop, and blight and mildew and other plant diseases have been rampant, a compost rich in birch leaves, or actual soil that has been under birch trees, can be lifted and dug into the area in order to restore it, and in one season the difference can be seen. Supposing you are looking at leached soil under eucalyptus trees, jacaranda trees or pine trees where nothing will grow, once the offending trees are removed, plant a row or two or three of silver birches, widely spaced. Within two years the soil will be restored. Or if the trees cannot be removed, use birch soil and compost which includes birch leaves, and dig it in under the trees as much as possible, and soil fertility will be generally improved and often restored.

Farmers in Europe and America made a practice of "brushing" a ploughed field with birch branches lashed together, or small birch trees tied behind a horse or a tractor, and these were pulled over the soil to impart nutrients to the soil. Surprisingly, this made a huge difference with seeds that germinated quickly, easily and strongly.

Birch leaves can be composted or fermented, and laid into seed boxes or beds, covered with sand and kept moist, the little seeds have a head start and produce excellent seedlings that can be transplanted easily and show no sign of wilt.

If you have space, consider a short row of silver birch trees. They do not have a very long life and they are so valuable in the compost heap I am awed.

They are tough, heat resistant, tolerant of dry conditions and seem to do well in most soils. They thrive near the compost heap the way they do at the edges of the forests in their native Europe and Asia, and give a gentle light shade and protection over winter bulbs.

Not only are birch leaves valuable in the compost heap but a delicious tea of birch leaves will ease muscular aches and pains, remove toxins, clear waste products from the kidneys and bladder, help in weight reduction, invigorate poor circulation, reduce fluid retention, soothe rheumatism and arthritis, soothe skin and scalp dryness, itchiness and irritations, reduce and disperse swellings and will even help to break up bladder stones. To make the tea use ¼ cup fresh leaves in 1 cup boiling water, stand 5 minutes, strain, sip slowly with either honey or a slice of lemon added, or both.

To make a facial cleanser and toner, boil up a big pot of silver birch leaves, twigs, sprigs and catkins with enough water to cover, add two or three big comfrey leaves, and simmer for 1 hour covered. Top up with water if necessary. Then cool and strain. Pour some into a spritz bottle and use to clear skin oiliness and spots – and use the rest as a spray on ailing plants, especially pot plants.

USES
Fertiliser, compost maker, medicinal, cosmetic

Borage

BORAGE IS VITAL IN THE GARDEN — ITS RICH MINERAL CONTENT MAKES IT A POTENT NATURAL BOOSTER NOT ONLY TO THE COMPOST HEAP, BUT AS A LIQUID MANURE AND AS A COMPANION PLANT IT IS SUPERB!

Borage is an exceptional companion to most plants. It literally blends its powerful nutrients into the soil, it acts as a nourishing mulch just by laying down a blanket of stems, leaves and flowers around an ailing plant, and a tea made of the leaves and stems is a superb tonic. Take half a bucket of fresh borage sprigs, fill up with one bucket of boiling water and leave it to stand and cool overnight. Next morning strain, toss the old borage onto the compost heap and then use this tea to revitalise everything. Spritz spray it as a foliar feed, water it into pot plants, seedlings, new cuttings in the nursery trays and beds.

Borage encourages fruiting in strawberries, marrows, pumpkins and cucumbers, and strawberry growers plant a row of borage every 20 metres in their strawberry fields to not only give a better flavour to the fruit but to increase yield, and to give so strong a tonic effect to the fruit that its storage time can be increased.

Borage is rich in sustaining minerals – calcium, potassium and phosphorus particularly – and it is a superb green manure crop to grow in a field which has become depleted and unproductive. It grows very easily from seed – in fact, once you have it you will always have borage – and what a pleasure that will be! Transplanting seedlings is easy. They are tough and accept handling and transplanting well, often not even wilting, and they can be spaced one metre apart in full sun. Keep the little plants watered well in the beginning – once established, they'll grow with vigour – then water twice or three times a week depending on the weather. Once the flowers set seed, plough them in well. Within two weeks you'll be able to plant in that same field, and the crop will be improved immediately.

One difficult summer with very little rain, I experimented with borage along rows of vegetables planted north to south. I thought borage's rampant growth would be helpful in keeping the scorching sun off the rows of tomatoes, lettuce, strawberries, cucumbers, green peppers and brinjals. I trained cucumbers and green beans along teepees made of reeds, and the shade made the greatest difference with borage giving such surprising tonic boosts to the tomatoes and brinjals, we actually had a crop!

Borage has in its leaves a particular property – it is a refrigerant which lowers the temperature. Also over infected areas it will hasten the healing by cooling. Perhaps this is what saved the rows of vegetables – they were kept cool!

Borage flowers are loved by bees, and have a refreshing, cucumber-like taste. Those flowers are delicious in stir-fries, fruit salads and drinks, and it is a much-respected medicinal plant that stimulates the adrenal cortex to produce its own cortisone. It helps to clear skin ailments, to moisturise very dry skin, to ease menopause and varicose veins, and for so varied a number of ailments we need to take a fresh look at this precious plant.

USES
Culinary, medicinal, fertiliser, compost maker

COMPANIONS
Brinjals, cucumbers, marrows, pumpkins, strawberries, tomatoes

Kohlrabi

BRASSICA OLERACEA VAR. GONGYLODES

IF ANY VEGETABLE HAD TO BE A SPACE AGE ONE, KOHLRABI IS IT – A SORT OF SPUTNIK WITH LEAVES. IT'S NOT OFTEN USED NOR FULLY APPRECIATED, YET IT IS QUITE A MARVELLOUS VEGETABLE AND ONE WE SHOULD CONSIDER. IT'S FUN TO GROW AND SIMPLY DELICIOUS TO EAT, IT'S BURSTING WITH HEALTHY NUTRIENTS AND EASY TO GROW FROM SEED.

An excellent source of vitamins – especially vitamin A and vitamin C – a host of minerals – calcium, phosphorus, iron, potassium – and fibre, kohlrabi is actually a cabbage mutant which originally and presumably developed in Europe. Historic references vary: some state it came from Asia to Europe with Attila the Hun, some say it came from China along the silk route, and it was first described by a European botanist in 1550 as a turnip rooted cabbage, a close relative to the staple kale, and it was grown mainly as pig food and winter cattle food.

I grow kale, also called collard greens or borecole (*Brassica oleracea* var. *acephala*) with it

kale

and sow the seeds of both in early autumn. Kale is native to the eastern Mediterranean where it has been cultivated for over two thousand years. Cooked and served with a rich cheese sauce with nutmeg and paprika, it fills many a hungry tummy with delight on a cold winter's night! Both kohlrabi and kale need the cold winter weather to thrive, even in heavy frost, and both are superb in soups, stews and stir-fries. Besides, kohlrabi's leaves can be eaten as well.

Sow seed in trays in early autumn and prick out and plant where they are to grow, spaced 15 centimetres apart for kohlrabi and 45 centimetres apart for kale, in moist, deeply dug, richly composted beds in full sun. Keep them well watered to establish them well.

Interplant with rows of pretty lettuces like Lollo Rosso and oak leaf (both winter crops, too), a row of thyme and parsley, and watch them thrive. I plant beetroot, onions and spring onions up against them and I have no aphids and no weeds. The garden in winter is prolific. This year's bumper crop was: on the path edge thyme, kohlrabi, dark-red oak leaf lettuce, spring onions, kale, Lollo Rosso lettuce, beetroot, kale, onions, butter lettuce, kohlrabi, parsley. Everything seemed to enhance the companion's flavour. It has been a superb visual and gourmet treat!

Kohlrabi does not do well next to strawberries, nor green peppers, but I have found a row of fenugreek seed and a row of mustard seed sown directly next to kohlrabi later in the season will shade it from the hot spring sun, and so I can have it for a longer period crisp and cool before the throbbing heat of the summer makes it bolt and become woody.

Kohlrabi is something different, and thin slices in stir-fries with mushrooms, drenched with lemon juice and butter and sprinkled with sesame seeds and served with crusty bread, makes a meal to remember. The Germans believe that if you eat kohlrabi daily throughout the winter you won't get flu or a cold.

kohlrabi

USES
Culinary

COMPANIONS
Beetroot, fenugreek, kale, lettuces, mustard, onions, parsley, spring onions, thyme

DISLIKES
Green peppers, strawberries

Turnip

BRASSICA RAPA VAR. RAPA

THE TURNIP IS A ROOT VEGETABLE THAT BELONGS TO THE BRASSICACEAE FAMILY, WHICH INCLUDES CABBAGE, BROCCOLI AND BRUSSELS SPROUTS. LIKE ITS COUSINS, IT IS MOST SUITED TO COOL MOIST CONDITIONS, SO AS A WINTER CROP TURNIPS WILL THRIVE.

Sow the seeds in late summer spaced thinly in a deep compost-filled trench in full sun, and cover lightly with compost topped with leaves to keep it cool and moist. If the seeds come up too thickly use a knife and very carefully and very gently lift one at a time out and immediately replant it in a soft moist hole where it can grow to its full potential. Turnip seeds are quite big, so when you sow them space them 13 to 15 centimetres apart to give enough room for them to develop into a luscious plant.

The young leaves can be reaped for a delicious spinach. Always leave at least three or four leaves on the plant – do not cut them all off at any one time – and steam the juicy leaves with lemon juice and salt and black pepper for literally 3 minutes, and serve with a little dot of butter. The young turnip can be pulled and eaten at any stage and as a child I can remember the excitement of finding purple topped turnips bursting with juiciness in the "soup row" my grandmother planted with kale, carrots, celery, peas, onions and leeks. Some were left to become tennis ball size, but mostly you just couldn't wait – they were so pretty and so juicy.

There is something about a turnip that makes an ordinary winter soup quite extraordinary! It must be the crispness, the pearly white glistening flesh and the beautiful purple "cloak" it wraps about its shoulders! No need to peel it – just cut off the root after it has been well scrubbed and grate it coarsely. To this day I still love winter soups and stews and I plant the "soup row" every autumn.

Lettuces, spinach, radish and chamomile do well next to turnips, and the winter vegetable garden gets prettier every year with rows of snapdragons, Californian poppies, red field poppies and calendulas. All these flowers can be eaten and should an aphid ever appear turnip peelings and roots can be chopped up into a strong brew – cover with boiling water and allow to cool. Once strained add a little soap powder and spray – it will also get rid of red spider and flies.

I also sow a new row of turnips in early spring, only because I love to eat the whole young plant – leaves and a golf ball sized turnip – steamed or in a stir-fry with new peas or smothered in a rich cheesy white sauce. The excellent blood building, kidney cleansing and revitalising tonic properties of the turnip clear away any remains of winter coughs and colds, and leave you energised and excited about the summer ahead!

USES
Culinary, medicinal, insect spray

COMPANIONS
Calendulas, Californian poppies, chamomile, lettuces, radishes, red field poppies, snapdragons, spinach

35

Cabbages

ONE OF THE MOST EXCITING, YES EXCITING, GROUPS OF PLANTS ARE THE CABBAGES, WHICH INCLUDE KALE, CAULIFLOWER, BRUSSELS SPROUTS, BROCCOLI, COLLARD GREENS, ORNAMENTAL CABBAGE, KOHLRABI, AND EVEN TURNIPS. ALL CAN BE GROUPED UNDER ONE HEADING AS ALL HAVE SIMILAR NEEDS.

Brussels sprouts

I have grown cabbages for many years. My favourites in the great Brassicaceae group are the kales and broccoli, and they're dead easy to grow. Rich compost-laced, well-dug soil in full sun is the first step, and if you always remember not to grow cabbages in the same place two years running, you'll never have a problem. I've had rows of cabbage between rows of potatoes with dill and chamomile between them, and the crop was excellent. The cabbages are a cool-weather crop, and so is dill and chamomile. Where aphids are a problem, a row of easily spreading pennyroyal under the broccoli or cauliflower or big Savoy cabbages is an excellent aphid chaser, especially if you walk on it to release its pungent scent.

Start off with seeds. I have found this to be best sown in late February. Transplant into moist, rich soil in rows as soon as the seedlings are big enough to handle, spacing them at least 50 centimetres apart. Alongside plant rows of celery, onions, dill, beetroot, chamomile, alternating with broccoli, cauliflower and kale. It looks simply beautiful, and the pickings for the winter stir-fries and soups and vegetable dishes are superb – you literally will eat off the garden all through winter with such flavours.

Around the edges of the cabbage patch plant rosemary, chives, sage, southernwood and thyme – these herbs will keep them free of that dreaded white cabbage butterfly that lays eggs in the cabbages. Slugs and snails love cabbages. So in order to protect your cabbages, especially in early plantings, save all the egg shells you can, then, after heating them in the oven for 15 minutes, crush them and sprinkle in a thin line all around the cabbage patch – the snails won't cross this line! Saucers of beer set into the ground will entice them away from the cabbages, and they'll drink and drown in the beer!

Picking the outer leaves of the cabbages and shredding them finely for stir-fries, makes a delicious dish, especially with mushrooms, sausages, onions and lemon juice.

If you remember the Brassicas have extraordinary natural antibiotics within them, as well as folic acid, calcium, magnesium, potassium, boron, beta carotene, vitamin C, vitamin E, vitamin K, phosphorus and iodine, you will understand why everyone says eat your cabbage or eat your broccoli – they are power packed with goodness.

It's worth growing a row or two of broccoli and letting it go to seed. Organically grown broccoli seed for sprouting is worth its weight in gold. The health benefits of this easy-to-grow plant are so important, broccoli sprouts will become the buzzword in the future!

cabbage

USES
Culinary, medicinal

COMPANIONS
Beetroot, celery, chamomile, chives, dill, onions, pennyroyal, rosemary, sage, southernwood, thyme

Pigeon Pea

I SIMPLY HAVE TO INTRODUCE THIS EXTRAORDINARY TREE PEA TO GARDENERS. FOR COMPANION PLANTING IT IS SUPERB AS IT IS A LEGUME, AND AS SUCH INTRODUCES NITROGEN TO THE SOIL. MOREOVER, IN OUR HOT AND OFTEN UNBEARABLE SUMMERS IT OFFERS SHADE TO NEARBY PLANTS AND IT ALSO ACTS AS A TRAP CROP FOR APHIDS!

The pigeon pea (much loved by pigeons!) is astonishing. It makes a slender, soft-branched shrub, up to 3 metres in height, and it bears a continuous and abundant harvest of precious, nutritious peas. The pigeon pea – also known as the cajun pea – is thought to have been cultivated in its native land, India, literally thousands of years ago. It is also indigenous to the top of Africa and to parts of Asia. The Malay name for pea or bean is kacung, pronounced katjung, and the name cajun comes from *Cajanus cajan*, the botanical Latin name. This name has become as well known throughout the world as *dhal*, the much-loved Indian ingredient.

It is mainly the green bean-like seeds that are eaten. Dried and split, the seeds are called *dhal*, but the immature pods are also eaten like green beans. Grow the little tree in a deeply dug and well-composted hole 2 metres apart and in full sun, and water well twice weekly. I usually sow three seeds together in spring and keep the strongest and biggest one. The leaves are slightly hairy and compound, and a loose cluster of small pea-like, yellow flowers at the ends of the branches produce the peas. It takes about 4 to 5 months to yield, and it is a commercial crop in several countries. Undemanding and a non-invasive feeder, the pigeon pea is used as a soil stabiliser and for contour banking in areas where storms erode the fields. Often vetiver grass is planted behind the pigeon pea trees to form living bands of contours.

It is both drought tolerant and will grow literally in any soil, and will even grow moderately in acid, infertile soil without much irrigation. In many areas it survives on rainfall only. I am thrilled by the resilience the pigeon pea has, and very impressed by its heavy infestation of black aphids – it's a superb trap crop – that make absolutely no impression on the actual pea crop! I spray the aphids with any one of the insect-repelling plant teas (see page 121 for recipes), and add extra soap powder, often only once. The aphids succumb, and the little tree with its light branches continues to produce abundantly as if nothing had ever happened!

Once the tree has been reaped, chop it up roughly and add the branches to the compost or plough them back into the soil. As a green manure crop it is excellent and with buckwheat – which thrives under it – you have a superb soil rejuvenator. Everything does well near the pigeon pea, and my best green peppers and brinjals and summer rocket have been grown in its light shade.

For something unusual and completely rewarding, this precious little tree will give you much interest and a sumptuous harvest.

USES
Culinary, green manure

COMPANIONS
Brinjals, buckwheat, green peppers, summer rocket, but will benefit most plants grown near it

Calamint

CALAMINTHA OFFICINALIS •
CALAMINTHA ASCENDEN • MICROMERIA SPECIES

TO MOST PEOPLE THIS IS A STRANGE AND RARE SORT OF PLANT, AND YES, IT IS UNUSUAL, BUT SO EASY TO GROW, SO PUNGENT AN INSECT-CHASING SCENT, SO PRETTY, SO USEFUL, I AM ASTONISHED IT IS RARELY USED.

Calamint or Emperor's mint originates in Europe and Asia, and was used through the centuries as a medicinal tea, as a detoxifier and cleanser, and a treatment for coughs and colds. As it induces sweating, it was used in medieval times as a treatment against the plague. Modern scientific research verifies that it contains a remarkable oil rich in pulegone which is a superb insect repellent much like pennyroyal.

Ancient cottages had bunches of calamint hanging over doorways, as it was believed to be a protective herb, safeguarding both the home and the occupants. Therefore it was also known then as the protection plant.

I started growing calamint about fifteen years ago, using seed I collected in England. It germinated easily and I was pleasantly surprised at its ease of growing and its self-seeding habits. I have come to love it! From that day I have never had to sow seeds again as it seeds itself so prolifically, and I have transplanted seedlings everywhere. It thrives in the most inhospitable of places. It came up in my tomato rows, I left it there. No aphids, no rust

happened to come about that year, and the ripening tomatoes nestled safely, protected in their leafy nests. It came up alongside the Florence fennel. No aphids settled on the fennel, and the bulbs tasted magnificent, and so it went on, coming up next to green peppers, brinjals, onions, lettuce, strawberries, and everything thrived. I was thrilled as I so enjoyed its tasty pepperminty tea taste. I made countless cups of calamint tea – just a thumb length sprig in a cup of boiling water, let it steep for three to four minutes, then remove the sprig and sip it slowly. I had no indigestion, no heartburn, no tension, no feeling of bloatedness and no flatulence. It was delicious, so I tried the fresh leaves in apple crumble, in fruit salads, on baked potato, in butterbean soup with celery and fennel, in icing for fairy cakes – it was delicious!

Research on calamint was patchy, but I learned that on excavating Hadrian's villa outside Rome, archaeologists found tiny seeds in the cracks of the floor tiles in the kitchens, the banqueting hall and the baths after a soft rain fell during the night. When the tiny seedlings were big enough to identify, the archaeologists took the plants to the Botanical Gardens and were told it was *Micromeria*. There are about eight species included in the genus *Calamintha*, which was used to flavour food, to make drinks, teas and medicinal brews. It was also used to wash with, and as a strewing herb on the floors to chase flies, fleas and mosquitoes. Hadrian had the right idea – I rub bunches on kitchen counters and windowsills, on the dogs, and tuck it into the dogs' beds. I let it grow everywhere, and I think of Emperor Hadrian.

USES
Culinary, medicinal

COMPANIONS
Brinjals, fennel, green peppers, lettuces, onions, strawberries, tomatoes

Peppers

IN THIS HUGE GROUP OF PLANTS THAT BELONG TO THE SOLANACEAE FAMILY, THERE ARE OVER TEN WILD SPECIES WORLDWIDE AND OVER FOUR DOMESTICATED SPECIES, WHICH ORIGINATE MAINLY IN SOUTH AMERICA. THE EXCITEMENT AT DISCOVERING THE POWERFULLY HOT AND SPICY PEPPERS WAS FIRST DESCRIBED BY A DR CHAUCA IN 1493, WHO WAS THE PHYSICIAN ON BOARD CHRISTOPHER COLUMBUS' SHIP THAT SAILED AROUND SOUTH AMERICA.

Peppers were first introduced into India and Africa by the Portuguese. Today China and Turkey produce the largest variety and quantity of chilli peppers, competing against the USA, Thailand, Hungary (for its paprika) and Central and South America.

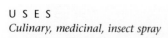

paprika

Virtually all cultivated peppers belong to the *Capsicum annuum* species, and can be divided into five main groups: cerasiforme (cherry shape), coniodes (cone shape), fasciculatum (red cone), grossum (bell pepper – common green peppers, also called sweet pepper) and longum (the elongated type like cayenne). All are rich in vitamin C, and the heat and pungency is derived from one extraordinary component called capsaicin – an alkaloid which is the therapeutic and flavouring gene. Just a single gene – if it is missing, there is no heat! Hot peppers are known as chillies throughout the world and they are rich in capsaicin, which stimulates the body's endorphins to promote a feeling of well-being. This is why chillies are so loved and cherished all over the world.

An annual, easily grown from seed, they need full sun and richly composted soil. A chilli collection is a fascinating gardening experience and companion plant to summer crops like radishes, lettuce, fenugreek, beetroot, parsley, carrots, beans and mealies. Grown in rows between mealies and pumpkins, superb crops can be reaped, and the birds stay away!

I space my chillies and paprika 50 centimetres apart, underplant with radishes, interplant with celery and parsley, and I pick baskets full! This is a real fun crop. My favourite is the helmet chilli as it is so pretty and prolific. The flesh is not too hot, yet the seeds are fire!

Medicinally, chillies have been used throughout the centuries added to food. Ground a red pepper for its tonic and antiseptic effects, which stimulates the circulatory system, eases the digestive system and increases perspiration. Interestingly, chillies stimulate the circulatory system by irritating the tissues, thus reducing sensitivity to pain. But use with caution! For sensitive systems chillies can even in some cases cause stomach ulcers. Chillies have been used for centuries for unbroken chilblains, neuralgia, lumbago, arthritis, laryngitis and pleurisy, but go gently and carefully.

A strong chilli and onion spray is a good insect deterrent, and crushed chillies or red cayenne pepper in ants' holes and around the patio will deter neighbours' cats and dogs as the smell irritates their noses without harming! For the spray, crush and mix equal quantities of chillies and pips with chopped garlic and onions, ¾ of a bucket, then top up with boiling water and leave to draw overnight. Next morning strain and add 1 cup of soap powder, shake and spray for aphids, flies, whitefly, etc.

bell peppers

USES
Culinary, medicinal, insect spray

COMPANIONS
Beans, beetroot, carrots, celery, fenugreek, lettuces, mealies, parsley, pumpkin, radishes

Caraway

CARAWAY IS AN ANCIENT HERB, RESPECTED, OFTEN REVERED, AND CHERISHED FOR BOTH ITS MEDICINAL AND ITS FLAVOURING PROPERTIES. CARAWAY SEEDS HAVE BEEN FOUND IN THE REMAINS OF STONE AGE ARTEFACTS AND THE EGYPTIANS THOUGHT SO HIGHLY OF CARAWAY SEED THAT IT WAS BURIED WITH THEIR PHARAOHS AS FAR BACK AS 5 000 YEARS AGO.

Caraway is to my mind a rather fragile herb, and in the heat of the African sun seems to do better in the cool months, so this is why I grow it with peas in winter. I sow both in the first week of autumn – early March – in richly composted, deeply dug, moist soil – first the row of peas, pressed in fairly deep about 2 to 3 centimetres, spacing 30 centimetres apart. (I soak the peas in warm water overnight to speed up germination.) On either side of this row I then sprinkle caraway seeds and rake them in gently. I cover with a light mulch of raked leaves, literally the first to fall at the end of summer, and I never let it dry out.

It is an excellent companion for peas, radishes, beetroot and sweet peas, but don't plant it near fennel or dill as they hinder each other's growth.

Caraway has the marvellous ability of its roots being able to penetrate compacted, heavy moist clay-like soils, and in its native Europe and Asia, it today still is used in reclaiming agricultural waste sites.

Just chewing a few caraway seeds will soothe colic, heartburn, cramps and indigestion, will disperse flatulence and tummy rumblings, and refresh the mouth. A tea of caraway leaves, flowers and seeds – ¼ of a cup to 1 cup of boiling water, stand 5 minutes – will ease colic, cramps, menstruation pains, bloating, and increase breast milk production. In the cosmetic world caraway is finding its feet as toner and cleanser, deodoriser and as a treatment for oily, spotty skins. Oil from caraway seed is used in mouthwashes and skin cleansers, and its deodorising properties are well documented.

If you cook a sprinkling of caraway seeds with cabbage or cauliflower or broccoli, it will reduce the typical cabbage odour, and also help the digestibility. Not only the delicious seeds are edible, but its feathery leaves and pretty white lacy flowers as well.

A summer crop of caraway is worth trying, especially if it is partially and lightly shaded. If you consider its properties as an antispasmodic, an expectorant and a diuretic, you need to make space for it. Rows of radishes, beans and mealies with caraway planted beneath the shade of the beans and mealies, could be the answer. A bean trellis tied at the top forming a long narrow tent gave me a cool tunnel last summer in which the caraway thrived. I was able to transplant the 10 centimetre high seedlings in the shade of the beans 30 centimetres apart, and I had fresh caraway all summer. It's easy to grow and prolific.

USES
Culinary, medicinal, cosmetic

COMPANIONS
Beetroot, peas, radishes, sweet peas

DISLIKES
Dill, fennel

Cornflower

CENTAUREA CYANUS

THE CORNFLOWER IN ITS INCREDIBLE BLUE IS A CHERISHED WILD FLOWER THAT ORIGINATES IN EUROPE. CORNFLOWERS ARE SO NAMED BECAUSE THEY GREW PROLIFICALLY IN THE CORN AND WHEAT FIELDS. I GREW CORNFLOWERS WITH MY GRANDMOTHER IN HER SEASIDE GARDEN IN GORDON'S BAY WHEN I WAS SEVEN. HER FAVOURITE COLOUR WAS BLUE, AND MY FAVOURITE COLOUR IS BLUE, SO YOU CAN IMAGINE HOW WE LOVED TO PICK BUNCHES OF CORNFLOWERS CIRCLED WITH WHITE DAISIES FOR THE BLUE GLASS BOWL ON THE DINING ROOM TABLE!

An easy-to-grow, cool-weather annual, I have loved cornflowers all my life and have used them in so many ways – in food, in medicine and in cosmetics – that I find its short flowering period was never long enough for all I want to do with the flowers. Most rewarding is that incredible ability cornflowers have of stimulating the growth of grains. Wheat, barley, rye and oats all benefit from the presence of cornflowers. This was known to farmers from medieval times, and the harvest thanksgiving wreath had cornflowers and red poppies woven in amongst the wheat, rye, oats and barley.

For bee keepers, especially in the dry winter months, cornflowers attract bees and provide enough nectar to keep them going – so do consider planting cornflowers for the bees too.

I am fascinated by the increased yields cornflowers undoubtedly stimulate, especially to grains. Some years ago I planted a small meadow with my grandmother's favourite winter annuals that she and I so many years before had collected: wheat, oats and barley, brilliant red field poppies, blue flax, chamomile, white ox eye daisies and agrostemma or "corn cockle" as she called it, and masses of our favourite cornflowers. I had dug in loads of good compost and watered it well as the cooler autumn days replaced a searing burning and relentless summer. I dug and re-dug the soil and watered it well, then raked and levelled it, and one morning I mixed all the seeds together in a bucket and scattered them far and wide, flinging them with wishes and blessings for soft moist landings and a breathtaking harvest. I then re-raked and set gentle sprays onto the little field and wearily trudged home with my dog. We inspected the field daily and were overjoyed to see the little spikes emerging.

Nothing is ever easy on a farm. The guineafowls loved the feast, the seed-eating birds joined them and the squirrels had great fun, but everything survived, and I added more wheat and barley seed from time to time which I covered well with soil. A green carpet emerged. It grew daily. My dog and I sat every morning and every late winter afternoon and watched it grow. By the first days of spring we could identify the first poppies, chamomile and thin ears of wheat. By midspring it was breathtaking and the dream was real. I cannot express the joyfulness my dog and I had walking and running in that magical, brilliant colour. The cornflowers, the most beautiful of all, made everything grow to perfection.

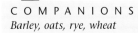

USES
Culinary, medicinal, cosmetic

COMPANIONS
Barley, oats, rye, wheat

Costmary

CHRYSANTHEMUM BALSAMITA
ALECOST • BIBLE LEAF

IS IT ONLY ME WHO LOVES COSTMARY? I HAVE OFFERED IT FOR SALE IN MY NURSERY FOR MANY YEARS, AND NO ONE IS INTERESTED! IT IS A TREASURE BUT IT DOES NOT HAVE SPECTACULAR FLOWERS. IT IS A CLUMP-FORMING, LOW-GROWING, PERENNIAL PLANT THAT OCCASIONALLY SENDS UP A SPRAY OF SMALL YELLOW BUTTONS. IT ASKS FOR NOTHING EXCEPT THE OCCASIONAL SPADE OF COMPOST, SEPARATION AND REPLANTING OF ITS NEAT RUNNERS, AND A GOOD WATERING.

But oh, the leaves! Rich in minty, camphory refreshing oils, it smells divine, tastes delicious and offers so much I am astonished so few are impressed! Let me extol its remarkable properties! Costmary is an ancient plant. In the Middle Ages it came into its own as a flavouring for ale (its common name then was alecost) and as a strewing herb on which one walked to refresh and cleanse the room. It was also known as Bible leaf, as leaves were pressed between the pages of the Bible to keep moths and fish moths away, and to scent the pages of the Bible with that minty fragrance that helped to keep the congregation awake during long and often boring sermons!

Used by the monks in ancient medicines, costmary was a respected and revered herb as the leaves could be used as a poultice over bee and wasp stings to reduce the swelling. A tea of costmary is still taken to this day in its native Europe and Asia to relieve coughs and colds, stomach upsets and fevers. Made with cloves and honey, "Sweet Mary Tea" was taken as a panacea for flu, bronchitis, indigestion and cramps, and all sorts of other ailments. The fresh leaves boiled up in water made superb hair rinses, washes and bath additions to soften the skin, and leaves were steeped in oil as a rub for aching feet and legs. Costmary was an important herb in the cloister gardens and can still be found there today.

I add the lovely fresh tender leaves – just one or two finely chopped – to salads, fruit salads, soups and custard, stir-fries and fruit tarts and cakes. The delicious spearminty taste is refreshing in cool drinks with lemon, and in hot teas with honey and lemon. My favourite way to use costmary is to stew a leaf with quinces or apples and chop a little into fresh cream poured over baked apples!

Add costmary leaves to the bath, to the laundry rinsing water, to the tumble drier – tie a handful of the soft fresh leaves in an old stocking or pantyhose leg and toss it into the tumble drier with some fresh lavender – the scent is simply beautiful!

Plant it in full sun in well-composted, deeply dug soil alongside beans, pumpkins, radishes and nasturtiums, and walk on it while you work in the vegetable garden. It will scent the air and chase whitefly, aphids and even voracious beetles. One of my favourite sprays, which is an excellent general spray, is to combine fresh basil sprigs – any of the basils will do – tansy leaves and southernwood sprigs with costmary leaves, roughly equal quantities of both, cover with boiling water and stand overnight. Next morning strain, throw the herbs onto the compost heap and for every bucket of brew add ½ a cup of soap powder. Spray liberally into ants' holes, on aphid infestations, onto whitefly, red spider – anywhere – and think about costmary.

USES
Culinary, medicinal, insect repellent

COMPANIONS
Beans, nasturtiums, pumpkins, radishes

Pyrethrum

PYRETHRUM HAS TO BE ONE OF THE WORLD'S BEST-KNOWN NATURAL INSECTICIDES. ORIGINATING IN EUROPE IN A SMALL AREA CALLED DALMATIA, IT IS NOW CULTIVATED COMMERCIALLY IN AFRICA, CENTRAL EUROPE, THE FAR EAST AND AMERICA, AND MANY COMMERCIAL INSECTICIDES CONTAIN THE POTENT PYRETHRINS AND CINERINS THAT ARE FOUND IN THE DRIED FLOWER HEAD.

Pyrethrum was used as an insecticide 2 000 years ago, and it controls aphids, codling moths, red spider, whitefly, and most leaf-chewing insects and ants and slugs. It can unfortunately be poisonous to bees and ladybirds, so always apply it late afternoon after the bees and ladybirds have flown away home. Dried, crushed and powdered fully mature flower heads can be sprinkled down ants' holes, and a row of pyrethrum grown near a patio interplanted with pennyroyal, will help to repel mosquitoes and flies.

Gardening 40 years ago on the farm was a great battle to just survive, and it was then, as a young bride, that I cultivated my first pyrethrum plants from seed sent down from Kenya. No one had ever heard of it and no one could tell me what to do. So I poured boiling water over the mature flowers with fresh rue added, let it cool, and then used that as a spray. Surprisingly, my unorthodox rue and pyrethrum spray was incredibly effective after only one application, and to my everlasting disappointment absolutely no one was interested. No farmers, certainly not my own farmer husband, and so I carried on walking my lonely path growing my little borders of pretty pyrethrum and using them in my organic garden. Forty years ago *no one had ever heard of organic farming!*

Pyrethrum did it for me. So I experimented with talc powder mixed with crushed pyrethrum flowers, and sprinkled this behind skirting boards and bookcases, and had no fish moths or cockroaches. I sprinkled this talc baby powder and pyrethrum along the paths under ferns and primulas and I could slay the slugs and snails. I started a whole programme of splashes and sprays and even dipping small bunches of pyrethrum flowers into saltpetre, the way our grandmothers did, and I lit these in a wide terracotta saucer and let the smoke chase the mosquitoes at an evening braai. (Never leave the saucer unattended.) We had no problems that night, nor did moths fly into the lamps. So I became even more impressed with pyrethrum and planted rows and rows of it. I still do, and it's easy to grow.

A cushiony tuft of perennial grey-green, finely cut leaves loves to be in full sun in a deeply dug, well-composted hole. I space the plants 40 to 50 centimetres apart. By the end of summer the first sprays of white daisies will appear. They are very showy and I snip off mature daisies as they begin to fade, and store them in a shallow paper-lined basket to dry. In this way I have a constant supply of potent pyrethrum which is safe for humans and animals. But when the active ingredients in the flower are extracted, those potent pyrethrins, these are also toxic to mammals. So in any case, always handle pyrethrum with care, and keep out of reach of children. The best part is that it doesn't accumulate in the environment. My trials in the Herbal Centre gardens show it is easy to grow in South Africa. What are we waiting for?

USES
Insect repellent

COMPANIONS
Used as a spray, it benefits most plants

43

Feverfew

ONCE KNOWN AS *MATRICARIA*, FEVERFEW IS ONE OF MY MOST USED AND FAVOURITE HERBS. ITS SHEER BITTERNESS NEVER FAILS TO ASTONISH ME! BUT IT IS EASILY CONFUSED WITH PYRETHRUM, OR CALLED CHAMOMILE, AS THEY ALL HAVE WHITE DAISY FLOWERS! THIS LITTLE BEAUTY IS ACTUALLY NOTHING LIKE EITHER PYRETHRUM OR CHAMOMILE, SO DO MAKE SURE YOU BUY THE CORRECT SEEDS TO START OFF WITH!

Originating is South East Europe, this lovely annual has been around a long time, and new hybrids have even produced a lime-green leafed one, which is equally effective as an insect repellent. It remains a loved garden self-seeding annual. The reason why I love it so much is that it is a gallant little guarding soldier wherever it is planted.

Modern research verifies it has analgesic properties and that it lives up to its ancient name as a "Woman's Herb" as it regulates menstruation, relaxes blood vessels, has an anti-inflammatory action and promotes menstrual flow. It also expels worms and eases migraine and arthritis. Often known as the Migraine Herb, its sheer bitterness makes it impossible to eat, so ask your doctor to prescribe capsules or tablets. *But there is a warning:* Those on blood-thinning medication, like Warfarin, should not take feverfew.

Altogether feverfew is a remarkable herb, and has been loved and cherished and even revered through the centuries. It was grown in medieval cloister gardens and used by the monks as a wound healer, a pain killer, a poultice for bites and stings, for aching arthritic joints, bruises and sprains, and for its ability to chase insects like cockroaches and moths and lice, and even slugs and snails.

Our grandmothers would have pressed fresh feverfew leaves and sprigs between sheets of thin tissue paper sprinkled with talc powder and lined drawers and shelves with this in order to keep woollen jerseys and blankets moth free. In the kitchen they hung bunches of feverfew and crushed the leaves every now and then in order to chase flies and mosquitoes. They even rubbed feverfew over windowsills and tabletops to keep the flies out. It was also used under foot in stables and storerooms where grain was stored, and the dried sweepings were crushed and spread under the lettuce and cabbage rows to keep cutworm, aphids, slugs and snails away. The slugs and snails would pick up the crushed leaves under their slimy bodies and literally curl up and die.

Feverfew's pungent smell and taste make it repellent to any insect it comes in contact with. If it is planted between rows of spinach, lettuce, beans, radishes, peas and squashes, it does a valiant job of keeping them insect free. Not even ants come near it, and the pretty sprays of daisy flowers make bees and butterflies hover excitedly over it.

Easily grown from seed, it will self-seed itself everywhere, and you will welcome it happily. Space the little plants, which transplant easily, 30 centimetres apart in full sun. They thrive in any soil, but can reach up to 60 centimetres in height in well-composted, well-dug, well-watered soil. The flowers are lovely and long lasting in the vase.

USES
Medicinal, insect repellent

COMPANIONS
Beans, cabbages, lettuces, peas, radishes, spinach, squash

Tansy

TANSY IS A TOUGH, RESILIENT, SHOWY AND VERY AROMATIC PERENNIAL THAT HAS BEEN KNOWN THROUGH THE CENTURIES AS A NATURAL INSECTICIDE. IT HAS BEEN USED FROM THE EARLIEST CENTURIES FOR THIS PURPOSE. ITS NATIVE HABITAT IS EUROPE AND ASIA, AND DRIED TANSY WAS SOLD OR EXCHANGED IN THE MARKETS AS A FLY, FLEA AND BEDBUG REPELLENT.

Being virtually indestructible, it has always been found in ditches and along the roadsides, in monastery cloister gardens and in every cottage garden, so great was the demand for it. Forty years ago I brought the first tansy seeds into South Africa in order to plant under my peach trees, and to use as a strewing herb, the way it was used in medieval times as a floor covering in court rooms, public places, churches and halls, to walk on – but I wanted to use it in the stables on the farm to chase the flies!

In the early centuries, apples, pumpkins, onions and nuts were stored on layers of tansy to keep them insect free, and to extend their life – as tansy acts as a protective barrier.

Tansy is so easy to grow – it literally flourishes everywhere! It takes full sun as well as partial shade, and sends up a metre to a metre and a half flowering spikes with bright little yellow buttons, which are lovely in the vase. A big vase of tansy flowers will keep the room free of flies – especially if the leaves are crushed every now and then to release its pungent smell.

Many years ago I urged nurseries to sell a tansy plant with every peach tree (or plum, pear, pecan nut or walnut tree they sold) as instant companion planting, but that was too much for them to think about. So it never happened. They kept telling me I was before my time with all my weird ideas! Some years later an old Swiss farmer visited me and told me how he used tansy to keep his blackberry and raspberry vines productive. With tansy they bear well and it keeps them insect free.

So I edged tansy around my vegetable garden in a wide, very prolific row. This included my beautiful roses with which I make rose petal syrup and rose petal jam, and there were no aphids nor mealie bug nor whitefly.

Tansy branches and leaves covered in boiling water and cooled overnight make a superb spray. Add ½ a cup of soap powder to every bucket of strained and cooled spray, and ants and aphids will be dealt with immediately. Also use this brew to wash down kennels, chicken houses, aviaries and pens.

Propagate tansy by dividing the clump in winter, and space the new little plants 60 centimetres apart in well-dug, richly composted soil that is kept moist. The new crop will be ready to do its insect-repelling job within a month, and its strong root system improves the soil's structure in both sandy soil and heavy clayey soil. Tansy is actually quite an incredible herb!

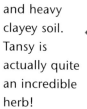

USES
Insect repellent

COMPANIONS
Blackberries, fruit trees, raspberries, roses

Citrus

NO ONE SHOULD BE WITHOUT A LEMON TREE! IT IS SUCH AN INCREDIBLY USEFUL, VERSATILE FRUIT AND SO BEAUTIFUL IN THE GARDEN THAT I CANNOT DO WITHOUT IT!

lemon

caffea or makrut lime (Citrus hystrix)

Growing a lemon, orange, lime, kumquat, tangerine or a naartjie tree is so easy that no garden should be without at least two of these fabulous fruits. It needs full sun, protection from frost, and at least 4 metres around it. In the colder areas it can be planted 2 metres from a warm north-facing wall. It needs a really huge and deep hole filled with good old compost. Set a wide plastic pipe, about 1 metre long, into the hole so that you can water right down to the roots. All citrus needs a deep watering twice a week in very hot weather.

Plant comfrey near it as comfrey fixes nitrogen in the soil, and all citrus trees thrive with nitrogen in the soil. Leaf curl is often a problem but if the infected leaves are carefully snipped off and burned, the new growth is usually back to good health again.

All the peels of the citrus can be added to insect-repelling sprays, and lavender planted between rows of citrus is a superb companion, as it keeps aphids and whitefly away. I grow kumquat trees next to lavender plantings and have never had even a suggestion of an insect on the kumquats, and we reap basket after basket of perfect little fruits every winter.

Lemon and orange leaves and skins can be rubbed onto windowsills to chase flies and mosquitoes. I grow three types of lemons so that I have lemons all year round. Cape rough skin, the biggest tree, laden with incredible lemons all through winter and deep into summer, never has a problem, bears year after year and is robust, resistant to drought and heat and cold, and its juice makes an incredible and unforgettable lemonade! This is the toughest of all lemons and should be in everyone's garden.

The beautiful and heavily bearing smooth-skinned Eureka lemon bears lemons throughout the summer, and forms a small, beautifully shaped tree. The Meyer lemon is a small tree which has smooth-skinned lemons. It is the only lemon tree that thrives in a big pot. It bears lemons through winter and into summer. It is very attractive and decorative.

To make a good spray for mildew and aphids, chop up lemon skins and cover with boiling water, add some fresh chopped lemon leaves and cool overnight. Next morning strain, add half a cup of soap powder for every bucket of brew, and use as a spray. This spray will also chase flies, especially in stables and chicken houses.

kumquat

USES
Culinary, medicinal, insect repellent, potpourri

COMPANIONS
Comfrey, lavender

Coriander

CORIANDER HAS BEEN CULTIVATED FOR OVER THREE THOUSAND YEARS, AND JUST THAT ALONE SHOULD TELL YOU WHAT A POPULAR HERB IT IS! EVEN THE TOMBS AND SHRINES FOUND IN ANCIENT EGYPT DATING BACK TO THE 21ST EGYPTIAN DYNASTY (1085 TO 940 BC) HAD CORIANDER SEEDS CAREFULLY PRESERVED IN CLAY POTS IN THEM!

The ancient Romans combined coriander with cumin seeds and vinegar and used this to preserve meat and fowl and fish. In China during the Han Dynasty (202 BC to AD 9) coriander was used as a precious medicine to treat wounds, sores, burns, boils and all sorts of other afflictions.

Coriander originates in Europe, Asia and the Middle East, and its pungent-smelling leaves, flowers and seeds impart so delicious a flavour to whatever food it is cooked with, that it is one of the top five favourite spices in the world!

Easy to grow, prolific and very attractive in the garden, coriander umbels of pretty white or pale mauve flowers are much loved by bees and butterflies. A quick annual, it is best to sow coriander seed where it is to grow in a space in full sun that is well dug and richly composted. Sow the seed 30 centimetres apart, and if you sow a few seeds every fortnight, you'll be assured of continuous leaves and flowers for the summer. The first "rosette" of tender, very tasty primary leaves is known as *danya* in Indian and Mediterranean cookery. Some market gardeners only reap the primary leaves as the secondary, feathery leaves do not have the tenderness or the high flavour that those first leaves have. So the secondary leaves are not picked. But the flowers are delicious in salads and stir-fries, and the seeds, even when they are green, are filled with an exotic taste and tantalising smell.

It is the smell and the oiliness of the seeds that aphids cannot tolerate, and this makes coriander an excellent companion to nasturtiums, mealies, dill and tomatoes.

I have planted coriander in a thick row between tomatoes and summer squash with basil on the other side of the tomatoes, with flat-leaf parsley next to the coriander and spinach next to the parsley, and I did not see an insect or notice a bite out of any leaves all summer. Besides, it produced record crops, so much so that I added a row of sweetcorn on the western side to shade the tomatoes with coriander next to it. The sweetcorn was so prolific we got up to six ears on one plant – and no birds and insects dared to even look at the summer bounty. I often think of that small field with nostalgia – everything worked in harmony, each shading and protecting the other in spite of the dryness and the heat. The coriander seed was magnificent that autumn.

Plant coriander between and catmint under the roses. It will protect the roses and look charming at the same time. I grew coriander between a long walk of pink standard Simplicity roses with catmint, and it was simply breathtaking in its summer beauty. Besides, I never needed to spray for aphids once!

USES
Culinary, insect repellent

COMPANIONS
Dill, mealies, nasturtiums, roses, spinach, summer squash, sweetcorn, tomatoes

Melons

MELONS BELONG TO THE SAME FAMILY AS SQUASH, PUMPKINS AND MARROWS, THE FRUIT OF AN ANNUAL TRAILING VINE GROWING FLAT ON THE GROUND. WATERMELONS (*CITRULLUS LANATUS*) ARE NATIVE TO TROPICAL AFRICA, BUT LIKE THE ITALIAN CANTALOUPE (*CUCUMIS MELO*) ARE CULTIVATED IN TROPICAL AREAS ALL OVER THE WORLD.

Rich in minerals and mainly vitamins B and C, melons are an excellent diuretic flushing the kidneys. It is refreshing and cooling to the whole body.

Interestingly, most melons have been cultivated on a commercial basis since the 17th century, and with careful intercropping can be grown in the same field continuously, but be sure to change the green manure crop yearly. Melons are fun to grow! Give yourself a bit of interest and plant some seed in a deeply dug, richly composted hole about 75 centimetres in diameter. Sow 6 to 10 seeds in the circle. Keep it moist and shaded, and when they start to grow, keep the strongest six plants and train the vines where you want them to go. They are fast growers. Interplant with garlic chives and mint – especially peppermint – and on a tepee or a bit of trellis, plant an annual morning glory whose exquisite heavenly blue flowers will act as a trap crop. I plant the annual morning glories on the fence that surrounds the melon plantings.

It is a fascinating crop to grow; you'll be inspecting it frequently. It's so pretty with the morning glories and the clumps of white flowering garlic chives. I make khakibos nests for the forming melons, as well as planting pennyroyal under them. As they mature, I cover them with khakibos branches bent over them to protect them from wasps and fruit flies.

One year a long vine threaded itself along the surrounding fence, and the fruit hung heavy off the ground. I made slings of orange pockets to support the fruit, and found it blemish free with no stings, and I wondered if it was the pennyroyal beneath it that grew so well in its partial shade, or the fact that it had

morning glories almost covering it. So this could be a way of protecting the ripening melons.

Twice in the summer give a dressing of compost into which bone meal and a spade full of finely crushed egg shells is dug in around the edges of the circle where the roots go deep. This seems to give the melons a tougher skin and improves the shelf life of the fruit.

In a very hot, dry spell, cover the ripening fruit with a bit of shade cloth or twist the vines to cover it – this will stop the sunburn which whitens the skin and reduces the fructose or natural fruit sugar in the flesh. I found the melons that did best were the ones shaded by the vines.

Don't plant melons near potatoes, sweet potatoes or radishes or near citrus trees. They seem to dislike one another and each stunts the other's growth. Give this unusual planting a try and make notes. Melons are fun and who knows, you may become an expert.

USES	COMPANIONS	DISLIKES
Culinary	*Garlic chives, mint, morning glory, pennyroyal*	*Citrus trees, potatoes, radishes, sweet potatoes*

Cucumber

CUCUMBERS HAVE BEEN AROUND A LONG TIME AND HAVE NEVER LOST THEIR POPULARITY. THE ANCIENT GREEKS AND ROMANS USED THEM WITH VINEGAR AS A FOOD, AND THINLY SLICED AS A COSMETIC, ESPECIALLY FOR OILY, PROBLEM SKIN, FOR SOOTHING BURNS, SUNBURN, RASHES, GRAZES AND BLISTERS. CUCUMBER HAS BEEN CONSIDERED TO BE A SUPERB DIURETIC THROUGH THE CENTURIES. IT WAS ONE OF THE MOST TREASURED OF CULTIVATED PLANTS IN THE WORLD, AND WAS USED AS A BARTER THROUGH THE AGES.

High in potassium, beta carotene and an enzyme known as erepsin which aids the digestion and helps to dissolve the uric acid that causes kidney and bladder stones, it also regulates blood pressure and is a natural laxative. So cucumber has been considered to be an excellent health food in the past, and is still so today.

Cucumber sandwiches on rye bread are not only a delicious snack but a healthy one as well, especially if eaten with a stick of celery stalk! Cucumbers are simple to grow. They form an interesting part of the summer garden. They can be grown up fences, over pergolas, up sunflower stalks, and love to be near beans, lettuces, radishes and green peppers. Moreover, they release a root secretion which inhibits weeds!

One year I grew a most fascinating "tunnel" of five lattice arches with a wide mesh fence staked between them. The arches were spaced 5 metres apart, and the arch itself had a width of 60 centimetres, which gave the cucumbers lots of space on which to climb through the lattice. All five arches had cucumbers grown on each side. The fence in between was planted with runner beans and nasturtiums, and radishes were planted as a patch edging under the arches. Everything seemed to thrive, and by midsummer baby cucumbers were numerous and attractively suspended overhead, and the beans were requiring daily pickings. The colourful nasturtiums took to clambering up between the beans, and with the shade each gave the other it was soon a cool, green walkway under the arches. I then realised cucumbers enjoy a bit of shade in the heat of the midday, and the beans kept their roots cool.

The radishes and nasturtiums acted as trap crops for aphids, which were quickly hosed down with soapy water never to return again. I strung wires all the way up the sides of the tunnel. The beans clambered to the top of the eight-foot-high arches and the cucumbers climbed along the beans. We reaped masses of cucumbers, enough to make pickles for the year, as well as cucumber and radish salads daily, and nearby lettuces thrived in the thick shade the cucumber tunnel threw in the hot afternoons. We had a daily feast and everyone still talks of our beautiful green edible tunnel. We're going to plant one again!

USES
Culinary, cosmetic

COMPANIONS
Beans, green peppers, lettuces, nasturtiums, radishes

Pumpkin

THIS WHOLE GENUS INCLUDES A SPECTACULAR AND VIGOROUS GROUP OF 27 VARIABLE ANNUAL VINES THAT ORIGINATE IN TROPICAL AND SUBTROPICAL AMERICA. *CUCURBITA MAXIMA* – THE LARGEST PUMPKIN – WAS FIRST GROWN IN PERU, AND REACHED EUROPE AFTER THE SPANISH CONQUEST OF 1532. PUMPKINS AND SQUASHES HAVE BEEN AROUND FOR FIVE THOUSAND YEARS, AND IN THE CASE OF MARROWS (*CUCURBITA PEPO*) FOR EIGHT THOUSAND YEARS IN MEXICO.

marrow

Pumpkin seeds have been taken medicinally for centuries and are rich in zinc, oil, vitamins and minerals. They have been used to treat worms in both humans and animals through the centuries. Dehusked seeds are a delicious snack and can be added to breads, biscuits, stuffings and stir-fries, and the pulp of the pumpkin, a favourite vegetable worldwide, is full of minerals and vitamins – especially vitamin C, beta carotene, calcium, magnesium, phosphorus and potassium – and is a favourite ingredient in roasts, fritters and pies. Because all squashes, pumpkins and marrows are highly alkaline, they relieve acidity, ease the digestion, and act as a bland, easily digested baby food that can be mixed with other foods.

I thoroughly enjoy growing a variety of these easy-to-germinate and quick-to-mature vegetables, for not only are the pumpkins themselves delicious and can be cooked in so many ways, but the flowers are edible and can be stuffed with savoury rice or mince, or mashed butter beans and onions and served with a rich tomato sauce. The vine tips, succulent and tender, quickly steamed and served with butter and lemon juice, or with mint sauce, are a gourmet dish.

Gem squashes served young and tender with the Sunday roast have been a family favourite for as long as I can remember, and the long marrows, deseeded and stuffed with fried onions and mushrooms and rice, and roasted, are summer fare everyone loves. And what about pumpkin fritters in winter, and butternut soup on a rainy autumn evening? Comfort food, part of family gatherings and food for homecomings, I can't do without pumpkins. They're exciting and so rewarding to grow.

They all need full sun, and deeply dug and very well-composted soil with good twice-weekly soakings. I plant groups of seven seeds in a circle in a little "dam" with a raised rim to retain the water, covered with leaves and grass to keep the soil moist and cool. Then I add around them their protectors – their companions – mealies, beans and radishes. These are all summer annuals. The pumpkin vines that I train to go in certain directions, cool the soil for the beans and mealies. Even in a tiny patch of garden you can grow marrows and pumpkins. I also plant garlic chives near them as this helps with mildew.

USES
Culinary

COMPANIONS
Beans, garlic chives, mealies, radishes

pumpkin

Cumin

NATIVE TO EGYPT, CUMIN IS A HERB THAT GOES BACK INTO ANTIQUITY. LOVED AND CHERISHED THROUGH THE CENTURIES, CUMIN SEED HAS BEEN FOUND IN TOMBS AND BURIAL CHAMBERS. THE ANCIENT CHINESE, INDIANS AND ARABS GREW IT IN CAREFULLY PROTECTED FIELDS TO USE AS BARTER, AND DEVELOPED TREASURED RECIPES THAT WERE HANDED DOWN FROM ONE GENERATION TO THE NEXT.

It needs moist, well-dug, well-composted soil in full sun, and if the soil is thoroughly raked and level, the seed can be sown right there, thinly scattered. Rake over and scatter a few leaves over it to maintain the moisture. Once the little plants are established, the long, thin leaves can be reaped and used in flavouring. The seeds can be left to mature on the fine umbels of pale flowers. The flowers are edible.

It is the seeds that are the most valuable, and these form an important part in curries and spicy pickles. They are still used in medicine today the way they were centuries ago when the monks cultivated medicine.

Cumin tea is a traditional drink for a new mother as it increases her milk and settles baby's colic. If fresh leaves and flowers are added to salads and stir-fries, it helps to clear toxins and to break down rich food, thus easing the digestion.

Cumin is without doubt quite a herb. It has a powerful taste, pleasant, stimulating. A cup of cumin tea will relieve colic, heartburn, bloating, arthritic pains, bring down a fever, ease the symptoms of insomnia, a cold and even soothe insect stings and bites if crushed and mixed with onion juice. It really is a remarkable herb, and is loved and cherished all over the world. Take 1 teaspoon of cumin seeds, pour over them 1 cup of boiling water and stir well. Stand 3 to 5 minutes, then sip slowly.

Try making a marinade of cumin and black peppercorns in lemon juice and olive oil for a steak or a chicken breast, and taste the exotic. You'll find place for a special jar of cumin on your spice shelf and you'll never be without it.

I sow cumin seed in early spring, and again in autumn. It does not enjoy the heat, so rather treat it as a cool-weather crop. It is a short-lived annual and it thrives if it is planted next to green peppers, chillies, paprika, radishes and brinjals. I make thin rows of cumin seed, spaced half a metre apart, and keep it moist and shaded. Then, when the green peppers are ready to be planted out with the brinjals I space them between the rows of now nicely maturing cumin. It's fascinating to see how each one thrives, and without doubt the bigger, stronger, more robust green peppers and brinjals give the cumin the protection it needs. The ripening peppers and brinjals are filled with extra flavour, deliciously strong and rich. I can imagine how cherished cumin must have been in Egypt and India's parched hot lands and can understand why they grew those protected fields. There's something about cumin ... I'm also developing incredible recipes ...

USES
Culinary, medicinal

COMPANIONS
Brinjals, chillies, green peppers, paprika, radishes

Carrot

CARROTS ARE ONE OF THE FIGHTING FIVE ANTIOXIDANTS (VITAMINS A, C AND E, SELENIUM AND ZINC), SO INCLUDE CARROTS DAILY IF YOU CAN IN THE DIET – FRESHLY GRATED, JUICED OR LIGHTLY STEAMED. SOW NEW BATCHES OF CARROTS EVERY THREE WEEKS TO BE SURE YOU ALWAYS HAVE SOME ON HAND TO PULL UP. THE FEATHERY LEAVES ARE SO PRETTY YOU COULD EVEN SOW CARROTS AMONGST YOUR FLOWERS.

Carrots are definitely one of the very best of all the health foods and are so satisfying to grow, as you are sure they are 100% organic. Rich in vitamin A particularly, and beta carotene, calcium, phosphorus, magnesium and potassium, raw grated carrot daily is a superb food for the liver, the kidneys and the entire digestive tract. It will also help to detoxify the whole body and act as a tonic to the blood. Moreover, it has antibacterial and antiviral properties. Imagine how your own home-grown organic carrots will boost your well-being!

Many years ago, during my research work in ancient herbals, I came across a picture of a carrot leaf, and next to it a picture of a man holding it in his mouth with a recipe below stating carrot leaf tea and the fresh carrot leaf held in the mouth would ease oral cancer. I have never forgotten it, for carrot juice and fresh carrot are recommended as treatments for cancer. It makes sense that the carrot leaf would be important in the diet too.

My most successful carrot beds – sown in light, well-dug twice over, richly composted beds in full sun – have been enriched with lime and wood ash and a prior buckwheat crop that was dug in with the compost. Slash the buckwheat crop thoroughly and leave it to wilt for three or four days first, then cover with compost and dig in as deep as you can. Soya beans or flax can also be used as a green manure here. I make a deep, wide trench for the carrots, 1 metre wide and as long as you have space for. In this way I can flood the bed twice a week. Next to the bed on one side I planted onions, and on the opposite side tomatoes edged with chives, then basil, then lettuce. Remember NOT to plant carrots next to cabbages, potatoes, fennel, broccoli and cauliflower. They all stunt one another's growth, but peas sown near carrots will thrive!

At the very edge of this part of the vegetable garden I had a row of wormwood – all the artemisias are valuable in the vegetable garden, and so is rosemary. Therefore, when you prepare your carrot beds, look where the neighbouring shrubby insect-repelling herbs are.

Interestingly, the wild carrot, a taller, more luscious plant than the cultivated carrot, grows a metre in height with a poorly developed root and beautiful heavy white lace flowering heads that are excellent as a cut flower. The monks and early herbalists used wild carrots extensively in the early centuries to treat many ailments, including cancer, tumours, ulcers, night blindness and kidney ailments. Through the centuries our beautiful orange carrots have evolved from this wild carrot. The more you eat them, the more you appreciate their deliciousness and healthful properties.

USES
Culinary

COMPANIONS
Basil, chives, lettuce, onions, peas

DISLIKES
Broccoli, cabbages, cauliflower, dill, fennel, potatoes

Carnation

I AM ALWAYS AMAZED THAT THE CARNATION IS SUCH AN ANCIENT HERB WHICH WAS USED BY MEDIEVAL MONKS AND HEALERS THROUGH THE CENTURIES. ONCE KNOWN AS "GILLY FLOWER", THE FLOWERS WERE USED TO MAKE "CORONETS", GARLANDS AND WREATHS, AND FROM THE WORD "CORONET" THE "CORONATION" WAS DERIVED, WHICH, IN TIME, BECAME CARNATION. AND INDEED, THERE IS NO OTHER FLOWER THAT CAN BE SO BEAUTIFULLY MADE INTO A CROWN OR A WREATH AS THE LONG-LASTING CARNATION. IT IS NO WONDER IT WAS SO POPULAR.

Today scentless stiff hybrids, the florists' standby, have replaced the incredibly fragrant, sprawling clove carnation once so vital a part of every cloister garden, every cottage garden and every castle garden.

The first soaps were made of carnation petals. The whole plant contains saponins which, when boiled in water, softens and foams very gently, and were used as a skin cleanser and wash. The petals were also used to flavour wines, drinks and cordials, syrups and confectionary. Carnation cultivation has been going strong for over 2 000 years!

Because of their exquisite clove-like scent, fresh petals can be crushed and pounded with cloves and clove oil as a superb insect repellent, which our grandmothers used to keep toilets and cupboards smelling fresh.

Originating in Europe, the Dianthus family is still a favourite garden subject, and although the old-fashioned, highly scented clove carnation can rarely be found today, keep searching, it does still appear, and for all its sprawling habits it remains one of the most beautiful of the scented flowers.

The saponins in the leaves are high in minerals, and this is what makes carnations so important as a companion plant. Their fragrance attracts bees and butterflies who then visit all the other vegetables in the garden, and pollination is hectic! I have planted carnations between green peppers, garlic, strawberries, mustard and soya beans, and I have had bumper crops. It seems the minerals it draws from the soil benefits everything nearby.

Give the row of carnations space – 70 centimetres – and plant the carnations 30 centimetres apart. Dead-head whenever you can to encourage more flowers, and whenever a long stem becomes woody and tufts of leaves form along it, pull off the tufts with a small heel, strip off the lower four leaves and plant in wet sand. This is a new plant! In this way you will increase your stock!

Do not over water the little plant. Keep it shaded and sheltered and moist, and it will root gradually. Once established, it can be planted into a compost- and soil-filled bag to mature and strengthen in the sun. My latest plantings between garlic, potatoes and brinjals look good. It's worth experimenting, and the petals are edible and delicious on cakes, in drinks, salads and ice cream!

USES
Culinary, cosmetic, insect repellent

COMPANIONS
Brinjals, garlic, green peppers, mustard, potatoes, soya beans, strawberries

Echinacea

THIS WONDERFUL MEDICINAL PLANT IS AN AMERICAN PRAIRIE PLANT, AND IS SO EASY TO GROW, SO STRIKINGLY SPECTACULAR AND SO IMPORTANT, EVERYONE SHOULD HAVE A ROW OR TWO IN THEIR GARDENS, NOT ONLY FOR ITS MEDICINAL USES BUT FOR ITS ABILITY, VERY LIKE COMFREY, TO ACT LIKE A FACELIFT, A NATURAL TONIC, TO PLANTS THAT GROW NEARBY.

Several years ago I tried this experiment with two farmers. Both grew paprika and green peppers through the summer. The one farmer had quite depleted soil, and short of adding strong chemical fertilisers which he was afraid to do as he had established himself as an organic grower, he needed to boost his yields. So he agreed to plant a test run. Comfrey was too big for between the rows and would hamper his ploughing as he planted twice a season, but the more compact echinacea, although perennial, could be ploughed out and replanted quickly and easily. So for every five rows of green peppers, he planted a row of echinacea with five rows of paprika on the other side. He also ploughed in a light spread of freshly cut comfrey leaves with his usual compost and cow manure, five rows green pepper, one row echinacea, five rows paprika, one row echinacea, and so on.

The other farmer on a nearby farm 2 kilometres away, just used chemical fertiliser between his rows of green peppers and paprika. They both had similar summer temperatures and rainfall, and they both watered twice a week. Within two months the echinacea farmer was starting to reap the first tender paprikas, and within three months he took his first huge green peppers and ruby red paprikas to market, almost twice the size of his neighbour's crop, that could only be reaped three weeks later! It was astonishing! And best of all, you could taste the difference!

Comfrey around the edges of the field or vegetable patch is vital so it can be reaped often, and after this wonderful experiment echinacea gained quite a reputation. Its pretty pink daisy flowers attracted a lot of attention and its ripened bristly seed heads were distributed among neighbouring farmers. One farmer reaped the flowers for the market. He removed the pink petals, and the "cones" in greenish golden-brown fetched good prices as cut flowers.

Echinacea can be grown as a rewarding perennial cut flower. My own experiments of it next to sacred basil and honesty were wonderfully successful – each seemed to set the other off beautifully, and they looked simply marvellous together. Brinjals grown next to echinacea have a brighter skin, grow quickly and do not have any bitterness if they are reaped while still tender.

Sow the seeds in trays of moist sand, and plant the little seedlings into bags of compost once they are big enough to handle. Keep them in partial shade, moving them further into the sun for longer times each day until they are hardened off and ready to plant in the field. They need full sun and compost-enriched, well-dug soil. Space the plants 40 centimetres apart.

Use the flowers and leaves in a tea: ¼ to 1 cup of boiling water, stand 5 minutes, then strain and take 1 cup daily for boosting the immune system as it has antiviral, antibiotic properties. Do not take it all the time, only when you are fighting flu or bronchitis. Use the cooled tea as a wash for skin ailments and a hair rinse, and add some to the bath. Echinacea is an incredible plant!

USES
Medicinal, cut flower

COMPANIONS
Benefits most plants grown near it

Buckwheat

BUCKWHEAT REALLY IS AN ASTONISHING PLANT. IT GROWS EASILY AND IN THE POOREST OF SOILS, IT GROWS QUICKLY AGAINST HEAT AND DROUGHT AND COLD WINDS AND STORMS, AND IT STANDS UP BRAVELY AGAINST ALL BUFFETING AND JUST KEEPS GOING – THE MORE YOU PICK, THE MORE IT GROWS, THE MORE YOU CRUSH IT, THE MORE IT PERKS UP. IT YIELDS SUCH AN ABUNDANT AND LUSH CROP OF TENDER, DELICIOUS LEAVES AND FLOWERS FOR SO MANY MONTHS, YOU CANNOT BUT HELP TO GIVE IT A SALUTE! BUCKWHEAT IS A SURVIVOR!

A quick annual, buckwheat is native to Northern Europe and Asia, and has been China's staple food for over 1 000 years. It is still Russia's staple food today. It is an excellent source of protein, thiamin, iron, niacin, calcium, magnesium, potassium and sodium, and the rare and very important rutin which tones the walls of the blood vessels.

For centuries it has been grown as the companion plant to corn (maize) in Europe, and it is possibly one of the most easily grown of the cereal crops as it loosens clayey, compacted turf soils which it penetrates and makes friable. It is a perfect green manure crop as it stores calcium, potassium and magnesium so effectively in its leaves it immediately enriches and sweetens the soil once it is dug in. Often it is used purely as a green manure crop, especially if the land has been over-worked. It grows so quickly, and often only needs six or seven weeks before it is slashed back into the soil.

Buckwheat does well next to barley, oats and rye, but is strongly antagonistic towards wheat – so never plant them together. I grow buckwheat next to globe artichokes, as each enhances the other's growth. The fresh leaves and flowers of buckwheat are delicious in salads with artichoke hearts and lots of fresh lemon juice. Add the flowers to soups, salads, stir-fries, drinks and stews – the little soft green-and-pink heart-shaped seeds can be eaten fresh too.

Buckwheat helps to clear haemorrhaging in the retina of the eye, and will warm cold hands and feet. It also assists in lowering high blood pressure.

Sow buckwheat in shallow drills – a furrow scraped out

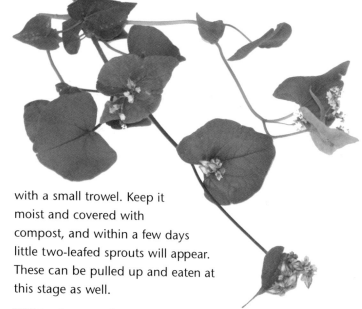

with a small trowel. Keep it moist and covered with compost, and within a few days little two-leafed sprouts will appear. These can be pulled up and eaten at this stage as well.

Within three weeks the plants are substantial and the tender leaves are delicious, waiting to be eaten in pretty salads. Last winter I grew, in full sun in lightly composted soil, a most fascinating crop, and each seemed to boost the one next to it. I chose barley, buckwheat, rye, blue flax (linseed) and oats. All grow to the same height and the blue flax flowers and the white buckwheat flowers had the winter bees humming. I had red Flanders poppies on each end of the rows which framed it all in brilliant red. It was simply beautiful, and visitors watched in amazement as we picked green oats for teas, buckwheat flowers, flax flowers and poppies for salads and stir-fries, and big bunches of barley and rye to fill the urns as winter flower arrangements. Try it – it's so easy to grow.

USES
Culinary, medicinal, green manure

COMPANIONS
Barley, globe artichokes, flax, maize, oats, rye

DISLIKES
Wheat

Fennel

NO GARDEN SHOULD EVER BE WITHOUT FENNEL! IT IS NOT ONLY AN EYE-CATCHING, BEAUTIFUL, FINE-LEAVED PLANT, BUT THE BEES, BUTTERFLIES AND LADYBIRDS LOVE IT! FENNEL IS A SUPERB HEALTH FOOD AND MEDICINAL AND COSMETIC HERB THAT STANDS ALONE IN ITS SIZE, ITS VIGOUR AND ITS EASY GROWING ABILITIES.

Be aware of the different fennels that are all easily grown from seed: ordinary fennel (*Foeniculum vulgare*) is a tough biennial and in warmer parts of the country even a perennial. It grows to 1 metre in height and often width, and is a mass of fine feathery leaves, thick, prolific and weather resistant. The yellow umbels of flowers are edible, deliciously chewable and will sweeten the breath, as will the seeds, which are abundant most of the year.

ordinary fennel

The Florence fennel (*Foeniculum vulgare* var. *dulce*) has a thick, bulbous, succulent base to the stem which is delicious in cooking, and this is the fennel that is mostly grown for the market in many countries. The bulb can be shaved thinly into soups, salads and stir-fries. The leaves of Florence fennel can be used in teas, or cooked with fish, mushrooms and chicken. This fennel is grown as an annual.

Then there is bronze fennel (*Foeniculum vulgare* var. *purpureum*), a dark, wine-red fennel that is an eye catcher in the garden. This, like the ordinary fennel, is more a perennial as it can be cut back vigorously and it will come up again and again. This fennel is hardy, easy to cultivate and it takes the heat, the cold and the drought. Like the other fennels it needs full sun, deeply dug, richly composted soil, and it propagates by seed only. Sow the seed in trays at any time of the year except in the coldest months, and plant out 1 metre apart when big enough to handle. Keep the plants moist until they are well established.

All the fennels are used in cooking. It is also the slimmer's herb and ¼ cup fresh leaves in 1 cup of boiling water, stand 5 minutes, then sip slowly, is a standard tea to help flush toxins from the body. It is an excellent diuretic – two cups of this tea are taken daily for three to four days in a row, then give it a break for two days, then continue, but not for more than a month. Thereafter have fennel tea two or three times a week. Chewing the seeds will ease flatulence, heartburn, colic, over-indulgence, as will the tea sipped slowly. The tea is an excellent laxative as well. The cooled tea makes an excellent lotion for skin ailments. As a spritz for refining pores and freshening, our grandmothers found fennel a great beauty aid.

Fennel is a strong herb and should not be planted near dill, tomatoes, beans, kohlrabi, caraway or coriander. They really dislike one another, but it is pretty enough to grow far away from the vegetable garden among the flowers where it will protect and strengthen them.

bronze fennel

USES
Culinary, medicinal, cosmetic

COMPANIONS
Calamint

DISLIKES
Beans, caraway, coriander, dill, kohlrabi, tomatoes

Strawberry

THE STRAWBERRY IS AN ANCIENT MEDICINAL PLANT AND LOVED AND CHERISHED THE WORLD OVER, NOT ONLY AS ONE OF THE MOST DELICIOUS FRUIT, BUT AS A MEDICINAL PLANT OF NOTE!

The original wild strawberry from which all the masses of varieties have arisen, is native to Europe, and plants have been traded, sold and experimented with from every hothouse in the snow to searing desert heat. This wonderfully adaptable little plant has spread and acclimatised and adjusted to every manner of change. It is a true gallant little soldier, and I love its tenaciousness!

I grew my first strawberries at about the age of five, and have never ever stopped growing them wherever I have lived! Nothing beats the thrill that engulfs you when you find those bright and juicy berries under the leaves, soft, sweet and perfect, and served with sugar and cream it is true food for the gods!

As path edgings in the vegetable garden I never cease to experiment, and this whole year quite by chance I had a double row of spring onions next to my usual strawberry path edging, and never had an aphid anywhere near the strawberries, nor did I have snails – surprisingly! I have done well with beans, spinach, lettuce and even roses, and the perennial sun-loving strawberry thrives with a bit of shade given by the taller lettuce and spinach even though the weather has been unbearably hot and dry.

Interestingly, strawberries don't like the soil in which cabbages, Brussels sprouts and cauliflower have grown. The beautiful ornamental kale, and the multi-leaved green kale didn't do as well as usual with strawberries close to them.

Strawberries themselves find rosemary, thyme and the mints too strong for them and they will not spread with their vigorous runners if these three herbs are near

them. They will still grow, but will definitely not thrive, not continually fruit, and will not set runners! The worst of all is gladioli – strawberries will literally die if they are planted anywhere near gladioli, even 20 metres away!

To propagate strawberries, dig over a bed in full sun to which lots of compost has been added. At the end of summer, carefully snip off the attached runners and immediately plant them out, spaced 30 centimetres apart. Water thoroughly and keep them moist until they are well established. Then lay straw and pine needles, and if possible some of the scrapings of the soil from under pine trees, as a mulch under the strawberries. This will protect the berries and keep them free from insects and cutworms and form a safe place for the berries to ripen.

A tea made of the leaves will treat diarrhoea, diabetes and kidney infections, liver problems and digestive ailments. The fruit is the best skin treatment for sunburn and acne, and the berries help to whiten the teeth! Give strawberries a chance – they're worth it!

USES
Culinary, medicinal, cosmetic

COMPANIONS
Beans, lettuces, roses, spinach, spring onions

DISLIKES
Gladioli, mint, rosemary, thyme

Soya Bean

THE SOYA BEAN IS ONE OF THE MOST IMPORTANT FOOD CROPS IN THE WORLD TODAY. IT CONTAINS A RARE SOURCE OF COMPLETE PROTEIN AND ALL THE AMINO ACIDS NECESSARY FOR HEALTH. KNOWN AS "THE MEAT OF THE EARTH" FOR THOUSANDS OF YEARS, IT WAS FIRST RECORDED AROUND 2800 BC BY EMPEROR SHEN NUNG OF CHINA AS HIS COUNTRY'S MOST IMPORTANT FOOD CROP. FROM THERE IT WENT TO KOREA AND JAPAN AND REACHED EUROPE AROUND 1712.

The soya bean is an erect, bushy annual with pretty white or mauve pea flowers, which rapidly turn into small, hairy beans. These can be eaten whole while young, or the green beans can be shelled from the pods and steamed, or they can be left to mature and reaped when dry.

Used in Chinese medicine for centuries, it is fascinating to know that the soya bean has been used to treat headaches, insomnia, restlessness, colds, flu and measles. Its hormonal effects benefit the liver and the circulation, and it is a respected treatment for menopause. You could say the soya bean is a wonder plant, and I am continuously astounded that no one seems to grow soya beans in their gardens! When a plant offers this much health and so vast a number of benefits, we should all have our rows of soya beans.

Soya beans need full sun and deeply dug well-composted, moist soil. Plant the beans 2 to 3 centimetres deep, spaced 50 centimetres apart and cover with leaves and grass to maintain the soil moisture and to keep the birds from devouring them.

The little beans yield that superb protein, flour, oil for cooking and salads, and lecithin. The oil is further processed into margarine and printing inks, paints and linoleum. Its proteins are used in the manufacture of synthetic fibres, fire-fighting foam, soaps, detergents, adhesives and industrial cleaning materials, and if anything is left over, it is a vitamin-rich livestock feed!

Try the green "beans" as a daily salad with lemon juice – it is superb for treating late onset diabetes, for toning sluggish circulation, and for stimulating a sluggish liver and kidneys. Best of all, this simple salad helps to reverse the build-up of toxins due to medication and processed foods within the body. It lowers the risk of cancer and moves sluggish bowels. Heart problems and high cholesterol are significantly lowered with a bowl of soya soup daily – and it's delicious!

The whole plant is an exceptional soil builder, compost maker and green fertiliser. Soya grown as a "smother mulch" will choke out weeds, store minerals in its leaves as it grows between other plants like mealies and pumpkins, and at the end of the season can be ploughed in, so helping to recondition and rejuvenate depleted soil. Grown between rows of mealies, it will control mealie borer and several types of beetles, and will act as a tonic growth stimulant. It is a nitrogen fixer in the soil and benefits every plant it grows near. For the compost heap it helps to break it down quickly while adding all those superb nutrients to it.

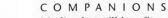

USES
Culinary, medicinal, fertiliser, compost maker, commercial and industrial products

COMPANIONS
Mealies, but will benefit any plant growing nearby

Sunflower

THE STATELY SUNFLOWER IS AN ENORMOUS ASSET IN THE GARDEN THAT MOST GARDENERS, SADLY, HARDLY THINK OF. IT IS THE MOST AMAZING SOIL IMPROVER AND A MARVELLOUS COMPANION PLANT TO MEALIES, AND OFFERS SHADE TO MANY OTHER PLANTS GROWN NEARBY. SUNFLOWERS ALSO ACT AS A TRAP CROP FOR WASPS, BEETLES AND STINKBUGS WHO ARE DRAWN TO THE BRIGHTNESS OF THE SUNFLOWERS AND THEIR POLLEN AND NECTAR, AND THEN THEY LEAVE OTHER PLANTS ALONE. THESE PLANTS ARE AMAZING!

Native to the Americas – North America and South America, particularly Peru and parts of Chile – they were grown 3 000 years before being introduced in Spain in 1514. Valuable as a source of food oil, in the 18th century Germany and Russia grew the quickly maturing sunflower crop in their brief summers for its seed, its oil and the young flower buds as a nourishing vegetable. It later spread to the Mediterranean and was used as a medicinal herb to treat malaria, to control cholesterol – by eating the shelled seeds and by sprouting the seeds which could sustain health over the long winters – to treat especially chest ailments and tuberculoses, muscular aches and pains and rheumatic conditions.

Sunflower oil does not go rancid, so it could be stored for long periods, and it has been used through the centuries as a massage and liniment oil. Cloths soaked in warmed oil and bound over the painful area were used by the monks in Europe by the end of the 18th century – and a more revered and respected plant was hard to find.

A folk remedy in Russia to treat malaria involved the maceration of chopped sunflower stems and flowering heads soaked and covered in vodka and left for 24 to 36 hours. Small glasses of the strained vodka, diluted with a little hot water, stimulates perspiration and thus soothes malaria symptoms. It is still used today in rural areas. The Russians also used fermented and sprouted sunflower seeds to make yoghurt and cheese.

Today the sunflower is still a vitally important crop and one that is cultivated in many parts of the world. I love growing sunflowers not only to eat those tender, young, secondary buds that form along the stems, but for the interest and the bright summer beauty they bring alongside the green mealies, and for the sheer brilliance they give to the midsummer garden that offers a mass of organically grown seeds waiting to be sprouted.

I watch carefully that they are never planted near potatoes, and although the odd bean does love to grow up a sunflower, I don't plant them together as they inhibit one another's growth.

For the organic farmer or gardener, chopped-up sunflower stalks are superb in the compost heap once the sunflowers have been reaped, fully mature. As a mulch on top of the heap, the sunflower forms a nutritious blanket that quickly assists the heap to break down with speed. Sow seed everywhere in full sun, add lots of compost and watch the magic unfold!

USES
Culinary, medicinal, cut flower, compost maker

COMPANIONS
Mealies

DISLIKES
Beans, potatoes

Walnut

IF YOU HAVE EVER TASTED A FRESH WALNUT – PEELED ITS THICK GREEN OUTER HULL AWAY AND CRACKED THE PALE NUT INSIDE, THE CREAMINESS OF THE ACTUAL WALNUT KERNELS IS SO AMAZING IN ITS TEXTURE AND TASTE – YOU WILL NEVER FORGET IT, AND YOU WILL ALWAYS WANT YOUR OWN WALNUT TREE THEREAFTER. BUT THEY ARE VERY SLOW TO GROW AND SLOW TO FRUIT, SO THE TREE YOU PLANT TODAY WILL ONLY COME INTO FULL HARVEST FOR YOUR CHILDREN AND GRANDCHILDREN. BUT PLANT IT ANYWAY, IT IS AN INCREDIBLE TREE!

Walnut has been used through the centuries to treat asthma, constipation, chronic cough, eczemas, herpes, urinary conditions, diarrhoea, anaemia, and it even helps to dissolve kidney stones – all this is contained in the nut!

Walnuts cannot stand wet feet and waterlogged soil – so don't plant them near a sprinkler. They thrive in a deeply dug hole, never less than 1 metre wide and 75 cm deep, filled with rich old compost, and they need a really deep watering once a week. Nothing will grow under a walnut – so it really is not a companion plant, but it is those compound leaves that are so useful, rather like tomato leaves. They can be rubbed fresh and green over the dog's coat to expel fleas and flies, and placed under the dog's bedding in kennels, the strong "juglone" in the leaves will chase fleas and ticks.

Long ago a strong brew was made of walnut hulls or "skins", leaves and even the outer shell of the nuts. This was boiled up for 20 minutes, then allowed to cool, and finally it was strained and used to water into ants' nests and cracks between paving stones and around rose bushes and vegetable plantings to control ants and mildew and even worm infestation.

Interestingly old herbals warn against planting tomatoes or potatoes or brinjals near walnuts as the juglone in the walnut's root secretions inhibits their growth. Walnuts were often planted around stables and near cattle kraals and milking sheds – just their presence would repel stable flies, houseflies and the flies that worry cattle, particularly near dairies. The cattle are seen to actually brush against the walnut trees in order to chase the offending flies, and horses seek the shade and protection of walnut trees.

The tree itself grows wide and big and it doesn't like its low branches being cropped or pruned in any way. So for a small garden a walnut is too wide and too spreading, but it is such a fascinating tree to have in the garden, if there is space give it a go. I grew up with a walnut tree in the garden and for children's love of climbing, this precious old tree invited exploration and the ripening nuts were treasures to collect.

Swatches of branches were picked to thrash onto the kitchen table and countertops and windowsills outside as well as inside, and the pantry window often had a bunch of fresh leaves hanging in it – and I never remember a plague of flies.

USES
Culinary, insect repellent

COMPANIONS
Not really a companion plant due to its large size

DISLIKES
Brinjals, potatoes, tomatoes

Lettuce

NATIVE TO THE MEDITERRANEAN AREA, THE PERSIAN KINGS ATE LETTUCE AS FAR BACK AS 550 BC IN ORDER TO REMAIN STRONG AND UNWORRIED, ALERT AND CLEVER, AND THE GREEKS AND ROMANS THEN ATE IT WITH MEAT AND COOKED INTO GRUELS OR SOUPS TO GIVE THEM STRENGTH AND WELLNESS. THE GARDEN LETTUCE WE KNOW TODAY WAS EATEN IN CHINA IN THE 5TH CENTURY, AND THE OAK LEAF AND CURLY LETTUCES APPEARED AS LONG AGO AS 1387! EVEN COLUMBUS TOOK LETTUCE TO THE NEW WORLD – IT'S BEEN AROUND A LONG TIME!

Today there are many fabulous varieties to grow and to choose from. Try growing a few of each one. Create incredible salads with the many kinds. It's simply a delight to get the vegetable garden ready for the autumn and winter plantings. Dig in masses of compost and old rotted manure, dig deeply a second time, and keep the soil moist, and then work out a design – I grow the curly-leaf lettuce next to the almost wine-red oak leaf, next to a row of carrots, then butter lettuce, radishes, green oak leaf lettuce, a row of Lollo Rosso lettuce, then a row of drum head cabbages, a row of iceberg lettuce, next to that a row of beetroot, then another frilly green Sherwood lettuce, and Chinese cabbage with strawberries next to it, and so on. The rows look simply amazing, and the colours mark the lines beautifully.

The new cut-and-come-again lettuces are really worth growing as you pick off the outer leaves only, even when they are quite tiny, and the rest of it keeps growing. They all retain their shape well and they're tender and delicious. Before long you'll be a lettuce lover!

Unfortunately, lots of other things love lettuce too for its tenderness – slugs and snails are first on the list. So save every eggshell you can, and when you have a good quantity, turn them all onto a baking tray and push the tray into the oven after you've baked a cake or cooked a roast and the oven is switched off. The remaining heat will dry out the eggshells, making them easy to crush. Sprinkle the crushed eggshells around the lettuces to deter the slugs and snails – their slimy under-bodies pick up the crushed shells and they can't get rid of them so they don't go any further.

Water well two or even three times a week and pick frequently. Lettuce is an excellent source of all the B vitamins, as well as vitamins A and C. It is rich in beta carotene, high in calcium (containing almost as much calcium as milk), it contains folic acid, magnesium and potassium. The benefits of eating a large plate of lettuce daily is that lettuce has excellent antispasmodic properties, and the leaves contain silicon which strengthens the joints, the bones and the connective tissue. Lettuce also is calming, soothing and quietening. In the early centuries wild lettuce was boiled in milk and fed to babies to calm fretfulness and to ease colic. Medical science has found lettuce to have sedative qualities.

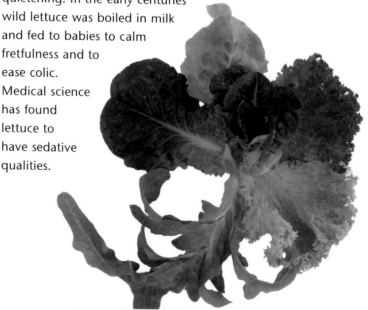

USES
Culinary, medicinal

COMPANIONS
Beetroot, cabbages, carrots, radishes, strawberries

Bay

ANCIENT, REVERED AND MAGICAL, NATIVE TO THE MEDITERRANEAN REGION AND SOUTHERN EUROPE, WHERE IT WAS SACRED TO THE GREEK GOD OF PROPHESY, POETRY AND HEALING, THE MUCH LOVED APOLLO, BAY TREES WERE PLANTED NEAR HOMES, CHURCHES AND FIELDS IN MEDIEVAL TIMES AS A PROTECTION, PRESUMABLY, AGAINST WITCHCRAFT, THE DEVIL, EVIL, ILLNESS AND EVEN THE FORCES OF NATURE!

Later it was established that bay actually is an extraordinary medicinal tree used through the centuries as an antiseptic, digestive, anti-rheumatic treatment. At one time pharmacists made ointments and salves, lotions and washes from bay leaves. Even veterinary ointments were made. My grandmother's bay sprig vinegar was splashed into the bath to ease aching muscles, to soothe sore feet and to remove excessive oiliness from teenage skin.

Through the centuries, bay sprigs were tucked into flour bins and into jars of lentils, split peas, barley, oats, rice – any grain that needed to be kept fresh for any length of time. Bay branches were frequently brought into the kitchen to replace the old ones submerged in the tins. In the days when refrigeration was rare, bay leaves lined the cooling coal box and outdoor "coal coolers" – wire cages with coals packed between two layers of wire mesh. The coolers stood outside to catch the breeze. Water dripped down the coals from a trough on top of the box with very small holes in it. The farmers nearby used a hosepipe tied high into the tree to dribble water over the coals, and inside it was packed with bay sprigs tucked into the coals and kept fresh for quite some time with the dripping water. It was quite effective, a marvellously ingenious device in the hot summers.

The bay kept everything sweet smelling.

Bay is much disliked by insect pests, and that is why bay leaves spread onto the pantry shelves, into linen cupboards, kitchen cupboards and even clothes cupboards, will chase moths and ants. If tucked into the dogs' beds will chase fleas and even ticks. A strange trick I learned as a young farm bride was from an elderly neighbour, a formidable lady who was meticulous in everything she did, and she ironed fresh bay leaves with a lightly warm iron to release the scent and oils before tucking them under tissue paper-lined shelves in her linen cupboards. Everything smelled fresh and no fish moth dared show its face, EVER! Bay and camphor trees are related, and she spread fresh camphor leaves picked from the huge tree in her garden under the paper as well. These she also lightly ironed! I was astonished!

Growing a bay tree is easy. It requires a good big compost-filled hole with a watering pipe 1 metre long placed deep into the hole so that the hosepipe can be inserted into it and the root area can be well soaked. Plant in full sun and give it a deep weekly watering, once it is established – twice a week in the hot months if necessary and while it is still young. Bay is susceptible in some areas to sooty scale, especially if it is in a moist area or if the season has been wet. Spray regularly with a strong hot soapy spray. Inspect it carefully and keep up the spraying – it will eventually loosen and dissolve the scale. If it is badly affected, prune off and burn the infected branches. Although slow growing, bay is a really amazing tree to have in the garden.

USES
Culinary, insect repellent

COMPANIONS
Bay gives dense shade and is a heavy feeder, so grow it away from the vegetable garden

Lavender

CONSISTING OF OVER 300 SPECIES, LAVENDER IS, WITHOUT A DOUBT, ONE OF THE WORLD'S MOST LOVED PLANTS. LAVENDER, IN ALL ITS EXQUISITE VARIETIES, IS THE TOP OF THE HIT PARADE, AND IT SEEMS THAT THIS IS WHERE IT WILL ALWAYS BE.

Our grandmothers used lavender oil to wipe over windowsills and inside cupboards to repel ants, moths, fish moths and mosquitoes. Bunches of lavender were tied to kitchen rafters to keep the flies out, and dried lavender sachets were in every drawer, in every linen and clothes cupboard, in every kitchen and pantry cupboard, and even under every mattress. In the laundry, great kettles of lavender water simmered, and when the water was scented enough, it was strained, cooled and used as a rinse for towels, sheets and pillowcases, and every item of clothing. Lavender bushes were grown nearby, and rows of lavender lined the paths. Picking was constant. Remember, the word lavender comes from "lavare", which means "to wash", and lavender water and lavender-scented linen was part of life just a century ago.

Think about it – how did they get rid of things like ants in the kitchen, moths in the winter woollies and blankets, mice and rats in the roof, even cockroaches, bedbugs and ticks and fleas? Lavender in particular and other strongly scented herbs were the fragrant solution!

My own grandmother showed me how to tie fresh lavender into thick hand-sized bundles tightly bound with string and to rub these over the steps and doorways to repel mice and cockroaches, how to tuck them into corners once those strong and pungent oils were released, behind cupboards, under the sink and everywhere a mouse or a cockroach could hide. I remember the beautiful fresh smell of lavender as part of my childhood as I pick bunches and rub the windowsills with it today, and I become seven years old again!

No garden can be without lavender! As an insect repellent, choose the English type of lavender like 'Grosso' or 'Margaret Roberts' *Intermedia* or spike lavenders such as "Grandmother's lavender". All of these are high in "camphorenes" which are good insect and rodent repellents.

Plant lavender around the vegetable gardens as a bee and butterfly lure, and mice, ticks and fleas will not come near! Interestingly, whatever plant is near lavender, you will notice it will be free of aphids, whitefly and even mildew, and if lavender circles vegetable gardens or chicken runs or aviaries, you can rest assured there will be no lurking mice or rats or fleas or any other insect around – they all hate the smell of lavender. So no wonder lavender was one of the best "strewing herbs" used to cover the floors of every castle and home and church in medieval times.

Lavender has antibacterial and antiseptic properties and is one of the most precious calming and quietening herbs ever known. Don't delay – grow it today!

USES
Culinary, medicinal, cosmetic, insect and pest repellent

COMPANIONS
Benefits all plants growing near it

Lovage

LOVAGE IS A FABULOUS PERENNIAL HERB TO GROW. I AM ALWAYS ASTONISHED AT HOW RARELY IT IS GROWN AND HOW LITTLE IT IS KNOWN. BUT ONCE YOU'VE GOT THE TASTE OF ITS RICH AND REMARKABLE FLAVOUR, YOU'LL BE AS THRILLED WITH IT AS THE ANCIENT GREEKS AND ROMANS WERE.

Native to the Mediterranean area and South West Asia, lovage was used both fresh and dried in the early centuries as a food flavouring and, importantly, as a medicine. The Romans preserved the leaves in vinegar for year-round flavouring, as it dies down in mid-winter in very cold areas. The medieval monks and priests grew it in the cloister gardens for treating the sick and to heal wounds and grazes, and as a tea for nausea, vomiting and particularly after over-imbibing! In Europe, lovage seeds steeped in brandy is still used today to treat aching joints, arthritic pains, colic, chilblains and poor circulation – but only 2 teaspoons of fresh leaves in half a cup of boiling water. Stand 5 minutes and sip slowly once a day!

Lovage acts as a tonic to plants grown nearby, and for convalescents, for the over-stressed and for those with chest ailments. Medical science proves those ancient treatments were indeed effective. Lovage is still used today to treat sore throats, chesty coughs, to ease fevers, clear spotty skins, soothe rheumatism and treat kidney and bladder ailments. Added finely chopped to the daily salad, lovage not only gives that rich distinctive delicious taste, but it forms the base for many commercial sauces, soups and dressings. So its common name, "The Maggi herb", is probably more familiar than the word lovage.

Growing lovage is a pleasure as it quite likes a little light shade where few other herbs thrive, but it is a deep-rooted heavy feeder, so it does need a lot of compost and a thorough watering (twice weekly, and three times a week in hot weather). Twice yearly give it a big bucket of rich compost dug in well, and trim off the tall (up to 1 metre high) seed and flower heads once the seeds have ripened and are drying out. Lovage only propagates from seed, so store the seeds in a screw-top glass bottle once they are completely dry.

I grow a row of lovage in the centre of a wide bed in my kitchen garden. I have a long fence for beans in summer and peas in winter on either side of it, and in this way its roots are kept beautifully shaded and the garden always looks neat and manageable, and the beans and peas, protected by the lovage, grow pest free and prolifically. Brinjals and green peppers and chillies do well in the vicinity of lovage, and its tonic action on all nearby plants is often quite evident, so it's worth growing everywhere. Commercial growers of St Joseph's lilies in Europe grow lovage near them to ensure many flowers. They plant one row of lovage seedlings every 8 to 10 rows of the lily corms.

The pretty yellowy-green lace flowers occur in double umbels and are delicious in pickles and sauces. So get to know this remarkable plant and add the fresh leaves to your cooking for that fresh celery-like flavour.

USES
Culinary, medicinal

COMPANIONS
All plants but especially beans, brinjals, chillies, green peppers, peas, St Joseph's lilies

Flax

LINSEED OR FLAX SEED IS ONE OF THE OLDEST KNOWN PLANTS IN THE WORLD. AN EXQUISITE, FRAGILE, GRACEFUL ANNUAL, A ROW OF LINSEED IN THE VEGETABLE GARDEN WITH ITS SKY-BLUE FLOWERS, WILL LIFT THE SPIRITS, AND AS YOU WATCH IT GROW YOU WILL BECOME AS FASCINATED WITH IT AS I AM.

I never cease to marvel that this easy-to-grow, simply beautiful crop has been around for over 7 000 years, and that in the Stone Age it was used to produce both food and cloth. Its slender stems were soaked and pounded with rocks, and the fibres were woven. In ancient Egypt it was grown to produce the linen cloth in which the mummies were bound.

The flowers and the seeds are edible, and grown in the vegetable garden it draws the bees who are entranced by its sky blue flowers, as are the butterflies – so yield and pollination of the vegetables are hugely increased by its presence.

My grandmother loved flax and grew it in her terraced sea gardens, reaping the seeds every autumn, which she crushed to clean. My sister and I helped her soak the slippery little shiny dark-brown seeds in warm milk and pounded them in her big china bowl with a china pestle for our oats porridge in the winter mornings. Once you've eaten linseed this way you'll be enthusiastically "addicted" to it, and yearn for it mixed into creamy oats porridge with honey and warm milk on winter mornings all through your life!

Dig a trench about 40 centimetres wide in full sun and fill it with compost. Moisten it well, rake it level and scatter the flax seeds into it, gently raking enough soil over them to cover. I scatter a light layer of leaves and grass over the seeds to keep them shaded and moist while they germinate, and I spray the whole area with a fine spray morning and afternoon until the tiny seeds push up sturdy growth through their cool blanket of leaves and grass. Thereafter I water once a day or even alternate days – the secret is never to let them dry out.

Alongside the row of flax I sow a wide row of carrots done in the same way – in a well-dug, richly composted trench and the seed scattered in at the same time. In this way I can water both together. A row of big, sweet carrots will be the reward. On the opposite side of the flax row, plant a row of potatoes, as the flax will keep potato beetle away and increase the size of the potatoes as it does the carrots.

The flax will ripen into round seedpods bursting with linseed which are rich in vitamins A, B, D and E, minerals and amino acids. Reap the seeds when the whole plant is golden and dry, and add them to everything – cakes, breads, muesli, yoghurt – and sprinkle into stir-fries, casseroles and desserts. The precious flax seed oil bought from health shops can be added to olive oil for a tasty salad dressing to treat a host of ailments including arthritis, bladder infections and chronic coughs, and the build-up of fatty deposits in the body. Sow flax at any time of the year all through the year – this is one of nature's miracle crops.

USES
Culinary, medicinal

COMPANIONS
Carrots, potatoes

Tomato

GROWING A TOMATO PLANT IS A MOST SATISFYING EXPERIENCE. NOT ONLY IS IT GRATIFYINGLY QUICK TO GROW, BUT IT BEARS PROLIFICALLY, AND A SANDWICH OF NEWLY BAKED BROWN BREAD, A THIN SPREAD OF BUTTER AND THICK, JUICY, VINE-RIPENED TOMATOES SPRINKLED WITH SALT AND FRESHLY GROUND BLACK PEPPER HAS TO BE ONE OF THE WORLD'S BEST LOVED COMFORT FOODS! IT CERTAINLY IS MY ABSOLUTE FAVOURITE!

When I come home too late, too tired and too worried to eat, this lifesaver sandwich and a good cup of tea put me into a calmer place, and within a short while I feel better. A friend who is a research biochemist said it is because of the high beta carotene in the tomato with its calcium, magnesium, phosphorus and folic acid content and its richness in vitamins A and C that calms and settles the anxiety, fatigue and tension. Whatever it is, I often gather with much gratitude enough little ripening tomatoes by torch light for just this sandwich.

The tomato is alkaline, not acidic, especially the home-grown ones! I have had this theory for a long time! If you are arthritic and fear eating tomatoes, grow your own organically. You will be able to enjoy them cooked with onions for a delicious pasta sauce with a pinch of crushed caraway and coriander seed and a teaspoon of fresh thyme – and you'll be amazed.

Tomatoes are also rich in lycopene, a powerful antioxidant, which is believed to be even more effective than beta carotene. So, for treating many debilitating diseases, including cancer, the tomato is all-important. It originated in South America, and the name tomato came originally from the Mexican word *tomatl*. It was spread into Europe by the Spanish and Portuguese in the early part of the 18th century, and from there through the rest of the world. At the end of the 18th century it was listed as an ornamental plant in the catalogues of a famous Parisian horticultural merchant. It took the world by storm and soon was grown in hothouses throughout Europe. Today there are many cultivars, and the huge beefsteak tomato still remains popular, as well as the ox heart and the tiny red cherries, those easy-to-grow little ones that every gardener should try just for the fun of it!

Tomatoes do well with onions, chives, parsley, basil and sage, and with marigolds, celery and carrots. With stinging nettles nearby, the tomatoes do exceptionally well as the stinging nettle root exudations stimulate the tomato vine into bearing more fruit. But don't plant fennel or kohlrabi near them – they will stunt the growth of the vines.

When tomato vines seem to be past their best, water in a strong nettle tea. Use gloves and pick a bucket full of nettles and add half a bucket of comfrey leaves. Cover with boiling water. Next morning water the whole bucket in around the plants, the leaves of the nettles and comfrey included. Lightly dug in around the roots. This often acts as a tonic, and a smaller new crop of tomatoes quickly appears. Tomatoes thrive with a mulch of their own leaves, and grow well in the same place year after year with a good, deep digging of compost and tomato leaves in between plantings.

cherry tomatoes

USES
Culinary, plant tonic

COMPANIONS
African marigolds, basil, carrots celery, chives, onions, parsley, sage, stinging nettles

DISLIKES
Fennel, kohlrabi

Apple

ALL APPLES, FROM THE SOUR LITTLE CRAB APPLES TO THE BIGGEST AND MOST SUCCULENT OF ALL APPLES, ARE ONE OF OUR MOST VITAL FOOD CROPS AND HAVE BEEN SO FOR MANY CENTURIES BEFORE CHRIST.

"An apple a day keeps the doctor away," our grandmothers used to say, and this was never more true than it is now, as the pectin in a well-washed or peeled apple (as most commercial varieties of apple are often heavily sprayed) helps to clear irradiation from the body, and its high vitamin and mineral content, especially vitamin C, makes it a marvellous health food.

Apple trees thrive in the cooler areas of the country, and prefer well-drained acid soil, yet even in a hot area it is worth experimenting, as often a crab apple will thrive – also requiring well-drained soil and a mulch of veld grass or hay roughly chopped up. Clover planted between apple trees was considered to be better than grass. Should the grass take over it needs to be kept mown or, better still, dug out, as grass is believed to inhibit bud formation.

A small apple orchard is a treasure you will never tire of, especially if it is underplanted with nasturtiums to lure away black aphids, with wallflowers, blue flax and foxgloves in spring, African marigolds in summer, and chives, which will all help to sweeten the apples and prevent apple scab, and to ensure even ripening.

A spray made of chives, crushed garlic and onions, tansy and our strong-smelling African marigolds is an excellent monthly treatment to keep aphids, scale, apple scab and brown rot away. Pour 1 large bucket of boiling water over 1 bucket of a mixture of any of the above. Leave it to stand overnight. Next morning strain, add 1 cup of soap powder, mix well, then splash or spray the whole tree.

A mulch or a strong tea of clover, particularly red clover, packed or watered well around the trunk, with a little apple cider vinegar – about 1½ cups – acts as a tonic. A blanket of leaf mould or leaf compost made only with rotted down leaves packed around the trunk helps to retain the acidity of the soil.

Don't plant carrots, potatoes or tomatoes near apple trees, as it is thought that the tiny amounts of ethylene gas that apples exude stunts their growth and spoils their flavour and the shape of the carrots and potatoes. Sweet peppers and brinjals also do not grow well near apple trees.

Wallflowers (Cheiranthus), are an excellent apple orchard flower, and act as a protection and a tonic to the apple tree. The Romans used crushed wallflowers as a bed on which to store apples for the winter, as the precious oils in the flowers protect the apples from rotting and also protect the apple blossoms.

wallflower

USES
Culinary, medicinal

COMPANIONS
African marigolds, blue flax, chives, clover, foxgloves, nasturtiums, wallflowers

DISLIKES
Brinjals, carrots, potatoes, sweet peppers, tomatoes

Chamomile

THIS MUCH-LOVED, VERY ANCIENT HERB FROM EUROPE HAS BEEN USED AS A SLEEP-INDUCING MEDICINE, A CALMING, PEACEFUL HERB, A NATURAL ASPIRIN AND AN ANTI-INFLAMMATORY, AS WELL AS A TREATMENT FOR COLDS AND FLU, ANXIETY AND FEAR. ITS COMPONENTS ACT AS A TONIC TO THE WHOLE SYSTEM, A TRUE TREASURE.

Chamomile is a plant doctor, and everything that it grows next to benefits from its protection. No insects breed near it and it literally keeps the plants whole and healthy, and stimulates their growth.

Chamomile is a cold weather plant and under the heat of the African summer sun it cannot survive, so grow it only in winter. Sow seed in March and as soon as the seedlings are big enough to handle, transplant them into a sunny site with well-dug, well-composted moist soil next to cabbages, broccoli, cauliflower, Brussels sprouts, kale, onions and even mint. The flavours are increased, aphids don't come near and its pretty tiny white daisy flowers are so appealing, you'll be enchanted.

Research has found chamomile has high quantities of lime in it. This makes it extremely valuable as a green manure crop. So, if you can bear to, dig the mature plant (save all the seed) back into the soil or pull up once the seed is harvested and toss onto the compost heap. It will help the compost break down quickly.

Tests have been conducted on winter wheat – 100 wheat plants to one chamomile plant – and the ears were fuller, longer and the wheat grew taller. So I experimented on my own crop of winter wheat. I grew chamomile around the edges of the field and was astonished to see the larger and fuller ears stretching four or five metres into the land in the proximity of the sparse rows of chamomile. Interestingly, if the chamomile grows thicker in some areas, it has the opposite effect. It actually inhibits the growth of nearby plants. So remember to plant chamomile fairly sparsely.

Chamomile tea is a superb tonic for watering onto seedlings. It helps against root rot and gives them added strength to grow quickly. Besides, it keeps many plant diseases at bay and keeps seedlings from damping off in the shade house or greenhouse. To make the tea, pour 1 bucket of boiling water over half a bucket of fresh or dried chamomile, leave to cool, strain and spray or water the tea over seedlings or young plants that show slow growth or yellowing or mildew. A cup of this tea for indoor plants is an excellent tonic. Wipe the leaves of indoor plants with a soft cloth dipped in chamomile tea – it acts as a foliar feed too, and it can be sprayed onto indoor plants as well.

Chamomile essential oil is the most incredible royal blue due to the presence of azulene, and if one or two drops are added to a massage oil, its calming soothing benefits are noticed immediately. This is truly an amazing plant, and we need to brighten our winter gardens with its charming presence.

USES
Medicinal, green manure, fertiliser

COMPANIONS
Broccoli, Brussels sprouts, cabbages, cauliflower, kale, mint, onions, wheat

Lucerne

I LOVE THE LANGUAGE OF FLOWERS, WHICH STATES THAT THE ANCIENT AND MUCH LOVED LUCERNE OR ALFALFA MEANS "LIFE". IT IS ONE OF THE RICHEST PLANTS IN ITS COMPLEX HEALING PROPERTIES, AND ONE OF THE BEST PLANTS IN THE WORLD FOR GRAZING CATTLE AND HORSES. IT IS ALSO ONE OF THE MOST IMPORTANT NITROGEN-FIXING LEGUMES, WHICH MAKES IT A SUPERB COMPANION AROUND FRUIT TREES – GRAPE VINES PARTICULARLY.

It has a massive rooting system. Some researchers say it can go down into the soil up to 10 metres, feeding on the minerals and trace elements more shallow rooted crops rarely, if ever, reach, and this is why it is so important for grazing.

Lucerne is a pretty, mauve-flowered perennial that is tough, undemanding, and will seed itself virtually anywhere. It sends it delicate branches out for the winds to toss, signalling its pure survival-against-all-odds. It can be cut literally to its base two or three times a year and up will come succulent and tender new shoots that are devoured with alacrity by cattle, horses, chickens, ducks, goats, and, if we're lucky, health-conscious humans as well!

Rich in particularly calcium and potassium, Vitamins A, B, E, D, K and U, and the best source of Vitamin B12, lucerne has to be the star health food of the century. Sprouted alfalfa seeds are literally bursting with easily absorbed energy, vitality and stamina-producing properties. It contains 19 per cent protein (equivalent beef has 16 per cent, milk 3 per cent), and the minerals calcium, potassium, sodium, magnesium, iron, chlorine and silica are amazingly high. This is what makes lucerne such a vital tonic.

Legends of lucerne's powers have been recorded through the ages. Pliny the Elder (AD 23 to 79), recorded that alfalfa was introduced to Greece by the King of Persia, King Darius the Great (550 to 486 BC), to feed his soldiers – in an attempt to conquer Athens – for strength and vitality and energy. Many wars were fought with lucerne in the diet of the horses as well as the soldiers, and wagons of bundles of lucerne were amongst the first foods to be taken by pioneering crusaders as they established new settlements. Broths and soups rich in the dried leaves or fresh, if they found them, were both a tonic and sustaining, and gave hope and courage in times of fear and anxiety.

Grown in the garden, lucerne is an undemanding pretty perennial with deliciously edible flowers and leaves – but do not let them wilt. Add to soups, salads and stir-fries, and have it often, especially as a health builder to fight coughs and colds, to treat menopause and menstrual problems – as it has excellent oestrogenic activity – or make a tea by pouring 1 cup of boiling water over ¼ cup of fresh lucerne sprigs and flowers, stand 5 minutes and then strain. *Warning:* Doctors suggest that those suffering from auto-immune diseases should not take lucerne too frequently.

Sow a row of lucerne near the vegetable garden. It will come up lavishly and quickly. A big bucket of lucerne tea can be made by pouring a bucket of boiling water over ½ bucket of fresh lucerne sprigs and let it stand overnight, then strain. Use this as a tonic for ailing plants and pot plants, or chop up fresh sprigs and dig them in around a plant that is not thriving and watch its quick revival. As a compost activator, lucerne sprigs are the best!

USES
Culinary, medicinal, green manure, fertiliser

COMPANIONS
Fruit trees and grape vines, but all plants will benefit from its ability to enrich the soil

Tea Tree

NATIVE TO AUSTRALIA, THIS IS THE REAL THING. ITS PUNGENT AND POWERFUL SCENT IS UNMISTAKABLE AND ITS SOFT, FEATHERY BRANCHES LOADED WITH PRECIOUS OILS ARE LIGHT GREEN, OFTEN GOLDEN-TIPPED AND DIFFERENT TO OTHER "TEA TREES".

The name tea tree was given to a great number of plants that were originally catalogued by Captain Cook on his voyages. His scurvy-ridden sailors were sent ashore wherever it was possible to search for any green plant with which to make "tea" in order to relieve their debilitating symptoms. So every plant they picked and tried was labelled numerically Tea Tree No. 1, Tea Tree No. 2, Tea Tree No. 3, and so on until they had a possible collection to treat their scurvy. Those tea tree names have stuck, and the pretty pink and cerise flowering shrubs in your garden that you know as "tea trees" actually are not!

Look carefully at the narrow, strongly-smelling tea tree leaf, and note how it joins the stem, one below the next, alternately left then right – hence its name *alternifolia*. The tree itself grows up to 7 metres in height, but in tea tree oil production it is cut down to between knee and hip height yearly. It grows up strongly with masses of new succulent oil-filled leaves.

I have trialled tea trees for South Africa for over a decade now and find they suit the climate well. They take heat and drought and dry cold winds, but do not survive unless protected below freezing point. Some of the trees I have grown have reached 7 metres in as many years. They look tatty and untidy, but after quite severe tidying up and pruning can be shaped to neat and interesting focal points.

They need to start life off in full sun in a deep hole filled with compost, into which a metre long piece of plastic piping at least 10 centimetres wide has been inserted at an angle. This is to get water down to its roots, and is wide enough to insert the hose. The tea tree will thrive with a deep weekly watering and is a wonderful water-wise asset in the garden.

You can pick sprays of leaves at any time of the year, as it is a tough evergreen. Sprays of fresh leaves tied into bundles can be used to thrash over kitchen counters, windowsills and patio furniture to chase mosquitoes, flies and fleas. Lay the sprigs in the dogs' kennels, on stable floors and around aviaries – ticks, bird lice, fleas and ants can't bear the smell. A strong brew made by pouring boiling water over a bucket of fresh tea tree sprigs and left to cool overnight, then, once strained and ½ cup soap powder added, makes an excellent spray for aphids, mildew, whitefly and even mealie bugs and red spider. It is superb for pot plants sprayed onto their leaves to keep them fresh looking, clear of mites, mildew, insects and even dust, and without the ½ cup of soap powder – which helps the spray stick – use the tea tree brew as a wash and spritz spray to revive and refresh tired-looking pot plants, and use clippings all round vegetables as a mulch – it protects everything and is a huge asset to have in the garden.

USES
Medicinal, insect repellent

COMPANIONS
Its insect-repelling qualities will benefit all plants

Lemon Balm

LEMON BALM OR MELISSA IS ONE OF THE MOST PRECIOUS AND BELOVED MINTS IN THE WORLD. MORE THAN 2 000 YEARS AGO GREEK, ARAB AND ROMAN HEALERS OR MEDICINE MEN PRESCRIBED LEMON BALM FOR INDIGESTION, OVER-INDULGENCE AND TO STRENGTHEN THE HEART, TO GIVE VIGOUR, PEACEFULNESS, TO RENEW YOUTH, AND TO CHASE AWAY MELANCHOLY! IT'S STILL ONE OF THE MOST IMPORTANT CALMING, SOOTHING AND DIGESTIVE HERBS EVER FOUND. IF YOU LOOK AT ITS IMPRESSIVE MEDICINAL VALUES, YOU WILL UNDERSTAND WHY EVERY GARDEN SHOULD HAVE LEMON BALM GROWING NEAR THE BACK DOOR. IT'S A LITTLE LIFESAVER!

A cup of lemon balm tea is one of nature's most incredible antidepressants. To make the tea, pour 1 cup of boiling water over ¼ cup of fresh lemon balm leaves and sprigs, leave 5 minutes, then sip slowly. It will soothe, calm and dispel fear, panic attacks, anxiety, restlessness, nervousness and irritability. It is a superb treatment for flu, muscular aches, pains and stiffness, headaches, spastic colon, colic, especially in babies, fever blisters, hyperactivity and over-excitable behaviour in children. It soothes chicken pox, helps high blood pressure, and it eases insomnia, overstress and plain desperation at life's circumstances. Moreover, it digests the food that sits in the stomach giving heartburn, flatulence, bloating and colic!

The list goes on and on, and it's a pretty, neat perennial, that can take both full sun and light shade. It asks for nothing except a good, deep watering twice a week, a barrow load of compost in late winter and midsummer, and a trim back of overgrown twigs to make way for the new spring growth once a year. The clump can be divided and planted out 50 centimetres apart in deeply dug, well-composted soil, and kept moist until it is well established. Thereafter water twice weekly.

Lemon balm's role in the garden is vital as it attracts bees that help with pollination. Lemon balm in Greek means "little bee" and if it is planted near hives and the leaves are rubbed into a new hive it will encourage the bees to make it their home.

A row of lemon balm planted between cucumbers and tomatoes, will increase the yield and the flavour in both, and although the bees are drawn to lemon balm, other insects don't like it – aphids and whitefly won't come near it.

Plant lemon balm near cattle drinking troughs. Milk cows in particular love it and after calving they seek it out. In orchards lemon balm does well in the light shade of plum and apple, peach and apricot trees, and in the colder areas under cherry trees. Its presence encourages the bees to pollinate the flowers, thus assuring a good crop of fruit. My plum trees are always so heavily laden I often need to support the branches on stilts. It's always on trees that have thick plantings of both lemon balm and tansy beneath them. For a suburban garden, give yourself the pleasure of a plum tree with lemon balm as a companion.

USES
Medicinal

COMPANIONS
Cucumbers, fruit trees, tomatoes

Mint

THIS ABSOLUTELY FABULOUS GENUS CONSISTS OF 25 OR SO, OFTEN VERY VARIABLE, SPECIES OF UNUSUAL PERENNIALS. THEY ARE MAINLY NATIVE TO THE TEMPERATE REGIONS OF EUROPE, ASIA AND AFRICA.

Most are rampant, heavy feeders, constantly seeking new ground. They spread by means of runners and love rich, moist soil in partial shade. Our own pointed-leafed *Mentha aquatica* is one of the most rampant, and reaches heights of up to 75 centimetres in its riverside habitat.

Many hybridise quickly, and I have personally been responsible for several hybridised varieties as, when I was a young farmer's wife, I found an ideal place for a mint garden and planted several long beds of mint together side by side. It was a feast for the bees and butterflies and the seeping furrow above the little field. I started with 12 varieties and ended with over 20! Naming them was chaos and even botanical experts threw up their hands in horror! So do separate the mints and grow them in beds edged with deep collars of heavy duty plastic to restrain them.

All the mints contain menthol that is the strong scent that has alerted humanity to its amazing properties. Mint's key actions are digestive, antispasmodic, pain relieving and antiseptic, and it stimulates the secretion of bile. It is at its most superb when it is taken as an after-dinner cup of tea. Just ¼ cup fresh sprigs to 1 cup of boiling water, stand 5 minutes, strain,

mint varieties

pennyroyal

sip slowly, and you'll be amazed at its quick and strong tension-releasing properties.

Grow it wherever you can and use it in a hundred ways – don't just stop at mint sauce. Serve it chopped with everything – salads, melons, fruit salads, lentils, mushrooms, rice. Just enjoy it! It is so good for you and there is such a huge variety to choose from. We base our famous iced fruit juices on mint tea and use corn mint or spearmint for fruit juice and fruit salads.

All the mints have the same uses. Two non-edible mints – pennyroyal (*Mentha pulegium*) and Corsican mint or jewel mint (*Mentha requenii*) – make superb "blankets" under tomato vines, green peppers and between roses, carrots and strawberries. I plant a large bowl of pennyroyal and place it next to my patio chair. Just rubbing your hands over it gently will release its marvellous scent, and mosquitoes will flee. Rub bunches of fresh mint over kitchen counters and windowsills, and make strong mint tea to mop kitchen floors to chase the ants and to spray onto aphids, mealie bugs and red spider. Pour 1 bucket of boiling water over ¾ bucket mixed fresh mint sprigs and cool overnight. Next morning strain, add ½ cup soap powder and stir well. Spray infected plants 2 or 3 days running. Experiment with the mints. All are excellent insect repellents.

USES
Culinary, medicinal, insect repellent

COMPANIONS
Carrots, green peppers, roses, strawberries, tomatoes

Moringa

THIS EXTRAORDINARY TREE IS EXTREMELY VALUABLE AS A NITROGEN PRODUCER IN THE SOIL. IN FACT, I WOULD GO AS FAR AS SAYING IT'S ONE OF THE MOST IMPORTANT TREES IN THE WORLD TODAY AS NO OTHER TREE OFFERS SO MUCH FOOD AND MEDICINE AND ITS EXTRAORDINARY USES PUT IT AT THE TOP OF THE LIST!

Moringa is a small, shrubby tree that thrives in semi-arid conditions, producing an abundance of pretty fern-like compound leaves (that make an excellent "spinach"), a mass of creamy-white, equally pretty small flowers that are edible and which mature into 30 centimetre-long pods that are bean-like and delicious. These pods mature and dry into winged seeds within their woody casing and these seeds are rich in an extraordinary oil, which burns without smoking and that can be used in cooking and as a skin cosmetic. The dried, crushed seeds are used to clear river water that is dirty with organic refuse.

I have trialled the moringa in the Herbal Centre gardens for almost a decade, and find it tough, resilient and easy to grow, but it is consistently eaten by mousebirds, monkeys, baboons, squirrels and anyone who fancies a tasty morsel. So my dreams of making a forest of moringas dissipate easily, but I keep trying, for this is an absolutely amazing plant!

What other plant has the ability to treat heart ailments – the root freshly grated and added to hot water? The seeds treat rheumatism, arthritis and gout, the juice of the crushed leaves and stems treats skin ailments, and leaves and flowers taken in a tea will gently stabilise blood pressure and clear and cleanse the blood, prevent and clear chest ailments, build strong bones and teeth, ease colic and indigestion, soothe stomach ulcers, and strengthen the heart.

What other tree can offer so much food and so much so continuously? The long, juicy bulbous root is deliciously pungent and can be grated into food rather like horseradish to stimulate the digestive system. The tender young green pods can be pickled with onions and chillies and are rich in a mass of vitamins and minerals, specially vitamin C and calcium. The seeds can be roasted and salted and eaten like peanuts, or roasted and crushed to release the simply amazing oil!

To add to this list of wonders, is the moringa's marvellous companion ability to plants like summer lettuce, spinach and tomatoes that grow well beneath its light and airy shade, as to jugo beans, those extraordinary luscious underground beans that grow like peanuts!

It's a feast growing moringa, and my astonishment at the speed with which it grows never ceases. All it needs is a deeply dug, compost-filled hole in the sun and with twice a week really deep watering. One rainy year I measured up to 4 metres in growth on one succulent shoot. It grows from seed which needs to be protected as rats and mice love it, but it transplants only when it is small.

USES
Culinary, medicinal, fertiliser

COMPANIONS
Jugo beans, lettuce, spinach, tomatoes

Myrtle

MYRTLE IS AN ANCIENT HERB – LOVED AND REVERED AND RESPECTED, NOT ONLY AS A MEDICINE, BUT ALSO AS A STREWING HERB IN MEDIEVAL TIMES. SPRIGS WERE LAID ON THE FLOORS TO KEEP THE HOME AND THE CASTLE FREE OF FLEAS, BEDBUGS AND LICE, AS WALKING ON IT WOULD RELEASE THE PUNGENT OILS AND THUS KEEP ALL INSECTS AWAY. ANCIENT LEGENDS DEDICATE MYRTLE TO VENUS, THE GODDESS OF LOVE, AS THROUGH THE CENTURIES BRIDES HAVE CARRIED MYRTLE IN THEIR BOUQUETS AND WORN MYRTLE SPRIGS IN THEIR HAIR AS A SYMBOL OF LOVE AND DEVOTION, FOR THIS IS WHAT MYRTLE MEANS IN THE LANGUAGE OF FLOWERS.

Myrtle is easily cultivated and it makes a strong weather-resistant hedge. It takes heat and drought, strong winds and rains, and hail and bitter winters. It responds beautifully to clipping, pruning and sculpting, and every precious piece can be utilised in insect-repelling sprays and potpourris and bath additions, as well as for medicinal applications.

I have planted myrtle around my vegetable gardens through the years, as its pungent and strong oils deter insects and the flowers encourage bees and butterflies which are so necessary for pollinating both the fruit trees and the vegetables.

I am mad about myrtle, specially the small leaf varieties *Myrtus communis* and *Myrtus communis nana*. They clip so easily and so excellently into topiary balls, and their abundance of exquisite white, multi-stamened flowers are breathtaking. I plant them 50 centimetres apart for a thick hedge, and 1 to 2 metres apart for topiary balls, which need air and space between them.

I make oily sprays with the clippings by pouring a bucket of boiling water over ½ a bucket of sprigs. I leave it to stand until comfortably warm, then I add 1 cup of any cooking oil I have – usually sunflower cooking oil – and ½ to 1 cup of garlic powder. I mash everything together in my hands (wear dishwashing gloves), literally rubbing the garlic powder with the oil into the sprigs. The warm water helps to disperse it, and then after everything is well mixed, I leave it well

covered to cool completely. Next morning I strain it out, add the sprigs to the compost and use the now very robustly pungent brew as a splash or spray for aphids and whitefly. It acts as a marvellous insect repellent and I shake and stir frequently so as to disperse the oil, which suffocates the insects instantly.

Myrtle sprigs in the bath after a hard day's gardening are soothing to tired muscles. Use the fresh sprigs tied into a facecloth with lots of grated soap and really massage it into the skin. You'll emerge refreshed and wonderfully clean. Myrtle is antiseptic and antibacterial, so all those little spots and scratches will clear up and if warmed myrtle sprigs are placed over bruises and sprains and strains, the gentle soothing oils in it will bring quick relief and relaxation. Tuck myrtle sprigs into cupboards to chase fish moths and moths, and to keep the cupboard smelling fresh!

USES
Culinary, medicinal, insect repellent

COMPANIONS
All plants will benefit from its insect-repelling properties

Catmint

CATMINT OR "CATNIP" AS IT IS SOMETIMES KNOWN, IS A PRETTY, PUNGENT-SMELLING PLANT THAT IS NATIVE TO EUROPE AND ASIA, AND HAS BEEN INTRODUCED AND NATURALISED ALL OVER THE WORLD. IT IS MUCH LOVED BY CATS WHO ROLL ON IT, SLEEP ON IT, EAT IT AND ECSTATICALLY ENVELOP THEMSELVES IN IT.

Catmint is becoming an all round favourite with gardeners who are aware of its excellent insect-repelling qualities, and who are planting it around roses as a pretty mauve and grey ground cover (*Nepeta mussinii*), around fruit trees (*Nepeta cataria*) and edging paths in the vegetable garden.

The taller-growing *Nepeta cataria* with white flowers is excellent with garlic as a spray for aphids, and it's worth growing next to tomatoes and between cabbage and cauliflower rows. In the early centuries, *Nepeta cataria* was planted around crops of wheat and barley to chase rats and mice that invaded the fields of ripening ears, and sprays of the pungent sprigs were used as a mat on which to pack the bundles of wheat or mealies to await threshing.

Both the catmints thrive in well-dug, moist, richly composted soil, and both can be propagated by cutting off the outer rooted sprigs and replanting them immediately. I find that after a year's growth, catmint begins to look untidy. So in the late winter cut back all the old flowering sprays and add them to the compost. They break down beautifully, and then dig in compost all around the clump. Divide when the new sprigs start to grow.

Tomato crops can be quite spectacular with the low-growing

Nepeta cataria

catmint (*Nepeta mussinii*) planted as a ground cover. The pretty sprays of mauve flowers entice the bees and butterflies, so the tomato plants benefit, and with basil or cabbages next to the tomatoes, the productive rows are bursting with a continuous supply of aphid-free leaves. In the cooler months, plant catmint under ornamental kale with pennyroyal and broccoli in the next row. Aphids will not even dare to come near. Walking on the low-growing catmint does not harm it, but it releases the strong scent and all the vegetables planted nearby get the benefit.

Nepeta mussini

Sprigs of the tall *Nepeta cataria* can be pruned off and placed in the dogs' kennels under their blankets to chase fleas and ticks, and rub the fresh sprigs all over the dogs' coats when they return from a walk in the fields to keep them tick free. A handful of khakibos with the catmint works wonders, and the dogs actually smell good!

To make a general spray of catmint, cut a bucketful of sprigs – both varieties have the same properties – add ½ to ¾ bucket of khakibos, and cover everything with boiling water. Stand overnight, then strain. Spray onto aphid-infested plants and water it down into ants' holes and into the dogs' kennels, or once you bathed the dogs add 3 cups to the rinsing water.

USES
Insect repellent

COMPANIONS
Cabbages, cauliflower, kale, tomatoes, but all plants will benefit from its insect-repelling properties

Basil

BASIL IS A HUGE ASSET IN THE GARDEN. YOU LITERALLY CANNOT HAVE ENOUGH OF THIS MOST SATISFYINGLY DELICIOUS AND BEAUTIFUL HERB. THERE ARE ABOUT 35 SPECIES OF ANNUAL AND PERENNIAL SHRUBS IN THIS GENUS, AND MOST CAN BE FOUND IN THEIR NATURAL HABITAT OF WARMER MORE TROPICAL COUNTRIES. THE GREEKS AND THE ROMANS LOVED THEIR BASILS FROM THE EARLIEST CENTURIES AND USED THEM AS MEDICINE TO CLEAR POISONS FROM THE BODY, AND INDIAN PHYSICIANS HAVE USED THEIR INDIGENOUS BASILS AS COMPRESSES, DETOXIFIERS AND HEART MEDICINE FOR CENTURIES.

High Hopes basil

Basil's taste and smell chases flies, aphids, mosquitoes, whitefly and even red spider. It is powerful planted around fruit trees, around the vegetable garden between rows of tomatoes, and it has been a favourite herb worldwide for centuries, but never more than it is now, as it surpasses itself as a favourite culinary herb everywhere.

One of the most precious herbs of all is holy basil or sacred basil, also known as tulsi (*Ocimum sanctum* now *Ocimum tenuiflorum*). Tulsi's strong clove scent, released from the leaves if rubbed over kitchen windowsills and counters and over patio furniture and blankets, will chase flies and mosquitoes, and if placed in the dogs' baskets will keep them free of fleas.

Basil is literally a wonder plant, and its use as a spray for fungus, mildew and scale is making every gardener sit up and take notice. Boil fresh basil sprigs, flowers and leaves for 30 minutes in enough water to cover them, then cool. Strain and add ¼ cup cooking oil, for example sunflower cooking oil, and ½ cup vinegar to every 2 litres of basil brew. Pour into a spritz bottle and spray onto plants affected by scale or fungus, or pour down ants' holes or around shrubs. Remember to shake, shake, shake as you spray to disperse the oil. You can pour the cooled tea without the oil but with the vinegar, down ants' holes between the paving, and although you can add rue to the mixture, don't plant basil and rue together – they are serious antagonists!

Try growing a number of varieties as even the fragile annual ones are superb as insect repellents and deodorisers. The relatively new giant perennial basil I have named High Hopes basil, is so vigorous and so pungent in the trials in the Herbal Centre gardens that I am astonished at its huge presence! Butterflies and bees love it, but aphids and black fly and scale hate its strong presence. I make buckets of basil tea for drenching the garlic chives coated with black aphids, and after two days of splashing with basil tea it is all over. Dried basil sprigs tucked under roses and used as a mulch keep them mildew and black spot free. It's worth adding basil leaves to other sprays you make and it's worth experimenting with. Basil is awesome!

sacred basil

USES
Culinary, insect repellent

COMPANIONS
Tomatoes, but all plants will benefit from its insect-repelling properties

DISLIKES
Rue

Marjoram & Oregano

ORIGANUM MAJORAN • ORIGANUM VULGARE

RICHLY SCENTED AND UNDEMANDING, THESE PRETTY LITTLE PLANTS ARE PART OF A GROUP OF FRAGRANT PERENNIAL SUB-SHRUBS THAT MAKE UP THE GENUS *ORIGANUM*, WHICH IS DISTRIBUTED ACROSS EUROPE, ASIA, CRETE AND NORTH AFRICA. ALL HAVE THE DISTINCTIVE STRONG, AND OFTEN, THE MOST DELICIOUS SCENT AND TASTE THAT SETS THEM APART, AND FOR OVER THIRTY YEARS I HAVE TRIALLED AND TESTED MANY DIFFERENT ONES WHICH MADE UP ONE OF THE FIRST *ORIGANUM* REGISTERS IN SOUTH AFRICA.

All have strong insect-repelling abilities and their rich flavonoids and volatile oils like thymol and carvacrol suggest they are increasingly important as natural insecticides. They are very easy to grow and prolific companion plants.

Oregano or wild marjoram (*Origanum vulgare*) is extremely variable in growth pattern, and many are flat ground covers which are marvellous for growing under tomatoes, green peppers and brinjals, and not an insect will venture near them. I have experimented through the years and find the tougher, dark-green leafed varieties are better in the heat than the more tender, white-edged leaves of Country Cream oregano and the lime green *Origanum aureum*, which both do well in the cooler areas and even survive light frost. Any of the *Origanums*, like the tall Greek oregano, do well with pumpkins, cucumbers, calabashes and loofahs. One year my radishes and carrots and strawberries were overrun by creeping oregano, and I had a bumper crop of exceptional sweetness.

The entire vegetable garden will benefit with this lovely group of plants, and a row of marjoram will remain neat, prolific and effective even between the roses and summer annuals. It will encourage bees to pollinate nearby fruit trees.

Interestingly, all the plants in the *Origanum* genus have excellent medicinal qualities taken as a soothing tea – ¼ cup fresh sprigs in 1 cup of boiling water, let it stand 5 minutes, then strain and sip slowly. This fragrant tea will ease indigestion, anxiety attacks, menstrual cramps, nausea and exhaustion, and soothe the aches and pains and fever of flu and heavy colds. Marjoram is particularly soothing, both as a compress over bruises and sprains and a stiff neck. A cup of marjoram tea, especially after a fall, will settle and calm. A warmed compress of fresh sprigs steeped in hot water and placed as hot as you can comfortably bear over the haematoma, will disperse and soothe quickly. The cooled tea makes a superb face wash for oily, spotty skin, and after a really busy day gardening, I make a marjoram scrub by tying a big bunch of fresh sprigs into a cloth with a handful of non-instant oats which I toss under the hot tap. Then, after a long soak, I use this bag of fragrance as a scrub with soap all over, and I again lie back in the hot water. All the aches and sunburn and rough skin disappear and I emerge soothed, refreshed and glowing.

marjoram

oregano

USES
Culinary, medicinal, cosmetic, insect repellent

COMPANIONS
Brinjals, calabashes, carrots, cucumbers, green peppers, loofahs, pumpkins, radishes, roses, strawberries, summer annuals, tomatoes

Scented Geraniums

INDIGENOUS TO SOUTH AFRICA, THESE EXQUISITE AND VARIED AND DIVINELY SCENTED PELARGONIUMS, COMMONLY (AND INCORRECTLY) KNOWN AS THE SCENTED GERANIUMS, ARE A WEALTH OF FRAGRANT OILS THAT HAVE BEEN USED FOR DECADES TO TREAT STRESS, TENSION, HEADACHES, INDIGESTION, NERVOUSNESS, CRAMPS, STIFF MUSCLES, ACHING JOINTS, TEARFULNESS, ANXIETY, SKIN AILMENTS, SLEEPLESSNESS, PREMENSTRUAL TENSION, DEPRESSION AND GRIEF, TO NAME ONLY A FEW OF THE VIRTUES MANY OF THEM ARE USED FOR.

The biggest favourite remains the rose-scented geranium. It even tastes delicious in drinks and cakes, and desserts and sweets. And a cup of rose geranium tea last thing at night will give you peaceful dreams!

Easy to grow in a sunny spot in the garden and becoming more and more popular to make fascinating collections of the scented pelargoniums, there is much to choose from – nutmeg-scented *Pelargonium fragrans*, *Pelargonium* 'Attar of Roses' or rose oil pelargonium, *Pelargonium scabrum* or citronella geranium – and there are apple-scented, peppermint-scented and lemon-scented pelargoniums, and all are excellent insect repellents!

In the Herbal Centre gardens we have planted and trialled through the years a vast number of scented pelargoniums, and used them in cosmetics (like *Pelargonium capitatum* – the wild rose pelargonium that creeps over rocky places), hand creams, room sprays and massage creams. So this beautiful group of plants remains a great favourite of ours – most of all for their incredible oils!

We make an easy and very quick spritz spray for flies and aphids in this simple way: Crush 2 cups of scented geranium leaves in a pestle and mortar with ¾ cup of sunflower cooking oil (do a little at a time). Keep the oil-rich fragrant leaves (and you can mix varieties here) in a screw top jar overnight. Next morning take ½ a cup out and pour over this 1 litre of hot (not boiling) water. Shake and cool. Then when lukewarm, strain and discard the leaves. Pour into a spritz bottle, shake frequently and spray onto aphids and whitefly.

A big pot of rose geranium sprigs and leaves simmering on the stove with enough water to cover them will clear the house of smoke and cooking smells, and if you add comfrey leaves you use the scented tea as a foliar feed for pot plants, tender annuals and salad crops – as both rose geranium and comfrey are edible.

Plant next to cabbages to repel the white cabbage butterfly, and edge the vegetable garden with any of the scented geraniums – their wonderful scent will lure insects away from the fruit and vegetables – and crush their soft leaves as you walk by to fill the air with fragrance. Mosquitoes, flies and horseflies can't bear the smell of any of the scented geraniums, so rub leaves and sprigs onto counter tops and windowsills and over blankets and pillows, and go to sleep with a sprig or two crushed under your pillow.

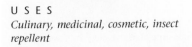

USES
Culinary, medicinal, cosmetic, insect repellent

COMPANIONS
Cabbages and other vegetables, fruit trees

Russian Sage

PEROVSKIA ATRIPLICIFOLIA

ORIGINATING IN WESTERN ASIA AND THE HIMALAYAN REGION, THERE ARE SEVEN SPECIES OF DECIDUOUS SUB-SHRUBS IN THIS EXCITING GENUS. ALL HAVE WHITE STEMS, PUNGENTLY AROMATIC GREY, FINELY CUT LEAVES COVERED IN GREY FELT AND ALL GROW 1 TO 1,5 METRES IN HEIGHT. THE FLOWERING SPIKES OR SPIRES IN PARTICULARLY RUSSIAN SAGE ARE SPECTACULARLY BEAUTIFUL. HUGE MASSES OF SKY-BLUE PANICLES WITH TOUCHES OF MAUVE FORM SPIRES OF TINY FLOWERS AND FILL THE GARDEN TWICE AND EVEN THREE TIMES A YEAR WITH SUCH ABUNDANCE IT TAKES YOUR BREATH AWAY.

Perovskia is simply stunning, and was only introduced to South Africa in the last decade or so. Our trials with Russian sage have been ongoing through the years, and our incredible plantings have inspired visitors to seek it out for their own gardens. A long-lived perennial, Russian sage needs full sun and thrives with a twice-yearly barrow load of compost. After flowering, cut right back to the base, dig in more compost and water twice weekly. It will thrive in most soils, and survive drought, heat, bitter winter winds (it is dormant in winter) and heavy frost – remember it comes from Russia! Propagation is from side-rooted cuttings from the clump, planted into compost-filled bags. It is easy to grow and propagate, and is loved by bees and butterflies.

We use it as a border next to trellises of sousou squash, melons, and calabashes, and it keeps them free of aphids and whitefly all through the season. The Meyer lemons growing in big pots nearby benefit as well.

Russian sage is planted between our rows of lavender, and this gives that incredible colour to the lavender plantings. We keep the Russian sage bed 50 centimetres wide only, and when we planted it out we gave it 50 centimetres spacing in between rows. It quickly fills that, making a continuous and vigorous row.

There is very little information on Russian sage – this here is based on our decade-long trials. A visiting Russian plant pathologist told us it is planted alongside fields of sorghum and potatoes in the warm months in Russia, and that most vegetable gardens in Russia have it as a border plant.

The long spires are cut and used in the winter barns where cattle, sheep and goats shelter, as a floor covering, which is frequently raked out and used in steaming compost heaps, and then fresh and dried spires and branches replace it with straw bedding to keep the animals warm and the fleas, ticks, ants and weevils away.

I make a superb spray for aphids with it and combine it with any other insect-repelling herbs like rue, khakibos, winter savory, basil, lavender, rosemary – whatever you have abundance of. I find it particularly helpful in the hothouse to keep mosquitoes away. We also add the exquisite dried flowers to our lavender potpourris as moth chasers and air fresheners, and we never seem to have enough. Walkways of Russian sage are so spectacular, you'll become as addicted to it as we are!

USES
Insect repellent, potpourri

COMPANIONS
Calabashes, lavender, lemon trees melons, potatoes, sorghum, sousou squash

Parsley

PETROSELINUM CRISPUM

THIS MUCH-LOVED, MUCH-RESPECTED, WELL-KNOWN HERB HAS BEEN AROUND FOR CENTURIES, AND HAS BEEN USED FOR SO MANY AILMENTS, WHOLE BOOKS COULD BE WRITTEN ON PARSLEY ALONE.

Parsley became hugely popular in Roman times during which the Romans ate it as a deodoriser. The ancient Greeks believed that the plants grew from the blood of their heroes, so it was fed in abundance to their chariot horses and their athletes! During the Middle Ages, the monks grew parsley in their cloister gardens in order to treat the sick, and it was taken to treat everything from hair loss to cracked heels and everything else in between!

Strangely enough, parsley has never lost its popularity – both the moss curled and the flat leaf parsley are equally popular, and whole farms are devoted solely to parsley production. I have always treated it as an annual, but it is really a biennial in cooler areas. It does need full sun, and it also does well in wide and deep compost-filled pots – the more you pick, the more it grows.

The only propagation is from seed, and I continuously sow seed in trays for constant use, planting them out 30 centimetres apart when they are big enough to handle. I planted borders of parsley everywhere, and through the years I have made notes and observations. You'll soon find yourself so involved in the pleasures of parsley that you'll find new companions next to which it thrives. Planted under roses in a circle around its base, it keeps aphids off, and I am certain now that black spot is not nearly so prevalent if parsley surrounds the roses. I have rows between beans, strawberries, broccoli, carrots, tomatoes, asparagus and spinach – it definitely boosts their growth and enhances their flavour.

This last winter I edged the paths all over the vegetable garden with parsley, then planted strawberries, then radish, then oak leaf lettuce, then parsley again, then celery, then kale, then parsley again, then rocket, then butter lettuce, then parsley again – I had a feast for six months.

Never underestimate the power of parsley. It is a superb diuretic, it enhances every dish it is added to (always add at the last minute), it clears toxins from the body, it is an ancient cure for arthritis, gout, rheumatism, cystitis, fever, acidic aches and pains and delayed menstruation, and it gently helps to control high blood pressure. It soothes prostate problems, the digestion, flushes the kidneys, sweetens the breath and acts as a skin cleanser, toner and tonic. A cup of parsley tea taken once or twice a day is a wonderful treatment. Take ¼ cup fresh parsley leaves and pour over this 1 cup of boiling water. Stand 5 minutes, then strain and sip slowly. Its rich vitamin A, B, C and E content and all its wonderful properties will quickly soothe the problem. Remember to chew a bit of parsley often – it will freshen the breath and tone the gums. Grow it close to the kitchen door for quick pickings.

USES
Culinary, medicinal

COMPANIONS
Asparagus, beans, broccoli, carrots, celery, kale, lettuces, roses, spinach, strawberries, tomatoes

Petunia

LONG AGO THERE WAS A SONG ABOUT A LONELY LITTLE PETUNIA IN AN ONION PATCH, AND ALL IT DID WAS CRY ALL DAY! I REMEMBER THINKING THAT IT WAS THERE FOR A REASON, AS THE PETUNIA IS A RESILIENT, TOUGH AND QUITE REMARKABLE PEST DETERRENT. IT ACTS AS A BEAUTIFUL AND VERY SHOWY COMPANION IN THE VEGETABLE GARDEN TO BROCCOLI, CAULIFLOWER, CABBAGE, BROAD BEANS AND LETTUCES. EVEN THE NEW, FRILLY, CUT-AND-COME-AGAIN LETTUCES DO EXCEPTIONALLY WELL WITH PETUNIAS, AS DOES THE ONION PATCH!

Petunias are part of the tobacco family and originate in Brazil. From the original trailing varieties that were rosy-purple in colour (*Petunia integrifolia*), to a breathtaking variety of hybrids has made these very showy and rewarding annuals a great favourite with gardeners all over the world.

"Petun" means tobacco, and petunias are a close cousin to the showy nicotianas. Both have an almost sticky leaf, and the leaves have a similar narcotic effect on humans. I have often wondered if the South American Indians smoked petunias in the early centuries, and why my grandmother always grew a row of pretty purple petunias (always purple) along the path next to the cabbages.

Because petunias are related to nicotiana, I have also grown the white and lime-green flowered compact flowering nicotianas as a trial companion to cauliflower and broccoli. In the milder winters, which we now seem to get, I have noticed everything benefits around the row of fragrant nicotianas. No whitefly, no aphids, no cutworms, and no beetle infestations appeared anywhere, and the vegetable gardens looked stunning with all the colours.

Petunias do best in winter plantings, I always thought, but in the past couple of years I have planted new young petunias and few new nicotianas in July, both in the vegetable garden, and mainly in the lavender rows, as we have a lavender festival in spring every year. To my astonishment, I have the most beautiful rare and very-tricky-to-grow young *Lavandula angustifolia* and *Lavandula intermedia* plants thriving between a vivid spread of mauvy-pink petunias. Their roots are shaded and protected, and the rows directly next to them where there are no petunias, are battling in the intense heat and dryness. It's such an amazing difference I intend to have petunias in both winter and summer in the future!

Two decades ago I was told by an old English colonel that he always grew petunias in his garden, as his grandmother had told him the old wives' tale that petunias in the garden will calm badly behaved children, and he had a group of very active and noisy grandchildren! I asked if he thought it helped, and he replied, "Oh yes – I dare not be without them!" Children love the scent of petunias, especially at the end of the day when the sun goes down. So perhaps there is some truth in that old wives' tale! I just love the colour and the prolific flowering of one of the world's easiest to grow annuals.

USES
Insect repellent

COMPANIONS
Broccoli, cauliflower, lavender, onions

81

Beans

BEANS ARE ONE OF THE WORLD'S MOST POPULAR AND MOST FAVOURITE VEGETABLES. THEY COME IN MANY SHAPES AND SIZES. ALL HAVE A HIGH PROTEIN CONTENT, ARE RICH IN VITAMINS AND MINERALS, AND ALL THE FLAVOURS AND TEXTURES MAKE THEM A DISH NO ONE EVER TIRES OF.

Beans were used as medicine, and the water in which they were cooked was saved and taken to rid the body of poisons. Every country has its own special type of bean, and these were eaten fresh and green in summer. Some of the pods were left to ripen and dry on the plants, and the inner bean was often kept as a staple food for the winter months. Interestingly, most beans are high in vitamins A and C – the raw runner bean has three times as much vitamin C as the cooked bean – and they contain iron, fibre and folate, as well as a substantial amount of niacin, riboflavin, potassium, thiamine, calcium and phosphorus. Mung beans (*Vigna radiata*) grown as sprouts are little bundles of jet fuel, and are exceptionally high in potassium. All round, beans are one of the best health foods and are very easy to grow.

Bush beans' (*Phaseolus vulgaris*) best companions are cabbages, cauliflower, kale, kohlrabi, carrots, cucumber, beetroot, leeks, celery and celeriac, potatoes and strawberries. Runner beans (*Phaseolus coccineus*) do well with mealies and popcorn, and our easy-to-grow African summer marigold is a superbly strong fighter of aphids, scale and mildew and even whitefly. As a bonus, all beans fix nitrogen in the soil, thus benefiting neighbouring plants.

Beans definitely don't like fennel and dill, and any of the

green bean

onion family – chives and garlic chives included. All beans love both winter and summer savory, and if they are interplanted with these two strong-tasting herbs – or cooked with fresh sprigs of both or either savory, specially the shelled beans – there will definitely not be so much gas produced.

The cool-weather-special broad bean (*Vicia faba*) is a stunning plant to grow. Firstly the shelled beans, once mature, are simply delicious. Cooked with a sprig of thyme, and served with lemon juice, butter, salt and black pepper, steaming hot, tender and succulent, they make a meal of their own. They grow to about 60 to 70 centimetres high, and the tops of the branches, and the flowers can also be steamed. Best of all, the old plants, once they have aged and stopped bearing, can be slashed and dug back into the soil. In this way they act as a superb green manure and soil builder. Planted with parsley and celery and strawberries between the rows, they all give each other such boosts of flavour you will become a broad bean lover.

broad bean

All beans thrive with well-dug, well-composted soil in full sun, and it's an interesting hobby to grow all sorts of beans and taste the difference. Try yard-long beans, butter beans, perennial beans, the little succulent brown and white beans, and black-eyed beans.

USES
Culinary, green manure

COMPANIONS
African marigold, beetroot, cabbages, carrots, cauliflower, celeriac, celery, cucumber, kale, kohlrabi, leeks, mealies, potatoes, strawberries, summer and winter savory

DISLIKES
Dill, fennel and all members of the onion family

Anise

ANISE IS A CHARMING LITTLE EASY-TO-GROW ANNUAL. IN THE VERY HOT MOUNTAINSIDE AREA WHERE MY HERBAL CENTRE IS SITUATED, I FIND IT DOES BETTER IN THE WINTER MONTHS, BUT IN SUMMER IT QUICKLY GOES TO SEED. IN SPITE OF THAT, I STILL SOW IT BETWEEN ROWS OF GREEN PEPPERS, BRINJALS AND COURGETTES, AND FIND THEY PROTECT EACH OTHER WELL.

Anise is so strongly aromatic that it chases most pests, and no slugs or snails go near it. So circle it around lettuce and kale and cabbage seedlings, and be surprised by the wonderful flavour in the vegetables it protects!

One of the most fascinating things I have discovered about anise is that coriander is its guardian! I found a reference to it many years ago in the American Prevention magazine and since then have planted them together, often with startling results.

Sprinkle a thin row of aniseed in a shallow furrow of moist well-dug, well-composted soil in full sun. Half a metre away sow a similar row of coriander seed. Rake the soil gently over to cover the seeds and keep them moist until they sprout. Then plant beans and lettuce seedlings and mustard lettuce on either side of the two rows and repeat. Not only will you have a fascinating garden of butterflies, fragrance and pretty umbels of delicate white and mauvy white flowers, but the seeds of both anise and coriander will give you a bonus crop filled with such superior taste you will be astonished. Remember that both anise and coriander have deliciously edible flowers and leaves, it's not just the seeds!

When the plants have reached maturity, watch carefully as the seeds ripen, so you can reap them before they scatter (wait until they turn dry and pale brown). Save the plants, chop up roughly and add equal quantities of khakibos leaves and tops, enough to fill a large bucket. Cover with boiling water and leave it to stand overnight. Next morning strain, add 2 to 4 tablespoons soap powder (I use Sunlight soap powder) to help the spray stick. Pour into a spritz spray bottle and use for aphids on roses, or red spider, or whitefly. The discarded stems and old flowers can be tossed onto the compost heap. Pour any leftover spray down ants' nests or around shrubs where ants are busy.

Never underestimate the power of aniseed – it is a really remarkable little plant and the seeds germinate easily. Those same little seeds were once used as a payment instead of taxes, and as a superb digestive which clears heartburn, colic, nausea, bloating and indigestion, but don't take in any form during pregnancy. It soothes and eases respiratory ailments, spasmodic coughing and pneumonia, and increases breast milk. Pour 1 cup of water over 1 teaspoon aniseeds, stand 5 minutes, stir well, sweeten with honey and sip the tea and chew the seeds.

USES
Culinary, medicinal

COMPANIONS
Brinjals, cabbages, coriander, courgettes, green peppers, kale, lettuce

Pine

A VAST AND VARIED GENUS WHICH INCLUDES 120 SPECIES OF EVERGREEN CONIFEROUS TREES AND SHRUBS, AND WHICH ARE NATIVE TO MOST NORTHERN HEMISPHERE TEMPERATE REGIONS OF THE WORLD, THE PINE HAS BEEN A RESPECTED AND OFTEN REVERED TREE THROUGH MANY CENTURIES.

Rich in resins and camphor-scented oils, and the precious antiseptic pinene, the pine has been used medicinally since early times, and was one of the first plants to have its oil extracted. Originally, the young tips of the branches and the needles were boiled in water for several hours, and cloths dipped in the strongly scented brew were used, warm and comforting, as a poultice as hot as could be applied without burning, to aching muscles, to strains, sprains and arthritic joints. The oil was skimmed off and mixed with lard and used as a massage oil, and a tea was made of the needles to treat coughs and colds, heart disease and urinary tract infections.

A number of pines produce edible seeds. The Gordon's Bay pine cones were treasures to pick up, just waiting to have the winged seeds cracked with a smooth beach stone on the cement steps, and gently and slowly chewed while looking at the sea – a childhood memory I go back to whenever I eat a pine nut!

But best of all it is the needles that make that quiet carpet and which can be raked and stuffed into baskets and bags, and transported back home to the strawberry beds! Pine needles have a high acidity – so do not use them as a mulch around alkaline loving plants. But mixed with grass clippings and leaves they make the most invigorating mulch around azaleas, ensuring a long and spectacular flowering period.

The long-needled pitch pine (*Pinus palustris*) was once a popular garden pine, and can still be found today in spectacular avenues. Native to America, this is the pine from which oil of turpentine is distilled (not to be

Pinus palustris

confused with petroleum-based turpentine), and so it was grown for commercial purposes but mostly for its timber.

I have struggled to grow the Scots pine (*Pinus sylvestris*), which needs the snowbound winters of its native Europe to thrive – Africa is too hot and too dry. I was enchanted to learn that its young branches produce tar and oil and resin, and that it was so impressive a medicinal tree. The pine oil used in aromatherapy is from this pine, and many years ago as a practising physiotherapist I used this oil to massage aching backs and arthritic legs and for poor circulation, and found it gave such relief that I have loved and respected it ever since.

Most pines are too big to grow in the average garden, but on a farm or smallholding the pine is a great asset. Our ancestors used raked pine needles, mixed with well-rotted manure and grass mowings for the best potatoes and tomatoes. Most precious of all you can taste the difference. My quest is to reintroduce the deliciousness of the tomatoes we ate as children to the tasteless beauties we grow today, and pine needles could be the key!

USES
Culinary (pine nuts), medicinal

COMPANIONS
Potatoes, strawberries, tomatoes, acid-loving plants

Peas

EVER THOUGHT ABOUT GROWING A CROP OF PEAS JUST FOR THE FUN OF IT? NOT ONLY IS IT A DECORATIVE CROP WITH THEIR PRETTY SMALL PINK, MAUVE OR WHITE FLOWERS, BUT THEIR JUICY LEAFY TIPS ARE DELICIOUS IN STIR-FRIES AND SALADS. BEST OF ALL, THEY ARE ONE OF THE BEST NITROGEN FIXERS FOR THE SOIL, MAKING IT AVAILABLE TO NEIGHBOURING PLANTS.

If peas are ploughed back into the soil once they have matured but not dried, they act as a superb green manure. I have re-established overgrazed, depleted fields with first, in summer, a buckwheat crop ploughed in when in full flower, followed for the winter by a pea crop. It's quite miraculous, and the crops that followed after my peas were rich and vigorous.

I really love peas. It was one of my very first gardening experiences with my dad – I must have been four or five years old. Every autumn he dug a trench in full sun, the width and length of his spade. He filled it with pure compost, first lining it with newspaper four pages thick. I held it in place as he spaded in the rich compost. Then he covered the trench with soil, raked it over and soaked it with a slow-running hose. A fortnight later he made a shallow slit in the trench and we set the little hard peas in it, a mere thumb-length apart and about 2 centimetres deep. (We first soaked the peas in warm water for three or four hours before planting.) Then he neatly raked it over and we carefully spread a wide ribbon of lawn mowings and leaves over the trench to fool the birds. Then we set up the chicken wire frames tied sturdily to strong fencing poles at either end of the long bed. He cleverly folded over the bottom edge of the wire making a 15 centimetre "cuff" over the ground where we sowed the peas to stop the birds scratching. In time the peas would grow through it.

Training the peas through the mesh was quick and easy as their tight tendrils eagerly looked for supports, and the growth is so quick and so rewarding you'll find yourself checking the pea bed every day, like we did. Next to the peas we sowed a bed of carrots and behind them a big wide row of potatoes, edged with radishes and onions. All winter we had this marvellous crop of succulent vegetables, and in spring the peas were abundant.

Eat young peas, pods and all, to get a good dose of calcium, magnesium, phosphorus, folic acid, B vitamins, potassium, zinc and iron, all of which act as a tonic, a liver cleanser and booster for liver function. The little tips of the vine and the flowers are delicious too. Try them chopped and sprinkled over stir-fries and salads, served with lemon juice and home-made mayonnaise.

The crop is abundant and you'll not be able to eat them all, but never forget, dried peas are simply delicious. Through the years I have had an extra large glass screw-top jar in which the dried peas have been safely stored. Just a handful in a soup or casserole adds flavour and thickening, and my grandmother's recipe for pea soup with onions, celery and a little ginger made with either fresh or dried peas, remains infinitely satisfying and a delight to make.

USES
Culinary, green manure

COMPANIONS
Carrots, onions, potatoes, radishes

Apricot

ONE OF THE PRETTIEST OF ALL FRUIT TREES TO GROW, THE APRICOT USED TO BE FOUND IN EVERYONE'S GARDEN. ITS WIDE-SPREADING BRANCHES MADE A PERFECT PLACE UNDER WHICH WE PLAYED AS CHILDREN, ITS CLOUD OF WHITE BLOSSOMS IN SPRING CAN TAKE YOUR BREATH AWAY IN ITS SHORT-LIVED BEAUTY, AND THE BARE, DARK, KNOTTY BRANCHES IN WINTER HAVE A BEAUTY OF THEIR OWN.

Native to Northern China, the apricot has been cherished through the centuries. The Romans were the first to make liqueurs from the ripe fruits. The medieval monks used the oil-rich pip kernels and the ripe fruits to treat coughs and chest ailments, as well as asthma and emphysema. In recent years, apricot kernels have been used in cancer therapy, and the rich oil in cosmetics.

Growing apricots is an exciting adventure as the trees grow steadily fairly quickly. They look beautiful at all stages of their development. A huge, deep, compost-filled hole is the first step. Set a metre-long piece of wide plastic pipe into the ground at an angle with a short piece sticking out above the ground and the other end set deeply in at the bottom of the hole when you plant the tree. This is a watering pipe – the hose is inserted into the protruding end, soaking the bottom of the hole so that the roots will grow down into it and it will have deep, moist roots.

Surround the tree with nasturtiums, southernwood and tansy, and have perennial basil and rosemary planted nearby once the tree matures and it blossoms abundantly. Make a "tea" of tansy, basil, rosemary and nasturtiums, and spray the young, green, marble-sized fruit with it once a week to prevent fruit flies. Fill a bucket with sprigs, leaves and flowers of all three, pour a bucket of boiling water over the sprigs so that they are all covered. Leave it to stand overnight. Next morning strain, add ½ to 1 cup of soap powder, depending on the size of the bucket, and mix well.

Discard the herbs and spray the fruit with the pungent-smelling tea.

Fruit fly bait can also be effective for apricots, peaches and plums, and jars can be hung in the trees, filled with a mixture of bran, molasses, Marmite and hot water, or mix mashed banana and beer with orange slices into another bottle. The fruit flies will descend into it and hopefully drown!

Do not plant brinjals, potatoes, tomatoes or the luscious fruit salad plant (*Solanum muricatum*) anywhere near your apricot trees – they impede each other's growth. Nor must you use the autumn apricot leaves as a mulch around tomatoes and potatoes. Even the leaves contain elements disliked by the *Solanum* genus, as does planting oats and barley and wheat near apricot trees – the growth of both is inhibited, and farmers have been aware of this for centuries – but buckwheat does well planted between the trees, and so does blue flax (linseed), peaches and plums.

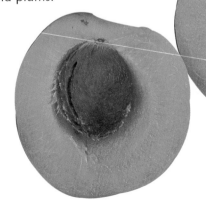

USES
Culinary, medicinal, cosmetic

COMPANIONS
Basil, blue flax, buckwheat, nasturtiums, peaches, plums rosemary, southernwood, tansy

DISLIKES
Barley, brinjals, fruit salad plant, oats, potatoes, tomatoes, wheat

Peaches & Pears

PRUNUS PERSICA • PYRUS COMMUNIS

I HAVE GONE THROUGH YEARS OF DESPERATION WITH MY PEACH AND NECTARINE AND PEAR TREES THAT ONCE FRUITED SO HEAVILY TO ALMOST NO CROP WHATSOEVER. MORE THAN ANY OTHER FRUIT, IT IS THESE THAT HAVE LITERALLY MADE GARDENERS GIVE UP AND LET THE FRUIT FLIES, WASPS AND BIRDS TAKE OVER.

As a child I remember watching peaches, plums and nectarines ripen in incredible beauty, and I can still feel the heaviness of the laden baskets that we picked so carefully and nestled the ripe fruit in soft leaves and little cups of grass. It was summer, and the scent was indescribable. Every neighbour had peach trees, a pear tree, a plum tree, a fig and a pomegranate too, in their back gardens, and everyone pruned, nurtured and watered them. They exchanged notes and recipes for making jams, jellies, plum pudding and peach ice cream, and all those other summer specials. It was just a way of life, we didn't really think about it. I thought I could create that lifestyle for my children on the farm and I kept trying – I even grew masses of borage all around them to help with blossom pollination.

I learned early on never to plant a peach tree in the same hole as the one that had died. I learned to chase birds and monkeys, I became a crack shot with a catapult, and I fought all the farmers nearby for using heavy chemical sprays. I still do, and I keep trying. Some years I am successful, other years the birds, monkeys and squirrels defeat me.

Tansy is the first line of defence – plant it thickly around the bases of the fruit trees. The second line of defence is rows of onion and garlic between the trees, and the third defence is a strange one which some farmers find excellent. It certainly lessens fruit fly and to an extent the wasps (it's the squirrels, birds and monkeys I can't beat yet!)

Hang a narrow-necked bottle in the trees, half full of a mixture of ½ cup of molasses, ½ to 1 cup beer, 2 teaspoons Marmite, 1 tablespoon sugar and a banana peel roughly chopped. Shake up well. This is a bait that is loved by fruit fly who will crawl into the bottle and get stuck in there and drown!

Even more strange, buy a bottle of Lennons Entress from the chemist. Bore a pencil-thin hole about 3 to 4 centimetres deep into the tree at the point where the trunk divides into branches. Bore it at a downward angle and inject the Entress into it in midwinter before the blossom starts. It will take only a thimble full at a time. Cover and seal the hole with a little dab of mud. Repeat this after a week, using the same hole, the muddy doorway scratched out. Again seal it in the same way. Do this every five or six days until the whole bottle of Entress is used up – a bottle per tree. In the third year of doing this, several farmers testified to its efficacy.

I also drench the trees, even the apricot tree, with a pungent tansy, onion and garlic spray: ½ bucket of fresh tansy and ½ bucket of chopped onions and their leaves, and about 2 cups of chopped garlic. Cover with a bucket of boiling water and stand overnight and cool. Strain next morning and spray heavily as the little fruits start to form. The secret is to keep at it when the fruits are thumbnail size. What a battle for these health-filled fruits – but for all those vitamins and minerals they contain, it's worth the struggle!

USES
Culinary

COMPANIONS
Borage, garlic, onions, tansy

87

Oak

THE OAK GENUS IS HUGE – THERE ARE OVER 600 SPECIES OF THESE GREAT, DECIDUOUS AND SOMETIMES EVERGREEN GIANTS THROUGHOUT THE NORTHERN HEMISPHERE. VARIOUS SPECIES HAVE BEEN LOVED AND CHERISHED THROUGH THE CENTURIES FOR BUILDING SHIPS, SLEIGHS, HOUSES, KISTS, BEDS, BARRELS, RAFTS AND FURNITURE. THERE IS EVEN ONE VARIETY THAT PRODUCES CORK, BUT THE MOST COMMON AND MOST LOVED OF ALL IS THE ENGLISH OAK, OR COMMON OAK.

This precious, long-lived, massive and magnificent tree has been used through the centuries as the medicine that controls bleeding, reduces inflammation, soothes haemorrhoids, sore throats, bleeding gums, eczema and ringworm, scratches, grazes, skin rashes and chafes. It even clears up diarrhoea and dysentery, all in the form of a tea made with the bark, which the monks of the local monastery dispensed. The ripened acorns were ground into a flour, roasted and made into a coffee-like drink. The leaves were used dried and neatly packed to fill pillows and mattresses.

In ancient times the oak was dedicated to Thor, the god of thunder, in the belief that he would protect them and their cattle and goats during the storms. Oaks were planted to protect fields from the storms and bitter winter weather. Oak leaves were carved into the door lintels and over the fireplace as a sign of protection, and acorns were carved for drawer and door handles and hung on blinds as a sign of safety and protection all around the house.

In the fields through the centuries, the oak leaves were raked and spread as mulches around apple and chestnut trees, and in Germany and Austria small oak leaf bonfires were made around ant and aphid infestations. If the leaves were fairly damp, they would burn slowly and smoke out any insect in the proximity. In Italy, citrus groves were always surrounded by oaks and to this day the oak leaves gathered in early autumn are used as mulches to chase snails, cutworms, ants and slugs. The mulch is extremely rich in calcium, and through the centuries gardeners and farmers would collect the leaves for compost and mulches or dig them directly into the soil.

The 1820 Settlers brought acorns with them from Holland and France into South Africa, and planted those tiny acorns around the homes they built so far from their native Europe. I love to think that the two huge oaks in the Herbal Centre gardens come from those original oaks that the French Hugenots planted centuries ago. We gather every fallen leaf in the early winter for our great compost heaps, and we spread the leaves under the winter lettuces and cabbages to deter snails. I can hear my grandmother's voice telling me "that storms make oaks take deeper roots", and I can still feel the excitement when I was 10 years old of a saucer full of little sprouting acorns on a sunny windowsill, knowing that from that tiny beginning a mighty oak will grow, and wondering if I will walk under it someday ...

USES
Medicinal, compost, mulch

COMPANIONS
Cabbages, citrus trees, fruit trees, lettuces

Radish

RADISH IS A LITTLE DO-GOODER! EVERY PLANT BENEFITS FROM HAVING RADISHES GROWN NEAR IT! STRONGLY PUNGENT AND WARMING, RADISH ROOT SECRETIONS AND LEAF COMPOUNDS LITERALLY DETER ALL SORTS OF INSECTS AND ACT AS A GOOD TONIC TO ALL KINDS OF DELICATE, NON-HARDY PLANTS.

I think radishes were the first vegetable I grew when I was four years old, and to this day I love radish and mayonnaise and brown bread sandwiches more than any other! Radishes develop in front of your eyes. There is nothing more rewarding than pulling up your own bursting-with-flavour radishes, so fresh, so crisp, so perfect, and did you know that you can steam the whole plant, leaves and all, and serve it with a touch of butter, a squeeze of lemon juice and a grind of coarse salt and black pepper as a gourmet delight?

As long as I can remember, I've planted a row of radishes winter and summer between lettuce rows, next to carrots, squashes, melons, cabbage and kohlrabi, between peas and cucumber vines, next to rows of tomatoes, strawberries and with green beans and mung beans and chickpeas. I keep experimenting and I keep making lists of how well radish does as a companion to really unusual things, like being scattered all over dormant asparagus beds in winter before the tender shoots come up in spring – and both taste extra delicious! Also, I've recently planted radishes with beetroot, close and prolifically, and have pulled them both up to steam, baby beets plus leaves, peppery mature radishes plus leaves, and served them together with a mustard vinaigrette and black pepper. It was delicious!

Sow the row of radishes in full sun in well-dug, richly composted moist soil, rake the soil over it and keep it moist by spreading a light layer of leaves over it. Don't let the bed dry out, and within three days you'll find the little seeds have sprouted. One of my favourite places to sow radishes is in the flower garden in the furrow between the lawn and the bed – right at the edge of the lawn, often wasted ground. A narrow row of radishes is so quickly reaped you'll still be able to keep the edges of the bed neat. But what a bonus! Especially if it is near delicate plants – the radishes will toughen them up!

Rich in calcium, phosphorus, magnesium, potassium, beta carotene, vitamin C and folic acid, this crunchy, crisp little explosion of goodness in the mouth will dissolve phlegm, open a blocked nose and clear sinuses, ease sore throats and a runny nose. If radishes are eaten with bread, potatoes, rye bread, rice or pasta, they will aid the digestion of the carbohydrates. In fact, the whole digestive system benefits from radishes, and I find myself adding them to everything – stir-fries, soups, casseroles – and I often sit in the garden for lunch with rye bread, cream cheese, freshly pulled-up radishes and a glass of chilled grape juice just to enjoy the moment. It's magical!

USES
Culinary

COMPANIONS
Asparagus, beans, beetroot, cabbages, carrots, chickpeas, cucumbers, kohlrabi, lettuces, melons, peas, squashes, strawberries, tomatoes

Rose

THE ROSE IS THE MOST LOVED AND PROBABLY THE BEST-KNOWN FLOWER IN THE WORLD! ANCIENT AND CHERISHED, ROSES HAVE BEEN USED AS MEDICINE LITERALLY SINCE TIME BEGAN, TREATING VIRTUALLY EVERY AILMENT. THE FIRST CLOISTER GARDENS GROWN BY THE MONKS IN EUROPE WERE FILLED WITH ROSES TO TREAT THE SICK.

A tea made of fresh rose petals was used to treat bladder ailments, coughs, colds, rheumatism, depression, grief, anger, over-excitement, fatigue, epilepsy, stress, indigestion, insomnia, period pains – to name but a few ailments. Surprisingly, medical science has proved the rose extracts, oils and teas definitely do have the properties that soothe and heal, comfort and strengthen, and do indeed help these ailments.

Everyone wants to grow good roses. Everyone would love to own a rose garden, and we all dream of roses around the door, and of lying on a bed of roses, and of gathering baskets of roses from our own gardens, scented and exquisite. We never seem to get enough of roses!

For organic growers, roses are often a treat and a challenge. In my dedication to all things natural, I have had to seriously experiment through the decades for the toughest roses that could survive in my strictly organic garden – without sprays or fertilisers – and survive in intense heat (we often go to 36 °C), mild winters, buffeting hail and wind, and frequent long periods of drought; and all this against the hot, tough, bright slopes of the great Magaliesberg mountains. Most definitely not the most embracing area for growing roses, but I manage to grow the tough survivor roses in beauty and abundance, and so I fill my baskets with fragrance and delight, and my pantry shelves with rose petal syrup and rose petal jam, and my cupboards with rose petal potpourris, and my bath with rose oils and bath salts, by companion planting and home-made sprays. I plant catmint (*Nepeta mussinii*) around the roses and lemon drop marigolds

the Margaret Roberts rose

all summer. In my kitchen garden potagers I grow my beloved 'Crimson Glory' at the ends of all the beds of herbs – thyme and winter savory, tarragon and oregano, rosemary and marjoram, parsley and strawberries, calamint and costmary and sage – and they thrive, unblemished. There is never a sign of an aphid or rust or black spot.

In the rose garden filled with the old-fashioned apothecary rose, the Margaret Roberts rose (which makes the most divine ice cream you have ever tasted), I grow lavender and petrea along the picket fence and I never spray. The huge and spectacular 'Abraham Darby', another apothecary rose, scrambles along the fence, surrounded by catmint. So far from its native England, it takes the heat and the drought, and enchants the visitors. We mulch twice yearly, two buckets of rich home-made compost per rose, and water deep weekly, and we foliar feed with comfrey and buckwheat spray every two months. Here is where companion planting really works!

USES
Culinary, medicinal, cosmetic, cut flower

COMPANIONS
Buckwheat, calamint, catmint, comfrey, costmary, lavender, marjoram, oregano, parsley, petrea, rosemary, sage, strawberries, tarragon, thyme, winter savory

Rosemary

A STRONG, PUNGENT, TOUGH AND RESILIENT HERB, ROSEMARY IS INDIGENOUS TO THE MEDITERRANEAN AREA AND SOUTHERN EUROPE. MUCH LOVED, MUCH RESPECTED AND MUCH USED, ROSEMARY IS A STURDY PERENNIAL HERB THAT HAS BEEN USED TO MAKE PROTECTIVE HEDGES AND SHELTERS FOR TENDER PLANTS THROUGHOUT THE CENTURIES. ITS WONDERFUL COMPANIONSHIP TO BEANS, CARROTS AND CABBAGES DISCOURAGES SNAILS, SLUGS, CATERPILLARS AND CUTWORMS, AND IT REPELS APHIDS. IN FACT, SURROUNDING THE VEGETABLE GARDEN, IT IS SUPERB!

Rosemary is actually quite an amazing herb. Through the years in the Herbal Centre gardens we have trialled many rosemary varieties, and at present we have fourteen stalwarts that do well in the heat and dryness of our mountain area. For some years we have put together a superb rosemary register for South Africa, finally whittling it down to the twelve or fourteen strongest and best, which we now propagate.

It has been a most fascinating exercise, and one which we will continue, we hope, as new rosemaries cross-pollinate in our gardens. (Rosemary belongs to the great Lamiaceae family like lavender and sage and basil, so cross-pollination often happens, and one needs to be constantly aware and on the look out for seedlings that come up in obscure places.)

Rosemary is actually an extraordinary herb, but one which we often merely take for granted. This is a pity, as it should be raised to noble status. Here is why: It is rich in superb oils and rosemary essential oil is one of the most powerful of all oils. It is an excellent natural insecticide, and branches rubbed on chair legs and over wooden tables, windowsills and countertops to release those powerful oils, will chase fleas, flies, mosquitoes, ants, weevils and moths. A strong tea of rosemary can be made by filling a bucket with fresh rosemary sprigs, then cover with boiling water, stand covered and cool. Strain, stir in half a cup of soap powder, and use as a spray on literally everything including roses, vegetables and the floors and mattresses. It will clear insects and put a fresh antiseptic scent into the room.

Rosemary was used during the great plague to act as an antiseptic, and to this day is used as a wash and lotion on wounds and grazes because of this excellent antiseptic action. It was also used as a strewing herb on the floors of castles and churches and public places in order to keep insects away. Medicinally it has been used through the centuries to treat epilepsy, arthritis, diabetes, chronic pain, as it has an anti-inflammatory action. It treats circulatory disorders and levels blood pressure, stimulates hair growth, restores energy and a positive outlook, treats depression, anxiety and improves memory and concentration. In today's frenetic world, rosemary is proving to be invaluable. A cup of rosemary tea – one small thumb-length sized sprig steeped in 1 cup of boiling water for 3 to 5 minutes and sipped slowly three times a week – is an exceptional tonic and a treatment for all the above ailments. It is proving to be so helpful we should all be planting this very easy-to-grow herb. A hedge could become a rare treasure!

USES
Culinary, medicinal, insect repellent

COMPANIONS
Beans, cabbages carrots

Raspberry

CONTRARY TO POPULAR BELIEF, RASPBERRIES ARE EASY TO GROW! CHOOSE GOOD FRUITING CANES SUCH AS AUTUMN BLISS, BUT BEAR IN MIND THAT, LIKE MOST BERRIES, THEY DO BETTER IN COOLER CLIMATES, ESPECIALLY WITH A GOOD SPRINKLING OF FROST.

I have found that a row of oats planted on either side of the raspberries protects and cools them and, as soon as it ripens, I cut the dry stems and push them through the shredder. Or you can roughly chop them up to make oat straw to use as a thick mulch around the raspberries. This mulch keeps the soil cool and moist and will increase the yield. In very hot areas the raspberries do best under 40 per cent shade cloth stretched high over them – at least 2 metres above to allow the circulation of air. Raspberry's companion crops of yarrow or tansy or wormwood – or any of the artemisias – also grow well in the 40 per cent shade. I have grown spring onions near raspberries, and garlic, and a row of big onions, and all have done well near each other, even enhancing the flavour of the raspberries, but don't plant near potatoes or near youngberries.

Raspberries do well if staked between a double row of wire stretched about 15 centimetres apart and 75 centimetres high. I tie the first canes up onto the wire supports with thick string at intervals of about 1 metre. The canes can be planted 50 centimetres apart, and this soon gets all the shoots going upwards.

Indigenous to Europe and Asia, this much-loved fruit has been a favourite food and a medicine herb through the centuries. Raspberry leaves made into a tea have been taken for centuries in late pregnancy to prepare for labour. (*Caution:* Use this only with your doctor's consent.) Rasp-berries have been taken to soothe sore throats, coughs, colds and chills, and to flush the kidneys and bladder, to treat rheumatism and mouth infections, and the leaves make an excellent mouthwash and gargle as well.

A precious much-loved fruit, raspberries need deeply dug, richly composted soil and a good watering twice or even three times a week. You will be rewarded with a crop of pure health-giving fruits! Raspberries are rich in vitamins A, B, C and E, and the precious vitamin B3, as well as calcium, magnesium, phosphorus and potassium, making this the most delicious health food ever.

Because raspberries act as a tonic to the whole system, and a natural detoxifier, they are included in drinks, syrups and over-the-counter medication. However, the most superb way of treating, toning and detoxifying the whole system is to eat them fresh (without sugar and cream!). Even more satisfying is growing them organically.

Seek out the varieties that do best in your area and persist. It is the most rewarding perennial crop you can grow. I propagate by pruning the whole plant literally to the ground in winter, I dig in masses of old compost and old manure, then I chop off new-rooted shoots and start a new bed every two years.

USES
Culinary, medicinal

COMPANIONS
Artemisias, garlic, oats, onions, spring onions, tansy, wormwood, yarrow

DISLIKES
Potatoes, youngberries

Blackberries

AN ANCIENT MUCH-LOVED FRUIT, EUROPE'S BLACKBERRIES, A PRECIOUS WILD FRUIT, HAVE REMAINED POPULAR THROUGHOUT THE AGES, NOT ONLY AS FOOD BUT AS MEDICINE AS WELL.

Rampant, invasive, thorny, in some places even difficult to control – why ever would we want to grow blackberries? Blackberries have the extraordinary ability to actually break down inhospitable soil, infertile soil, and can make even stony ground into a garden! They have fibrous, invasive roots, they dredge up and utilise minerals from deep in the soil, and their leaves are simply and amazingly "potent" as a mulch, in the compost heap and as a natural fertiliser in the form of a tea.

Like yarrow and comfrey, blackberry leaves and stems deep inside the compost heap will break it down and activate decomposition of tough grass mowings and old weeds.

Sunflowers and elderberries grown near blackberries will encourage the birds to leave the fruit alone. Tin cans and florist ribbons tied in the vines will rustle and move, and frighten the birds. If the blackberries are planted near apple trees with stinging nettle as a companion, the abundant crop of apples, as well as the blackberries, is filled with flavour and grows with vigour and vitality.

Plant all the berries – this includes loganberries, youngberries and Tay berries – in full sun in well-dug, well-composted soil (the compost must be turned and dug in twice). The rewards are huge, as the fibrous roots spread far and wide searching for food and storing the minerals in their roots as well.

Fresh berries served with honey and Bulgarian yoghurt are high in vitamins, especially vitamin C, minerals, calcium in particular, magnesium, phosphorus and potassium, and make a truly fantastic tonic for the whole circulatory system. Whenever they are ripe, be sure to serve this dish often.

If you dig up blackberries for transplanting, cut off portions of the roots for the compost heap and make a tea of unruly cut-back vines and leaves by filling a bucket with cut-up pieces covered with boiling water. Leave it to stand overnight. Next morning toss everything – "tea" and all – onto the compost heap or fill trenches with the brew and the bits of leaves and vine, and cover with compost for a row of runner beans or winter peas. You can virtually see the difference this mineral boost will give the seedlings.

Through the centuries, farmers have made this blackberry vine tea with stinging nettles, yarrow and lucerne clippings in equal quantities as a boost for precious, rare plants, ferns and fruit crops. It is potent, powerful, and so rich in minerals and nutrients, it will coax new life into old plants *and* old farmers, they say! Dilute half a cup of the brew with half a cup of boiling water, add honey and a slice of lemon, sip slowly, and put on your dancing shoes!

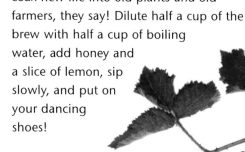

USES
Culinary, compost maker

COMPANIONS
Apple trees, elderberries, stinging nettle, sunflowers

Rue

RUE IS ONE OF THE STRONGEST SMELLING OF ALL HERBS – SO POWERFULLY STRONG THAT IT LITERALLY SHOCKS! IT IS AN ANCIENT HERB USED IN THE VERY EARLIEST CENTURIES IN ANCIENT GREECE AND ROME FOR MANY AILMENTS, BUT IT REMAINS A MOST DANGEROUSLY POISONOUS HERB AND MUST ONLY EVER BE TAKEN UNDER PROFESSIONAL GUIDANCE.

Never take rue nor even pick rue during pregnancy, fresh leaves can cause severe skin reactions. I have picked bunches of rue on a hot summer afternoon to use as an insecticide. I carried them across my arm and within minutes great, hot, red, itchy weals appeared and remained for about three hours, gradually easing as I applied masses of aloe vera gel and *Bulbine frutescens* gel. I washed the area immediately the weals appeared, with cool water into which I had added about half a cup of apple cider vinegar. I then dried the area and applied the aloe vera and bulbinella gel. So be very careful how you handle rue.

Nevertheless, rue is a hugely important herb in the garden, especially if planted near compost heaps (and stables, kennels and cattle stalls if you are on a farm). It chases flies, mosquitoes and ants, and has been used through the centuries especially for this purpose. Bunches tied together and used to brush and beat over the steps, sills and floors of the stables will send flies scurrying, and if the horses walk over it, the strong scent will even send ants scurrying.

Hang bunches over windows and doorways to keep mosquitoes out, and pour boiling water over one bucket of fresh rue, enough to cover it. Once it has cooled, strain and use this strong brew to water down ants' holes or to splash or spray onto aphids and whitefly. If a little soap powder is added – ½ a cup to every bucket – it makes an excellent spray for mildew, fungus or tough black aphids.

One year when there was a large infestation of cutworms and borers and my strawberry crop was badly affected, I cut rue branches and placed them over and under the ripening strawberries. I got an excellent crop, but the nearby basil died – so remember rue and basil don't grow well together.

A border of rue around the vegetable garden and orchard is a superb investment – especially for fruit trees – and if the rue is frequently cut and trampled on and packed around the trunk of the peach or nectarine or pear trees, fruit fly is also deterred. Tansy with rue works well, planted around fruit trees and if planted between tomato rows you literally have perfect tomatoes, and the birds are also wary of rue.

Branches of rue can be used as a platform on which to ripen apples or onions, and the fruit can be stored safe from any worms or beetles if rue is near. It takes extremes in temperature but thrives in the full sun, and withstands a lot of drought. Rue has to be one of the most powerful of all the insect-repelling herbs.

USES
Medicinal, insect repellent

COMPANIONS
Fruit trees, strawberries, tansy, tomatoes, but all vegetables will benefit from its insect-repelling properties

DISLIKES
Basil

Sage

THE ANCIENT EUROPEANS THOUGHT COMMON SAGE (*SALVIA OFFICINALIS*) ENHANCED HEALTH AND MENTAL CLARITY, PARTICULARLY IN THE AGED. MODERN RESEARCH PROVES SAGE IS IN REALITY AN EXCEPTIONAL PLANT THAT HAS ANTISEPTIC, ANTIFUNGAL AND DEODORANT PROPERTIES. IT IS EXCELLENT FOR THE DIGESTION AND MOUTH AND THROAT INFECTIONS, AND CONTAINS OESTROGEN, SO IS HELPFUL IN MENOPAUSE.

Sage is indigenous to the Mediterranean area mainly, but different sages are found in many areas in Europe. Sage belongs to the huge Lamiaceae family of which there are literally over 900 species in the genus, ranging from the pungent and showy *Salvia leucantha*, to the American prairie sage, *Salvia clevelandii*, and all have superb natural insecticidal properties. All sages are strongly scented and powerful, rich in intense oils and medicinal values. Throughout the world these precious plants have been utilised in many different ways, from flavouring to medicine. In the role as companions, growth stimulants and soil tonics, sage is one of the most respected plant groups in the world.

Salvia officinalis

All sage flowers secrete an abundance of nectar, so for bee keepers the sage varieties are important planted near the hives. Sage partners rosemary well, and rosemary honey is delicious. So plant the different rosemaries near hives with the sages as well.

I concentrate on the ordinary edible sage – *Salvia officinalis* – for food flavouring and teas, as well as a companion for carrots, tomatoes, cabbages, broccoli and cauliflower, and my winter kale partnered with

sage and lettuce had not a single aphid on it. But don't be tempted to plant cucumbers near sage – they will not thrive.

Both *Salvia leucantha* and *Salvia clevelandii* are so strongly scented, leaves and flowers can be scattered over floors and chicken coops, stables and kennels, and fleas, flies and mosquitoes will flee! The more these sages are walked on, the more they will exude their pungent scents so that even rats and mice depart – it's too strong for them too.

Long ago I learned that sage leaves act as a very remarkable "fertiliser" if dug in around grape vines, and will enhance the taste of the grapes. They grow in full sun and in well-drained soil, and reach 30 centimetres in height, but when they are more than five or six years old, they tend to become woody, so replace them and chop them up for the compost. Once we pulled up a long, thick row of very old sage bushes. We later found when we used this sage compost on new grape vines that it was extremely rich and invigorating. The vines grew quickly and so well, we now know what they mean when they say sage acts as a tonic!

Salvia clevelandii

USES
Culinary, medicinal, insecticide

COMPANIONS
Broccoli, cabbages, carrots, cauliflower, grape vines, kale, tomatoes

DISLIKES
Cucumbers, wet waterlogged soil

95

Elder

ONE OF MY FAVOURITE HERBS, THE ELDER, IS AN INCREDIBLE PLANT THAT HAS SO MANY USES YOU COULD SERIOUSLY BECOME A DEVOTED ELDER LOVER LIKE ME! IT'S ONE OF THE WORLD'S MOST LOVED HERBS! INDIGENOUS TO EUROPE AND ASIA, THE ELDER IS PROBABLY ONE OF THE WORLD'S MOST ANCIENT MEDICINAL PLANTS THAT HAD ALREADY BEEN INTRODUCED TO MOST COUNTRIES IN THE CIVILIZED WORLD BY THE 17TH CENTURY.

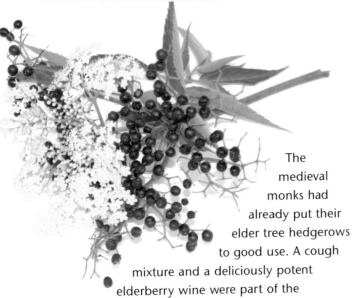

The medieval monks had already put their elder tree hedgerows to good use. A cough mixture and a deliciously potent elderberry wine were part of the monastery earnings, and to this day elderberry cough mixture is an important treatment for persistent coughs, particularly in children. The ancient Egyptians used the precious flowers, so plentiful in early summer, to beautify the skin and to improve its moisture content, to clear spots and greasiness, and to act as a toner. Today many commercial beauty products use elderflower extracts for skin repair and rejuvenation.

We may have forgotten or overlooked how important the elder tree is in the garden, as now only the occasional tree can be seen whereas in the days gone by every home owner grew one or two elders to protect the home, to keep witches away, to use as medicine, and, importantly, to use as an insecticide! Grow an elder near the compost heap if you can – it needs full sun and thrives near the warmth and moisture of the compost heap. It assists in breaking down the compost. It literally helps to break everything down as its roots penetrate under the compost.

The leaves of the elder are poisonous to insects including those tough peach tree borers, woolly aphids, whitefly, fungal diseases, and powdery mildew, and a general all purpose spray is extremely effective, but do not eat fruit or vegetables sprayed with elder for at least two weeks. Fill a bucket with elder tree leaves, prunings and clippings. Pour over this 2 buckets of boiling water, a few sprays of fresh rue and about half a bucket of marigold or khakibos sprigs and flowers. Stir with a strong stick, cover and leave to cool overnight. Next morning strain (add the discarded leaves and sprigs to the compost heap) and mix ½ to ¾ cup of good soap powder into the mixture. Stir well. Use as a spray – it is wonderfully health giving as a tonic to ailing plants too, and to pot plants.

Elder trees are really shrubs as they are multi-stemmed and reach not much more than 3 metres in height. They can take clipping and training, and make excellent windbreaks, hedges and focal points. Their exquisite white lacy flowers are delicious in cakes, fruit salads, as fritters, and made into teas and champagne they are stunning. The berries make fabulous jam, cordials, wines and cough mixtures with lemon and honey that everyone loves. As if that wasn't enough, you can make flutes and whistles from the hollow stems!

Make a space and grow this precious plant – it will intrigue you all year round and keep the garden clear of pests!

USES
Culinary, medicinal, insect repellent

COMPANIONS
Most plants will benefit from its insect-repelling properties

Salad Burnet

SANGUISORBA MINOR

THIS IS A STRANGE LITTLE HERB TO FIND IN A BOOK ABOUT COMPANION PLANTING, BUT I HAVE FOUND IT TO BE SO IMPORTANT A HERB AS A FODDER CROP AND A TONIC HERB, THAT I HAVE KEPT A SPACE FOR IT WITHIN THESE PAGES.

Long ago, in fact from the 16th and 17th centuries in its native Europe, this easy-to-grow small, short-lived perennial was grown extensively for sheep and cattle, as it is richly nutritious, far more so than grass, it grew literally anywhere, and it remained green all through the winter, even under the snow. So there was always food for the cattle and sheep, as well as for the community. Salad burnet and onion and dried pea or bean soup became a winter standby and a great health booster.

Salad burnet is a hardy, easy-to-grow, self-seeding and attractive little plant, and I am surprised no one grows it today, especially as it has so many uses. It is a tonic herb, not only to all who eat the mildly flavoured, fresh, almost cucumber-tasting leaves, but it is also important as tonic to the soil. On the compost heap the leaves break down quickly, donating a mass of minerals to the compost. Or it can be ploughed in as a soil revitaliser – a green manure crop – so vibrant and potent that if it were to be combined with buckwheat, which matures quickly and will give salad burnet a chance to develop under its cooling shade, the two can together be ploughed into the most depleted and poor soils, and within a season that area will be richly reimbursed.

Propagate salad burnet from seed sown in compost-filled bags and plant it out once it has matured 45 centimetres apart in a furrow so that it can remain cool and moist. Sow buckwheat on either side of this row. In the vegetable garden I am not only thrilled with salad burnet, but I am constantly astonished at its tough resilience and its support of broad beans, peas, lettuce, radishes, sunflowers, mint and thyme. It

literally thrives, sending out cushions of succulent and tasty leaves for salads and stir-fries, but the plants next to it thrive and grow with speed and aplomb! It is literally a little wonder plant and one I urge gardeners to experiment with for constant surprises! This summer it just happened to be near a cherry tomato plant. I picked an endless supply of very tasty cherry tomatoes from this plant – far more than any other of the tomatoes. So next summer I'll plant salad burnet between the tomatoes.

Add the tender leaves to soups and salads, stir-fries and casseroles, and relish it. It is a survivor plant. Make a lotion of it by pouring a litre of boiling water over 3 cups of fresh leaves and let it cool. Use as a wash or spritz spray over sunburn and dry, chafed skin, eczema, insect bites and rashes. Keep it in a spritz bottle while you're working in the garden and spray yourself frequently.

It takes both sun and light shade well, and thrives with a twice weekly watering and lots of compost dug in around it twice yearly.

USES
Culinary, medicinal, green manure, fertiliser

COMPANIONS
Beans, lettuces, mint, peas, radishes, sunflowers, thyme, tomatoes

Santolina

AN ANCIENT HERB GROWN IN MEDIEVAL TIMES AS AN INSECT REPELLENT, SANTOLINA IS FOUND IN DRY, STONY PLACES IN THE MEDITERRANEAN AREAS. IN THE 16TH CENTURY IT BECAME POPULAR FOR KNOT GARDEN HEDGES, AND ABOUT A DECADE AGO I SAW IT IN SPLENDID GEOMETRICAL DESIGN IN THE HAMPTON COURT GARDENS, ITS SILVER-GREY, NEATLY CLIPPED FOLIAGE CONTRASTING BEAUTIFULLY WITH EQUALLY WELL-CLIPPED BOX HEDGES (*BUXUS SEMPERVIRENS*).

Once used as a medicinal herb for worms, skin rashes and even for poisonous bites, medical research during the 1980s found it to be an effective anti-inflammatory to reduce inflammation quickly, aid digestion and to expel internal parasites.

It is seldom used today as its pungent taste and smell is too strong to make it popular, but as an insect repellent it is excellent. Its fine, grey leaves and round button petal-less flowers make it attractive in landscaping. One of my most spectacular plantings that gets visitors to the gardens ecstatic, is a long curved bed of *Briza* shaking grass next to Russian sage (*Perovskia*), *Agastache* 'Heather Queen' (Korean mint which has coral pink flowers), caffea lime trees (which are the delicious lime leaves used in cooking, finely chopped) edged and underplanted with *Santolina chamaecyparissus nana*, a round, small variety. Not only does it look breathtaking, but the only insects in the whole vicinity are the bees! No whitefly, no aphids, no red spider, no mildew. It's the most powerful army of insect guns you can imagine, and every plant is thriving despite erratic rainfall!

Known as "cotton lavender" in ancient times, santolina was cultivated in every cottage garden as a household insect deterrent. Sprigs were cut and laid on floors as strewing herbs to be walked on to chase fleas, ticks, bedbugs and weevils. Bags and sachets of dried cotton lavender were tucked into bedding, clothing, shawls and blankets, in cupboards and drawers and in kists, to deter moths and fish moths. This is where the word "cotton lavender" comes from – it was often combined with lavender as a moth chaser between linen and cotton clothing and bedding. In the moth-repelling sachets we make in the Herbal Centre studios, santolina still features as an important ingredient.

In the garden I plant it next to cabbage, kale, broccoli and my precious new cauliflowers, and it keeps insects off spinach, radish and peas, and most exciting of all, roses! A border of cotton lavender next to the roses looks stunning. Make it into an all-purpose insect-repelling spray by pouring 1 ½ buckets of boiling water over 1 bucket of mixed santolina sprigs, rue sprigs and Russian sage sprigs and cool overnight. Next morning strain, add 1 cup of soap powder and spray thoroughly, specially for aphids on roses and cabbages. I usually have to do it only once, but for very persistent aphids do it again the next day.

Santolina is rewarding and attractive in the garden. Propagate by seed and plant out in full sun once the little plants are sturdy. It is a neat perennial, but does not like wet feet.

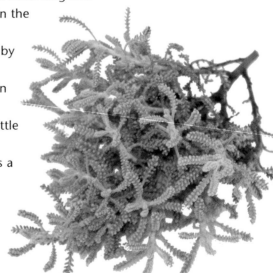

USES
Insect repellent

COMPANIONS
Broccoli, cabbages, cauliflower, kale, peas, radishes, roses, spinach

Soapwort

OF ALL THE PLANTS IN THE HERBAL CENTRE GARDENS, IT IS SOAPWORT THAT REALLY STEALS THE SHOW FOR THE VISITING SCHOOL CHILDREN. I PICK A HANDFUL OF SOME VERY ORDINARY GREEN LEAVES AND A PINK FLOWER HEAD, AND DIPPING EVERYTHING INTO A NEARBY BIRDBATH'S WATER, I START RUBBING THE HANDFUL IN CIRCULAR MOVEMENTS IN MY HANDS. WITHIN 30 SECONDS THE GREEN LATHER IS CLEARLY VISIBLE, AND THE DISBELIEF ON THEIR ASTONISHED FACES NEVER FAILS TO MAKE ME LAUGH! I SPREAD THE GREEN BUBBLY FOAM OVER WILLING LITTLE HANDS AND ARMS, AND THEY CROW WITH DELIGHT. I LET THEM PICK AND RUB THEIR OWN SOAPWORT LEAVES AS IT IS SO VERY PROLIFIC THERE IS ALWAYS ENOUGH FOR EVERYONE, AND IT MAKES THE GREATEST IMPRESSION!

Soapwort is a pretty perennial phlox often known as Bouncing Bet, and its origins are temperate Europe, Asia and North America. It has spread with ease throughout the world – it actually is a very invasive plant and once you have it you will always have it. So take care and control it constantly.

Soapwort was used by the Assyrians in the 8th century BC as a wash for everything, including fabrics. Today it is used to clean museum treasures as it is mild and safe to use, even on ancient tapestries, pictures and furniture. In England today, in places where old water mills can still be found, soapwort grows abundantly close by as a reminder of its importance. Soap, as we know it today, only began to be commercially manufactured in the 1800s, so soapwort was grown in every cottage garden. It was soft and gentle on the skin and hair, highly regarded and consequently nurtured well.

It is, however, poisonous to fish to an extent, so do not let it invade river and pond edges. Remember always, it is tough and invasive and resilient and thrives everywhere.

Why we grow soapwort so abundantly in the Herbal Centre gardens is because it is so useful in the natural sprays we make. Ants, aphids, whitefly, red spider and mealie bug are all eliminated by it, and a huge pot of soapwort sprigs, including stems, flowers, roots and leaves, boiled up for 20 minutes with enough water to cover it, will form a superb liquid soap that, when cooled and strained, can be watered down ants' holes, splashed and sprayed onto plants, and if used as a wash for horses, will even chase the flies to some extent, and condition and clean their skins. It really is the most extraordinary plant, and one that I have often used boiled up with khakibos, marigolds, rue, southernwood or pennyroyal, equal quantities of both. The resulting liquid is sticky enough to be sprayed onto fruit trees, roses and vegetables, and even aphid-infested cut flowers. I have experimented for years with soapwort and am constantly surprised by its strength and efficacy!

It can be harvested any time of the year, and is best used fresh. It propagates by rooted runners and it is virtually indestructible. It thrives wherever it has water and, in compost-rich soil, its beautiful eye-catching pink phlox flowers are showy enough to pick for the vase!

USES
Insect repellent, natural soap

COMPANIONS
Most plants will benefit from its insect-repelling properties, but it needs restraining

Winter Savory & Summer Savory

SATUREJA MONTANA • SATUREJA HORTENSIS

SAVORY IS AN ANCIENT, MUCH-RESPECTED HERB THAT HAS BEEN USED AS BOTH MEDICINE AND FOOD FLAVOURING FOR OVER TWO THOUSAND YEARS. ONCE IT WAS CONSIDERED TO BE AN APHRODISIAC AND WAS USED BY THE ANCIENT GREEKS AND ROMANS. IT WAS ALSO AN IMPORTANT INGREDIENT IN A VARIETY OF WINES!

The savories – both the perennial winter savory (*Satureja montana*) and the annual summer savory (*Satureja hortensis*) – belong to the great Lamiaceae family, and this genus has a vast number of species of annuals, perennials and sub shrubs, all used medicinally. They do well in sunny well-drained soils and grow to 15–30 centimetres in height and width.

Both are excellent digestives – sprigs of winter savory help to digest bean dishes and dissipate sour belching, flatulence and bloating often caused by beans. So they are unusually grown together. Winter savory has resins and tannins in its leaves and is strongly antiseptic, antispasmodic and astringent. It has expectorant and tonic properties, and so has been grown for centuries to treat many ailments.

The greatest power that the savories have is their simply incredible oils. Just crushing the sprigs will release that amazing fragrance. If you were to take a cup of freshly picked and well-crushed leaves and sprigs (do it with a rolling pin or pound them in a pestle and mortar) and stir them into one cup of good aqueous cream heated in a double boiler while it simmers,

winter savory

you'll be engulfed by the scent, and after 20 minutes the whole room smells of it. You'll quickly understand why it will soothe aching muscles and release neck tension if massaged into the area. Strain out the leaves first. Sore throats and colds can be eased by massaging the throat area with it, and a tea of winter savory will ease a cough and help to open the nose.

Planted in the garden in full sun and with good compost and well dug soil, it will form a low mat of solid dark green. Propagate by rooted cuttings dug off from the sides of the main plant and root in pots, kept in the shade until well established. Summer savory is a taller, more fragile annual propagated by seed, and it has the same uses.

Working in the garden with bites, rashes and scratches, and flies and mosquitoes all around, the savories become your friend and can be picked and rubbed over arms and legs and tucked into hats to keep the insects away.

Both beans and onions benefit from winter savory near them, but sowing any sorts of seeds close to them may result in poor germination – so give that a thought. I have had successful rocket, roses, tomatoes and brinjals with winter savory nearby, and even if it is planted in the corner of the garden it will keep whitefly, aphids and rust far away. A drench made of boiling water and winter savory in equal quantities and left to cool overnight, is wonderful for splashing onto roses – it acts as a tonic. Water it around them too.

USES
Culinary, medicinal

COMPANIONS
Beans, brinjals, onions, rocket, roses, tomatoes

100

Sesame

SURPRISED TO SEE SESAME APPEARING AS A COMPANION PLANT? YOU WILL BE EVEN MORE SURPRISED TO LEARN IT CONTAINS A FANTASTIC INSECT AND PEST-REPELLING INGREDIENT CALLED SESAMIN USED THE WAY THAT PYRETHRUM IS USED!

I am mad about sesame seeds! I sow them everywhere – between flowers, between vegetables, next to mealies and the sunflowers. All they need is full sun, well-dug, richly composted and well-raked soil, and moisture – enough to germinate. After that, slender spires will come up quickly, forming white and pinky flowers that quickly turn into precious little spiky seed cases. A tall annual, it will often top the sunflowers and the mealies, and is so fragile it's almost not there at all. It is intriguing. It can be ploughed or dug back into the soil at any time – even when it is dry – and it will pour into the soil masses of minerals and its insect-repelling sesamins, which inhibit cutworm infestations.

In order to reap your own organic non-hulled sesame, pull up the whole plant before the seed case is fully ripened – or it will burst and scatter the seeds far and wide – cover with a large paper bag and hang upside down. It will self-ripen, the pods will burst and the crop of tiny, highly nutritious and health-filled seeds will be safe!

Now this is the best part: chop up the stems and pods and dig them back into the soil to treat it for cutworms and nematodes – it will also return its high mineral content to the soil.

Sesame originated in North Africa and it has been a revered and respected crop from the earliest centuries. So valuable were the seeds that the pharaohs had the seeds buried in the pyramids with them, and some were found in Tutankhamen's tomb – so perhaps sesame was indigenous to Egypt.

The seeds are packed with vitamins A, B, E and iron, calcium, phosphorus, potassium and easily absorbed protein. Sesame is so important a food that its medicinal values are legendary.

Sesame was grown within the city walls, and was used in those early centuries as barter and trade. Then it was used to treat tumours, cysts, hard swellings, skin growths, scar tissue and slow-healing wounds. Its rich oil can be used as a treatment, massaged into scars, and it will help to heal an old wound. Just eating sesame will treat coughs, colds, eczema, kidney and bladder ailments, it will boost milk production in nursing mothers, strengthen nerves, lower blood pressure and treat coughs, colds, tinnitus, dizziness and blurred vision due to anaemia. The precious sesame oil can treat the scalp and dry skin, and can be rubbed into the skin to smooth wrinkles! It's quite a wonder plant!

Sesame loves mealies and sunflowers, and will boost their nutritional content and increase their growth. It acts as a magnet to wasps, and the wasps in turn feed on the mealie worms – but never plant it near sorghum as sorghum's roots exude a substance which inhibits sesame's growth and germination. Try growing sesame, it is great fun to watch and to think of the pharaohs.

USES
Culinary, medicinal, insect repellent

COMPANIONS
Mealies, sunflowers

DISLIKES
Sorghum

White Mustard

MUSTARD IS ONE OF THE MOST LOVED, MOST PRECIOUS OF HERBS KNOWN, AND TREASURED AND RESPECTED BOTH AS A MEDICINE AND A FOOD, AND AS A TRADE ITEM FOR CENTURIES. HAVE YOU EVER AS A CHILD GROWN LITTLE TRAYS OF MUSTARD SEED ON WET COTTON WOOL TO SNIP WITH KITCHEN SCISSORS AND EAT ON BREAD AND BUTTER WITH CUCUMBER? IF YOU HAVEN'T, I'D GO AS FAR AS SAYING YOU'VE MISSED OUT ON SOMETHING SIMPLY INCREDIBLE AND YOU NEED TO DO IT NOW! IT'S AN EXPERIENCE THAT MAKES YOU APPRECIATE THE WONDER OF NATURE.

Mustard is a quick-germinating annual that is one of the most valuable green fertilisers in the world. It will literally breathe life into depleted over-grazed, over-worked soil, and all you do is dig it in as soon as the flowers open and before it sets seed.

Mustard is a soil tonic, and the crop that follows it will be a bumper one. My favourite is to sow those strange ancient peanut-like beans from the top of Africa, called jugo beans, into a bed of mustard-enriched soil. The beans that emerge look like peanuts but are multi-coloured and you grow them on a circle of raised sand with a hollow in the middle. The mustard protects them and encourages their growth, and before long the vine matures and this exciting cluster of "beans" can be dug up.

The mustard keeps snails, nematodes and eelworms at bay – they can't stand it. Poultry and bird aviary farmers grow mustard inside the runs. The birds eat the mustard and it disinfects the soil as well.

Rows of mustard partner lettuce, mealies, cabbages, cauliflower, broccoli, tomatoes, fruit trees, tree tomatoes, potatoes, and grape vines with often quite amazing results, and the alkaline root secretions on mustard are so positive that it literally changes the soil balance from acid to alkaline. So don't grow mustard near acid-loving plants. I sow mustard throughout the year, it does well in winter too, where it acts as a trap crop for those defeating cabbage butterflies.

The more I grow mustard, the more impressed I am. The tender leaves give salads and stir-fries a bite and a zest. The bright yellow flowers do too, and the young seed-pods are stunning crushed with coriander leaves and garlic and butter as a spread on fish or toast or baked potatoes.

Medicinally, mustard boosts the immune system, it is rich in minerals, especially calcium, iron, potassium and phosphorus, and vitamins E, A, B and specially C. Mustard fights bronchial infections and pneumonia, it will ease constipation, arthritic and rheumatic aches and pains, and with its high alkaline content helps to dissolve painful deposits and stimulate the circulation. It is a true tonic herb and a valuable digestive herb, an antispasmodic and a good diuretic. Mustard tea for coughs and colds – 1 teaspoon mustard seeds, 2 teaspoons ground ginger, 2 teaspoons honey in 1 cup boiling water – is wonderfully soothing.

USES
Culinary, medicinal, fertiliser and soil tonic

COMPANIONS
Broccoli, cabbages, cauliflower, fruit trees, grape vines, lettuces, mealies, potatoes, tomatoes, tree tomatoes

DISLIKES
Acid-loving plants

Potato

THE POTATO IS PROBABLY THE BEST-KNOWN MEMBER OF THE GREAT *SOLANUM* GENUS. THERE ARE OVER 1 400 SPECIES, WHICH INCLUDE TREES, SHRUBS, VINES, PERENNIALS AND VEGETABLES. ALTHOUGH MANY SPECIES ARE POISONOUS, POTATOES AND BRINJALS AND THE UNUSUAL FRUIT SALAD PLANT (*SOLANUM MURICATUM*) ARE MUCH LOVED AND GROWN COMMERCIALLY ALL OVER THE WORLD.

Native to South America and the most widely eaten vegetable in the world, it's fun to grow potatoes not only in a neat and uniform row, but scattered through the garden in among the flowers! Easy to grow and very rewarding, a single small potato with a growing "eye" or little green shoot, planted 10 centimetres deep into richly composted, deeply dug, moist soil, will thrive, daily putting out new leaves into a succulent pretty bush! There is nothing nicer than digging up and cooking your own potatoes, organically grown and under your own eye!

Potatoes have been around a long time! It is believed that the South American Indians have been cultivating and eating potatoes for over two thousand years! The Spanish conquistadors arrived in South America in the 16th century and took the potato back to Spain and introduced it to Europe in the 16th century, and to the rest of the world by the end of the 17th century. Its popularity has never waned. It is rich in vitamins C and B3, folic acid and potassium; it is an energy booster, a strengthener and a muscle toner.

Growing potatoes organically, truly organically, is one of the most important aspects of organic gardening and the only way of getting the above elements out of a potato. It is now thought that chemical fertilisers and sprays are absorbed by the actual potato and that it acts as a sponge, reducing the nutrient value, and can cause a deficiency in the vitamins and the keeping ability of the potato. Under fluorescent lights potatoes will turn green, which is not healthy eating, and the better the organic composts and natural minerals in the soil, the better the crop and the healthier the potato.

If a band of mustard is planted close to the potato row and dug in around it once it starts to set seed, the mustard will act as a tonic to the potatoes. Grown next to mealies, peas, beans, strawberries, green peppers and marigolds, with horseradish close to the potato bush, you'll have an army protecting the crop, and the potato's proximity will keep the companions free of aphid and beetle attack, but they dislike raspberries, tomatoes, pumpkins and sunflowers.

Sweet potatoes (*Ipomoea batatas*), with their edible leaves, also benefit from these companions. If they are grown organically, they will help to bind heavy metals within the body to aid detoxification. There is extra magnesium and calcium in sweet potatoes, and they help to regulate menopausal symptoms.

No matter how small your patch of garden, give yourself the pleasure of growing potatoes!

USES
Culinary

COMPANIONS
Beans, green peppers, horseradish, marigolds, mealies, mustard, peas, strawberries

DISLIKES
Pumpkins, raspberries, sunflowers, tomatoes

Goldenrod

NATIVE TO EUROPE AND ASIA AND NATURALISED IN NORTH AMERICA, GOLDENROD IS A STRONG GARDEN PERENNIAL ALL OVER THE WORLD. IT IS AN ANCIENT AND MUCH LOVED HERB. I HAVE GROWN MANY DIFFERENT VARIETIES THROUGH THE YEARS AND HAVE ALWAYS BEEN ASTONISHED AT THEIR TENACIOUSNESS. MY FEW CANADIAN GIANT SOLIDAGO (*SOLIDAGO CANADENSIS*) CUTTINGS FROM A FRIEND'S GARDEN IN THE CAPE OVER 20 YEARS AGO, HAVE BECOME SO PROLIFIC I NOW ACTUALLY DIG THEM OUT AND DISCARD THEM, SO BE CAREFUL WHERE YOU PLANT GOLDENROD.

The original European goldenrod (*Solidago virgaurea*) has only a height of about 75 centimetres and a spread of 70 centimetres. This more delicate variety, as well as the cut flower varieties, are not so invasive. All are perennial and autumn flowering, and give so vibrant a splash of gold to the end of summer plantings, I am always intrigued.

All varieties offer similar medicinal values, and goldenrod tea has been popular since the Middle Ages when monks grew it in the cloister gardens for treating everything from upset digestive systems, sore throats, kidney ailments, urinary infections, cystitis, for healing wounds and to help clear candida and hayfever and rhinitis. Goldenrod tea is proving to be one of nature's gentle treatments for treating toxins, bladder stones, arthritic and rheumatic inflammatory conditions. To make the tea, pour 1 cup of boiling water over ¼ cup of fresh flowers, stand for 5 minutes then strain and sip slowly.

Goldenrod is a magnificent herb – it has antifungal and antiseptic qualities and is a superb antioxidant. Gout sufferers swear by the cup of goldenrod tea.

The flowers are the important part and can be dried for winter use, and when you really look at goldenrod's virtues you will give it the respect it really deserves.

Growing it is so easy. It needs a deeply dug and richly composted bed in full sun. Propagation is by means of rooted tufts dug off the mother plant in winter, and these small rooted pieces can be planted into compost-filled bags and left in a shady, sheltered place to establish. Once they are strong and vigorous, place the bags in the sun for daily increasing lengths of time until they have hardened off. Then plant the little plants about 50 centimetres apart and water 2 to 3 times a week, and control it. Remember it is invasive.

Farmers have used goldenrod for centuries to nourish their depleted soil, as it is so rich in minerals and enzymes. The long stalks of fully opened flowers were slashed and dug into the soil from bordering beds along the edges of fields. I have used a hammer mill to process my goldenrod and spread it onto the field and ploughed it in. I planted mealies and pumpkins in that field and had a bumper crop, and along the beds of goldenrod, green beans and squash of all varieties thrived. As an important "catch plant", goldenrod is simply amazing as it attracts ladybirds, hover flies, lace wings, praying mantises, who in turn devour aphids, ants, mealie bugs and caterpillars.

John Gerard, the Herbalist, wrote in 1597 that "Goldenrod is extolled above all other herbs". We should be sitting up and taking notice!

USES
Medicinal, cut flower, fertiliser

COMPANIONS
Beans, mealies, pumpkins and squashes

104

Comfrey

JUST THE WORD COMFREY MAKES ME FEEL BETTER – IT IS A HUGELY IMPORTANT PLANT IN THE ORGANIC GARDEN AND AN AMAZING PLANT TO USE IN MANY DIFFERENT WAYS. IT IS HUGE AND A PROLIFIC GROWER. IT LOVES MOIST COMPOST-RICH SOIL WHERE IT PRODUCES VAST QUANTITIES OF HUGE, HAIRY LEAVES AND THOSE PRETTY, CURLED, BELL-FLOWER STALKS THAT ARE SO SKIN SOFTENING IN YOUR BATH. I LOVE COMFREY! IT SAVED MY GARDEN AND ME FROM MANY MISHAPS, IT SAVED MY FARM ANIMALS, IT SAVED MY SANITY AND MY FINANCES, AND IT HEALED MY ACHES AND PAINS AND BROKEN BONES!

I was given my first comfrey plant by an Indian homeopathic doctor when I was a young mother living on an isolated farm. I read up everything I could and fed it to my chickens, and made soup of it for my elderly dogs with marrowbones and carrots. I gave it to the calves who were not drinking well, and I made it into ointments and salves and lotions and compresses and creams and poultices. (*Warning:* Do not take comfrey internally or eat it as a vegetable; do not apply leaves over broken skin.)

The leaves break down compost faster than anything I know – perhaps it's the high silica content and all the minerals and vitamins in the leaves, and the precious allantoin that helps to knit bones. Its high calcium, potassium and nitrogen content makes it one of the best natural fertilisers. I use the fresh leaves to line the holes and the trenches I dig for my food crops, and my sweet pea crop. You can cut it frequently and it comes back so quickly it is an investment in the garden.

I have it planted in abundance near my compost heaps, around my vegetable garden, near the drinking troughs at the stables and near the milking sheds so that the horses and cows can "help themselves" when they need it, and often it's eaten down to the crown.

I make liquid manure with it by filling a large drum with hot water poured over 2 buckets of chopped fresh comfrey leaves. I suspend a hessian bag of manure into the drum (about the size of a bag of oranges, which is equal to 2 buckets), and I cover the drum. Every day I give the drum a stir and swish the bag around to release the goodness of the manure into the water. It starts to really smell, so don't do this near the neighbour's fence! After three weeks it's really smelly and now is the time to try a little out. Dip in a watering can and water around an ailing plant. Check the next day to see if it has burned the plant at all. If not, hang on two more days, water the plant all around and over the leaves. The plant should by now have perked up, or if the manure mix is still too strong it will show unmistakable signs of burning. Then wait another week before using it.

Plant comfrey wherever there is space. It dies down in winter but comes up with a spade or two of compost in the spring. It is a magical herb – give it space!

USES
Medicinal, compost maker

COMPANIONS
Used as a soil tonic, it will benefit most plants

Marigold & Khakibos

PUNGENT AND RICHLY SCENTED, ALMOST OILY, THE HUGE VARIETY OF SPECTACULAR SUMMER-BEDDING PLANTS IN A COLOUR SPECTRUM FROM DARK COPPERY RED TO ORANGE TO PALEST YELLOW AND EVERYTHING IN BETWEEN, IS A FABULOUS GROUP OF NATURAL INSECT REPELLENTS.

I am mad about marigolds because they are my vegetable protectors. I plant them everywhere. I love their colour, their perky brilliance, their satiny shimmering and I love their deep, warm scent. There are so many varieties to choose from for summer gardening. When the voracious insects are at their worst, the Tagetes army will come to the rescue.

The *Tagetes* genus has around 50 species of annuals, which originate in the tropical warm parts of the Americas. Often known as Mexican marigolds, or our common garden variety *Tagetes patula*, the bedding plant now hybridised into different heights, colours and sizes, it originates in Mexico where it is burned as an incense to destroy bedbugs, lice and fleas. In Mexico it is used internally to remove intestinal worms, particularly in animals, and as a lotion and cream externally to treat insect bites and infections, and to relax sore spasms and tension in over-strained muscles.

Khakibos (*Tagetes minuta*) that amazing, tall 1 metre high summer weed, is used in the same way, and is ploughed into the soil to protect against nematodes and slugs. Bunches are hung in stables and chicken houses, or used as strewing herbs to cover stable floors and milking sheds to chase flies and ticks, or put under dogs' blankets and into kennels to keep dogs tick and flea free.

Khakibos, contrary to public belief, is native to Central and South America, and has become widely naturalised throughout the world. In many countries it is known as khaki weed or stinking Roger. It is thought to have come into South Africa in the straw bedding for the horses that came by ship at the time of the Boer War. What a gift Mexico has given many countries, as crushed, dried khakibos and marigold leaves can be crumbled and pushed down ant holes and spread along paths under succulent lettuce and spinach to deter slugs, and used as an effective, safe-and-easy-to-make spray.

Fill a big bucket with fresh khakibos or marigold leaves and flowers and cover with boiling water. Leave it to stand covered all night. Next morning strain, add ½ cup of soap powder and mix well. Spray or splash onto aphids and mealie bug, whitefly and even mildew and rust. Be lavish. Or, without the soap powder which helps it stick to the leaves of the plant, water the khakibos and/or marigold "tea" into ants' nests and all around the outside of the house to prevent ants and cockroaches entering. Use the tea to wash down floors in the kitchen, in the back yard and in kennels and aviaries, as well as milking sheds and stables. Whenever you see a khakibos seedling, leave it to grow to maturity – it is one of the most rewarding natural insecticides in the world.

Note: Overseas herb books call *Calendula officinalis* "Marigold". Do not confuse them, they are completely different plants. Calendula is a winter annual with no insect-repelling abilities.

USES
Insect repellent

COMPANIONS
All plants will benefit from its insect-repelling properties

Dandelion

WHO COULD HAVE THOUGHT THAT ONE OF THE WORLD'S MOST COMMON AND WIDESPREAD WEEDS COULD POSSIBLY BE IMPORTANT ENOUGH TO FIND A PLACE IN THIS SORT OF BOOK? WELL, HERE IT IS – NOT ONLY AS ONE OF THE WORLD'S MOST EXTRAORDINARY HEALING PLANTS, BUT ALSO AS A SURVIVOR.

As it is so rich in a number of important minerals, it makes a superb natural fertiliser, and it contains liberal amounts of copper, calcium and potash, which builds up the soil to ensure and encourage the plants to crop and mature well and to taste better. Wherever you can, dig back into the soil mature dandelion plants – for an organic farmer it's worth its weight in gold!

If you think that the leaves are shaped like the teeth of the lion (hence its name in French – *Dents de lion*) you'll not be surprised to realise its wealth of minerals, especially potassium and calcium, and its wealth of vitamins, especially vitamins A, B, C and D, you'll understand why eating dandelion will give you strong teeth, nails, bones and hair!

Fresh dandelion leaves, although slightly bitter, are delicious chopped with celery and parsley, mixed with lemon juice and then added to potato salad or couscous or rice. Sprinkled over roasts, soups, salads and stir-fries, it will act as a tonic, a blood builder, a joint strengthener, and will clear acne and help to flush the liver and kidneys. It is a marvellous plant and we should be eating it often. We most definitely should be planting it often – never mind that it comes up in the lawn – it's worth it. It exhales ethylene gas, which ripens nearby fruit trees. The young, full-of-minerals seedlings can be pulled up and added to the precious compost heap, as dandelion makes the most beautiful compost ever!

Many years ago when my children were small, like most young mothers I was seriously short of cash. I had just imported and sown my first dandelion seed of the largest and most prolific of all dandelions, and I had decided to plant a green manure crop that I could sell as an organic fertiliser. So I sowed a thick band of buckwheat down one side of a small field and next to it I sowed the dandelion seed in a wide band. Next to that I planted comfrey roots and pieces of root in a wide band. I had dug in the richest amount of compost I could find and I kept everything well watered and watched over my little field of dreams with an eagle eye.

Everything flourished. My crop was astonishing! By midsummer I reaped the first bags of my green manure, chopping off the leaves of all three with a scythe! I then put them through a small shredder and let the pieces dry out, spread on newspaper in the shade for two days. I then packed my still soft and fairly moist green manure in hessian bags the size of a potato pocket, and set off to sell it all on a farmers' day. I sold only two bags! Everyone laughed at me, no matter how much I explained and extolled the mixture's marvellous properties! No one understood anything about organic farming then. I must have been quite crazy, they thought. But I went home and emptied my unsold bags onto my vegetable garden and you should have seen the incredibly lush and rich crop that followed. Everybody came to see it with unbelieving eyes, and no one laughed as they bought my vegetables!

USES
Culinary, medicinal, green manure, compost maker

COMPANIONS
Fruit trees

Thyme

NATIVE TO THE MEDITERRANEAN AREA, THYME (THERE ARE ABOUT 150 VARIETIES) NEVER CEASES TO PLEASE, AND IT IS INDISPENSABLE FOR EVERY COOK. IT HAS AMAZING ANTIBACTERIAL, ANTISEPTIC QUALITIES, AND SOME RESEARCHERS SAY IT CAN KILL BACTERIA IN 40 SECONDS!

An easy-to-grow perennial, thyme makes a charming ground cover and path edging in the vegetable and herb garden. I literally cannot cook without thyme, and for the big, tender succulent stews that I have always cooked for my family, thyme features as a strong and simply delicious flavour. Thyme will grow anywhere! It is tough, resilient, undemanding, and will put up with searing heat as well as heavy frost, and in Europe even snow! A true survivor, it rapidly forms a good ground cover, gently mounding over uneven ground, and edging paths with softness.

Lemon thyme (*Thymus* × *citriodora*) and silver posy thyme (*Thymus varigata*) are equally as charming as *Thymus vulgaris*, the true culinary thyme, and I find all three invaluable under tomatoes, brinjals, green peppers, melons, squashes and especially cabbages. It does not mind being trodden on, and in medieval times thyme walks were planted to enable the ladies' dresses to be perfumed as they walked alongside the plantings, their long dresses and petticoats sweeping over the thyme and releasing the precious thymol oil, which also incidentally chases fleas, flies, mosquitoes and ants!

If you are lucky you might find the tiny creeping thyme with minute either pink or white flowers, Bressingham thyme (*Thymus coccineus* or *Thymus alba*). Some specialist nurseries may have it – it is simply beautiful planted between stepping stones, and gives an exquisitely strong scent, while at the same time sending ants scurrying. The ordinary creeping thyme (*Thymus serpyllum*), makes a strong spreading mat, and it grows so rapidly you can cut it back quite

heavily and use the cuttings on which to store apples or pears to ripen. I also make nests of creeping thyme for ripening pumpkins or tomatoes. Twisted with khakibos, you will have an insect-proof nest on which to ripen paw paws or avocados evenly and quickly.

Thyme planted along paths and all round the vegetable garden is a huge asset. It literally stops the creepy crawlies getting in. They don't like the smell!

During the Middle Ages, small thyme, rosemary and lavender posies were made for the ladies to carry and sniff as they walked in the streets with the open sewers and into public places to protect them from the unhealthy smells and germs. Those little posies are called tussie-mussies, and I have made them with my grandmother since I was about four years old. You start with a bunch of rosebuds, heads together tightly, then circle with thyme sprigs. Secure with a rubber band and then make the next circle of rosemary sprigs, then another circle of perhaps yarrow or violets or honeysuckle. Secure again with a rubber band and finally end with a double circle of lavender. Fasten securely, first with a rubber band, then tie a pretty ribbon around it. I love using the thyme when it is in flower – it makes a most loved present for someone special.

Thymus vulgaris

USES
Culinary, medicinal, insect repellent

COMPANIONS
Brinjals, cabbages, green peppers, melons, squashes, tomatoes

108

Clover

THIS IS A LARGE GENUS WITH AROUND 240 SPECIES OF ANNUAL, BIENNIAL AND PERENNIAL THREE-LOBED LEAF PLANTS FOUND ALMOST EVERYWHERE IN THE WORLD IN TEMPERATE AND SUBTROPICAL REGIONS. IT IS EASILY GROWN, IT SPREADS EASILY AND IS COMMON AS FORAGE CROPS.

The red clover (*Trifolium pretense*) has fascinating medicinal uses. During the 1930s, red clover became popular for treating several ailments, including cancer. Since then, medical research has been continuous. It is today used in capsules and tablets for treating an astonishing number of ailments. Some doctors prescribe it for menopausal symptoms and breast and ovarian cancer, and for treating arthritis, gout, psoriasis and eczema, bronchitis and chest ailments. For inflamed, aching sprains and joint strains, a compress of red clover, both leaves and flowers, is as popular now as it was in medieval times in its native Europe. It's really worth growing in every garden.

Clover fixes nitrogen in the soil, so it is an important green manure crop that has been used and respected by farmers throughout the world for centuries. Easy to grow and to cultivate, it is worth digging it back into the soil because of its high and vitally important boron content. Boron is a trace mineral that is often depleted in over-cultivated fields, and farmers noticing yellowing leaves and brittle stems on a plant would add chopped clover to the soil around it with compost.

I have used clover with great success on my poor mountainside soil, firstly as a mulch around plants in summer's heat waves, and also as a strong tea with comfrey to revive poorly growing plants. Pour 1 bucket of boiling water over ¾ of a bucket of roughly chopped fresh clover and comfrey leaves. Leave it to cool overnight. Next morning strain, add the leaves to the compost heap and use the clover and comfrey brew to water into and spray onto ailing plants. Use any clover, red or white. Plant red clover between rows of cabbages and broccoli and cauliflower, or use chopped fresh clover as a dense mulch. This encourages spurts of growth and those growing show specimens will find this green mulch, renewed every fortnight, an amazing tool for increasing both size and flavour.

In France and Italy, clover is grown under fruit trees and grapes, and mowed (with scythes in the past) to make a mulch all round the trees. Clover on the compost heap is amazing, especially if it is immediately dug in so that it is completely covered, and watered. Within a week it will have started its nitrogen action. The heap heats up and starts breaking down.

Refreshing clover tea is made by pouring 1 cup of boiling water over ¼ cup fresh red clover leaves and flowers. Leave it to stand 5 minutes, strain and sip slowly. It is a wonderful tonic for you, and if there is any left over, for your pot plants too.

USES
Medicinal, fertiliser

COMPANIONS
Broccoli, cabbages, cauliflower, fruit trees grape vines

Fenugreek

FENUGREEK IS ANOTHER ONE OF THE WORLD'S MOST ANCIENT AND MOST RESPECTED HERBS. NATIVE TO THE EASTERN MEDITERRANEAN AND NORTH AFRICA, IT HAS BEEN USED THROUGH THE CENTURIES BY MANY CULTURES, BUT IS MOST LOVED BY THE ARABS AND THE EGYPTIANS.

An Egyptian papyrus dating back from 1500 BC records its medicinal uses for treating childbirth, burns, wounds, and as a digestive. Interestingly, Dioscorides in the 1st century recommended fenugreek as a treatment for gynaecological ailments, and Hippocrates in the 5th century prescribed it for inflammations and infections and for treating ulcers both internally and externally. New and ongoing medical research proves that it is in fact helpful for all these ailments, and may even inhibit cervical cancer (it has been used for centuries in China for this). Its high vitamin A, B and C content, as well as its high mineral content, makes it an excellent health food, but do consult your doctor always and avoid if you are pregnant.

Crushed seeds warmed and bound over a boil or a suppurating wound will bring it to a head. It will also ease fevers, colic, stomach upsets and increase breast milk. New research is looking at it as a helpful diabetic herb, and one which will lower blood cholesterol. In the bath it is helpful in treating cellulite, clearing spots and rashes, and is one of the rare herbs that will aid anorexia to stabilise weight gain.

To make a tea, take 1 teaspoon of the seeds to 1 cup of boiling water, stand 5 minutes and sip slowly. Add the pungent, succulent leaves to stir-fries and salads, and grow the easy-to-germinate seeds as deliciously nourishing sprouts. And it is a superb curry ingredient!

Fenugreek is one of the easiest of all crops to grow. It germinates quickly – virtually every seed germinates – and a row sprinkled between lettuces, beans, cucumbers, tomatoes and squash of all types not only will come up and flourish in record time, but will shade the roots and stop moisture from drying out, act as a tonic and an insect repellent to the plants it grows beside, and it will chase aphids, whitefly, millipedes and beetles – specially if the leaves are lightly crushed.

I sow the seeds everywhere all the time directly into well-composted soil in full sun, and the little seedlings can be pulled up and eaten when they are even 3 centimetres high. They can be sprinkled over roasts and grills and stir-fries like a succulent mustard and cress. In fact, they grow well beside both mustard and cress on wet cotton wool indoors.

Fenugreek's most spectacular use is as a green manure crop, a natural fertiliser and compost builder. Scatter the seeds over the compost and over a field of well-tilled soil, preferably after a shower of rain. Let them mature for six weeks, then plough them in, or let them stand and make a fabulous foliar feed of the fresh leaves. Pour 2 buckets of boiling water over 1 bucket of fenugreek leaves, flowers and roots. Let it stand overnight to cool, strain, then add 3 cups of bone meal to the water, mix well and splash or spray onto pot plants, squash, cucumbers, beans, spinach and brinjals, and water some in around them. This spray will also act as an insect repellent without the bone meal.

USES
Culinary, medicinal, green manure, fertiliser

COMPANIONS
Beans, cucumbers, lettuces, squash, tomatoes

110

Nasturtium

LET'S RETHINK NASTURTIUMS! THIS WONDERFULLY OLD-FASHIONED, CHEERFUL AND PROLIFIC ANNUAL IS A VITALLY IMPORTANT TRAP CROP IN EVERY GARDEN, AND ITS JOURNEY ACROSS THE WORLD FROM PERU IS A TRIBUTE TO HOW MUCH IT IS LOVED AND ENJOYED AND HOW TOUGH A LITTLE SURVIVOR IT IS!

Think of its early beginnings – travellers eating the delicious leaves and flowers, and those spicy seeds pickled in brine and in vinegar, which gave flavour to meat and beans and fish, and how they would have shared the seeds, so easy and so prolific to grow, with strangers, who lovingly nurtured them and took them further and further from their native land, at times even using them as trade, until most temperate regions in the world have nasturtiums. Some have even become naturalised in moist ditches and waste ground all around the globe. What a gallant little soldier the nasturtium is, grown first as a cottage garden flower, then as a vegetable and now more and more as a trap crop for whitefly, aphids and red spider. So it has become a necessary companion for cabbages, broccoli, mealies, radishes, tomatoes, broad beans and cucumbers – even helping with mildew – and as an excellent companion to quince trees and pomegranates.

Everyone loves the dear little bright-faced nasturtium – so cheerful, so undemanding, so easy to grow and so simply satisfying – but did you know it has natural antibiotic properties within those quite bitingly hot circular leaves? Nasturtium has been used as a medicinal plant since the 17th century to treat scrofula – which is a tubercular infection of the lymph nodes – and fresh leaves, flowers and seeds are added to the diet to treat chest ailments, nasal congestion and even emphysema. A tea can be made of the leaves and flowers, taken twice daily. Doctors in the last century actually prescribed nasturtium as a sure cure, and so nasturtiums were cultivated in every cottage garden

and in the monastery gardens, so many were the uses. For wound washing, dressings over burns and grazes, and cuts, and to boost the immune system especially during the month before the winter sets in, fresh leaves and flowers were eaten daily, and pickled seeds and leaves were kept in every medicine chest to fight coughs, colds and flu, and for washing wounds.

Why I love it so much is that it is the greatest lure for black aphids, enticing them to come and suck their wonderful juices. Then, when it is thickly coated in aphids, the whole plant can be uprooted gently and very carefully – tuck a large sheet of plastic around the plant first so as to catch up all those aphids – then bundle it all up and toss it into a large hole in the middle of the compost heap and completely cover it over with soil. Soak it well and leave it to rot. If you live on a farm and can make a safe bonfire – in town it is not allowed – burn the whole plant.

Add the leaves and flowers to salads, eat on sandwiches with cheese, and grow this precious summer plant everywhere, it's a tonic herb, it's a survivor herb, and in the cycle of nature it is a huge asset.

USES
Culinary, medicinal

COMPANIONS
Broad beans, broccoli, cabbages, cucumbers, mealies, pomegranates, quince trees, radishes, tomatoes

Stinging Nettle Urtica Dioica

"STINGING NETTLE," I CAN HEAR YOU SAY INCREDULOUSLY. YES, STINGING NETTLE, ONE OF THE MOST UNBELIEVABLY INCREDIBLE PLANTS IN THE WORLD. IT IS A COSMOPOLITAN WEED THAT ORIGINATES IN TEMPERATE REGIONS WORLDWIDE, AND IT IS CALLED A "FAMILIAR WEED OF HUMAN HABITATION".

Nettle is a fibrous plant used since the Bronze Age for cloth manufacture, as a food, and as medicine. Ancient, respected and fully hardy, the nettle has been used abundantly over the centuries, and today it is still one of the best treatments for gout and arthritis ever discovered.

Rich in chlorophyll and nitrogen, nettle literally gives the compost heap and the soil it is ploughed into, a "turbo boost", breaking down organic matter quickly and efficiently. We gather barrows full of the lush leaves, which are laid under layers of grass mowings and clippings and raked leaves on the compost heap, and with a thin layer of manure on top of this potent heap and thoroughly watered, we are using the exceptional compost within 6 to 8 weeks. But always gather the nettles with long gloves, secateurs and great care. The sting, strangely enough, should you get stung, is good for you, moving sluggish circulation with speed, but apply immediately the soothing gel of aloe vera or bulbinella (*Bulbine frutescens*). Literally keep applying until the sting goes.

Propagation is by chopping off pieces of the perennial clump-forming mother stock. Plant them about 1 metre apart as the clumps form quickly. It takes full sun and thrives in deeply dug, well-composted soil, and it can be forgotten about, neglected, and not even thought about – and still it will survive and thrive!

Fresh leaves and succulent tips can be picked with gloves on and cooked as a nutritious mineral-rich spinach. Or brew a tea using ¼ to ½ cup fresh leaves to 1 cup of boiling water, then stand 5 minutes, strain and sip slowly for arthritis, gout, catarrh, retention of fluid, impaired kidney function, kidney stones, blockages in the urethra. It is non-allergenic and will soothe and clear hay fever. One cup of tea daily is taken for chronic conditions, 3 to 5 cups is taken for acute conditions for no more than 4 to 5 days, and stop once the condition has cleared.

In the garden, plant nettles near potatoes, tomatoes and horseradish for an abundant crop, and next to radishes and peppers, peppermint, sage and marjoram to intensify the taste. A bucket of strong nettle tea made by pouring one bucket of boiling water over ¾ bucket of fresh nettle sprigs, is both a tonic and a natural pesticide if watered around ailing plants or sprayed as a foliar feed and deterrent.

Nettle leaves are rich in vitamins and minerals, as well as chlorophyll, and in fact the leaves are processed commercially to extract the natural green colouring, which is used as a food colourant. Fresh leaves tied in bundles can be added to buckets of fresh milk to impart their valuable minerals and vitamins. The more you cut back the leafy sprays, the more it grows. Older leaves contain oxalate crystals, and this is what makes nettles so valuable for compost making and digging back into poor soil. We indeed need to re-think stinging nettles!

USES
Medicinal, fertiliser

COMPANIONS
Horseradish, marjoram, peppermint, peppers, potatoes, radishes, sage, tomatoes

Vetiver Grass

IT IS THOUGHT THAT THE PRECIOUS AND EXTRAORDINARY VETIVER GRASS – ALSO CALLED KHUS-KHUS GRASS – WAS ORIGINALLY INDIGENOUS TO INDIA, BUT IT HAS BEEN FOUND IN SO MANY COUNTRIES – LIKE RÉUNION ISLAND, MALAYSIA, INDONESIA, HAITI, SRI LANKA AND VIETNAM – THAT THERE IS SOME CONTROVERSY ABOUT ITS ORIGINS.

Its rich and remarkable oil, abundant in the roots, is known as "the oil of tranquillity" and is a valuable commercial crop, and its name vetiver is derived from the Southern Indian name "Vettiveri".

The root has an earthy, heavy aroma, and is an excellent repellent to moths, fish moths, flies, cockroaches and bedbugs, and has been used through the centuries as a moth repellent in clothes, and gives those exquisite finely woven Indian cotton clothes that distinctive smell.

Vetiver is a precious plant – every part of it is used – and its tough, robust adaptability to all climates, soil conditions and situations makes it invaluable as plant to control erosion. The fibrous and prolific roots hold the soil on steep banks, and as contours across sloping fields, vetiver grass is superb. The grass itself can be tied into small bundles and made into fly repelling natural air conditioning screens to hang over windows and doorways. Splashed often with water it not only cools the room but it has a pleasant unobtrusive fragrance that chases the flies and the mosquitoes. Hats woven from the grass itself with the fibrous roots, keep the wearer cool if dipped into or splashed with water, and free from flies and midges.

The grass itself slashed and chopped roughly and left to dry, can be burned over fields where severe insect damage has manifested – even its ash is an effective insect repellent and the ash can be scattered under ripening vegetables to deter slugs and snails. Dug into the soil the ash acts as a fertiliser and the burned roots as an insect repellent in the soil. Since using it in a bed that was thick with cutworms, just once, and by digging in a thick quantity of the ash, I have not had a cutworm since!

I have grown vetiver grass for forty years, and I often wonder why so few gardeners, even after my magazine articles, workshops and exclamations of delight, have not utilised it. This is probably the most valuable grass known to mankind! The incredible oil from the roots is a cosmetic ingredient and is used in bath preparations, skin softening soaps, men's colognes, aftershaves and muscle relaxant massage creams. The roots themselves are used in potpourris to fix the fragrant oils, and are tied in a face cloth with shaved soap and used for a body cleanser and muscle relaxant. A vetiver tea is taken for anxiety, restlessness, fear, depression, pain, burnout and tension, and is actually being researched at present as a natural tranquilliser. Take ¼ cup chopped leaves with a couple of little roots, pour over this 1 cup of boiling water, stand 5 minutes, then strain and sip slowly.

Plant the wonder grass in full sun 1 to 1 ½ metres apart in a big compost-filled hole, water deeply twice weekly and experience it!

USES
Medicinal, cosmetic, potpourri, insect repellent

113

Violet

THIS MUCH-LOVED GARDEN PLANT, THE SWEETLY SCENTED PERENNIAL, ORIGINATES IN EUROPE AND ASIA AND BOTANICAL RECORDINGS GO BACK IN HISTORY TO THE FIRST CENTURY AD WHERE IT WAS FOUND GROWING IN SYRIA, TURKEY AND NORTH AFRICA, AS WELL AS IN EUROPE. I LOVE THE FACT THAT THE VIOLET WAS GROWN COMMERCIALLY IN GREECE AS FAR BACK AS 400 BC AND IT BECAME THE SYMBOL OF ATHENS. THE ROMANS GREW VIOLETS TO FLAVOUR THEIR WINE FROM 65 TO 8 BC, AND EVEN NAPOLEON WAS UNDER THEIR SPELL – IT WAS HIS FAVOURITE FLOWER AND HE PLANTED THEM ON JOSEPHINE'S GRAVE.

Violets are tough, resilient, and can take extremes of temperature, but love the cooler months and the spring when their blooms are so prolific and their exquisite scent fills the air. Propagation is by runners that can be chopped off from the clump with a sharp spade at any time of the year, and if the piece is immediately replanted in moist richly composted soil in partial shade, it will literally not even turn a hair and will just keep going!

Violets are extremely valuable in the garden, they actually act as a trap crop for insects luring them away from other plants. I plant them next to lettuce and spinach, and the insects will leave these alone, preferring rather the taste of the violets! So next to cabbages and kale, the row of violets acts as a most wonderful companion!

Medicinally violets have a huge part to play as well. The leaves, flowers and even the rootstock have been used through the centuries in a tea, and eaten in salads, to treat coughs, colds, sinus, hay fever, blocked noses, and for bronchitis and flu a cup of violet tea is not only soothing and calming, but it is an excellent decongestant and expectorant, and it breaks down phlegm and eases asthmatic spasms.

Interestingly a cup of violet tea has been taken for centuries to ease hangovers – think of the Romans with violets in their wine! Make the tea by pouring one cup of boiling water over ¼ cup fresh violet flowers and leaves, stand 5 minutes, strain and sip slowly. For a cough add a little honey to sweeten it, and a squeeze of lemon juice.

Our grandmothers used to crystallise violets with egg white and castor sugar, and once dried they were the most charming cake and pudding decorations. Violet jam is something quite incredible, and I used to make it every spring, filling small glass jars with its exquisite taste. With lemon juice to thicken it, it is a very gentle process and very time consuming to pick all those spring violets to make only a few jars – but so worth it.

Use the violet flowers and leaves in soothing and softening skin creams and lotions and bath oils, and saturate your senses in the unforgettable and haunting fragrance. Try eating five flowers to soothe a headache, and think about the ancient treatment of violet flowers and leaves in teas, salads and puddings and even cool drinks to treat depression, anxiety and tumours. New medical research is confirming those ancient treatments for shrinking tumours and cancerous growths. Keep a sharp look out for violet essential oil – it is as precious as gold!

USES
Culinary, medicinal, cosmetic

COMPANIONS
Cabbages, kale, lettuces, spinach

Grapes

WHEREVER I HAVE LIVED ALL THROUGH MY LIFE, FROM MY EARLIEST CHILDHOOD, WE GREW GRAPES – GRAPES OVER PERGOLAS, OVER ARCHES, SHADING CAR PORTS, SHADING COOL ARBOUR AREAS NEXT TO THE HOUSE, TRAINED UP FENCES, ALONG WALKWAYS, AND SOME WERE EVEN TURNED INTO THE MOST BEAUTIFUL GARDEN UMBRELLAS GROWN OVER THOSE CIRCULAR WASHING LINES. RICHLY AND THICKLY COVERED IN LEAVES AND FRUIT, SHADY AND BECKONING ALL THROUGH THE SUMMER, AND BARE AND SUNNY IN WINTER, THE GRAPE ARBOUR INVITED A PLACE FOR REST AND CONTEMPLATION, AS WELL AS FESTIVITY AND CONVERSATION OVER THE HOT CHRISTMAS HOLIDAY FAMILY TIMES.

We used the young leaves in several dishes – wrapped around spicy mince, or around mushrooms and mozzarella cheese, and cooked in home-grown tomato sauce, and served on steaming mounds of green mealies cut off the cob, or brown rice. The vines and the exquisitely delicious grape juice they produced were part of my wonderful, safe childhood, and I continued that way of life for my own children and now grandchildren. Grapes mean summer and health and happiness, and to this day I still make that luscious grape juice that makes memories.

So I make gardens of grapes and I have planted sage and chives at the foot of each vine. I plant elder trees nearby and a long row of perennial basil beside the vines. In this way I ensure that the fruit will be extra sweet and the yield good, and the vine leaves will be mildew free. That's the way we've always done it.

Mulching the roots of the vines and keeping them free of weeds and grass is also important. I tuck in garlic cloves next to the chives and sow long swathes of chamomile in autumn as the leaves start to fall. The chamomile acts as a tonic to the whole vine, and at the end of spring I dig the entire row of chamomile into the soil between the vines. Then the chamomile acts as a tonic for the new spring growth. Compost is vitally important twice yearly, and a twice weekly deep watering directly onto the vine is essential for a good crop.

I do spend a lot of time tying up ripening bunches of delectable grapes in brown paper bags to protect them from the birds, wasps and later the bees. It is worth the effort. I use little wire ties so the whole bunch plus the bag can later be clipped off the vine and the bag torn off it once it is safely in the kitchen.

Use chopped tendrils and young leaves in salads and stir-fries, and should you want to go on a grape diet for a few days, include these as well as your own organically grown grapes for a real health boost.

If you think that wild grapes originated in the Caucasus and Western Asia, and that cultivation and wine making began around 3000 BC, you'll be astonished to realise grapes are probably one of the oldest foods, or should I say drinks, in the world. They have been treasured throughout the ages. Even the seeds give us grape seed oil, another bonus! What wealth!

USES
Culinary

COMPANIONS
Chamomile, chives, garlic, perennial basil, sage

Ginger

ONE OF THE WORLD'S BEST-LOVED SPICES, GINGER WAS CARRIED BY THE ROMAN SOLDIERS IN THEIR MEDICAL SUPPLIES WHEN THEY INVADED BRITAIN IN AD 43! NATIVE TO SOUTH EAST ASIA, GINGER HAS BEEN GROWN AS A CROP IN THE TROPICAL REGIONS ACROSS THE WORLD. TONS OF FRESH GINGER ROOT ARE SOLD IN MARKETS EVERYWHERE DAILY, AND IN JAMAICA IT IS GROWN TO ITS EXQUISITE BEST, THE WARMTH, THE SOFT GENTLE RAIN AND THE RICH SOIL AND SEA BREEZES GIVE IT THAT INCREDIBLE TASTE THAT MAKES IT ONE OF JAMAICA'S MOST SOUGHT AFTER EXPORTS.

Ginger is actually easy to grow. Its requirements are deeply dug, richly composted, loose, friable soil. It can take full sun and often thrives in light shade in very hot areas. It needs heat, a deep watering twice weekly and more compost in summer.

Select your ginger from the greengrocer in late winter and choose pieces that have pale greenish "eyes" starting to form. Prepare the area by digging in lots of compost, and keep it moist. As the spring starts to come, cut off the pieces of ginger that have the "growing eye" on each one at the natural neck and press it into the ground, spacing each piece 30 to 50 centimetres apart, as deep as your thumb will go. Cover with soil and leaves and keep the area moist. The leaves will keep it warm. Once it sends up the little stiff pointed shoot, water it twice weekly.

In late summer it will flower white, headily scented flowers, and as the autumn draws in, the lush green growth and thick stems will start to turn brown and die off. Wait until it dies down completely, then dig up your own rhizomes! Ginger will only taste good once it has matured and the top growth has died down naturally. Even then leave it in the ground for another three weeks to ensure its strong and wonderful flavour.

Quite by chance I grew St Joseph's lilies close to the ginger, and on the other side I grew taro (*Colocasia esculenta*), known in South Africa as madumbi. Both were the very best I have ever grown – the lilies reached well over a metre in height with up to eight flowers on a stem, and the air was headily fragrant for weeks, and the taro with its huge elephant ear shaped leaves was the biggest specimen I'd even grown. (Note that this is not the same as the decorative elephant ear, which is poisonous.) So my conclusion was all three benefited the other, and this year I have planted new daylily roots next to the ginger, and taro next to them. I am hoping for masses of white daylily flowers and buds for summer salads, and with ginger as a companion it should be a big and luscious crop!

Save the ginger roots for teas to treat nausea, flatulence, colic, poor peripheral circulation, lack of energy, diarrhoea and exhaustion. Slice four or five paper-thin slices into 1 cup of boiling water, stand 5 minutes, sweeten with a touch of honey if liked, and sip slowly. Add freshly grated root to stir-fries, sauces and marinades. Mix with ground cayenne pepper and sprinkle under precious plants to deter ants and cutworms, and mix ginger powder and grated pieces with cayenne pepper and coffee grounds to deter snails and slugs.

USES
Culinary, medicinal

COMPANIONS

Lilies, taro (madumbi)

Beneficial Weeds

Long ago I read a book called *Weeds – the Guardians of the Soil*, and how important they are. I had a field of vegetables and at that time I was almost defeated by the weeds, but I had the best pumpkins, mealies, beans and spinach I've ever grown – completely overrun by weeds. Being a busy mother and farmer's wife and running a pottery business, there wasn't time in the day, and I felt every day as though I was drowning. I would fight my way through the weeds into that field, my black Labrador at my side, carrying my basket at the end of a busy day to pick the vegetables for supper, and I had to open a path of weeds for him to get through. But my crop was amazing! I had always thought weeds depleted the soil of nutrients, but I had to agree with the author, whose name I have now forgotten, that weeds are the guardians of the soil.

When the summer was over and the field was reaped, I ploughed in everything in a double ploughing and let the weeds re-nourish the soil, and my winter crop of vegetables was equally abundant, strong and extra tasty!

The writer explained how weeds with long fibrous roots could aerate the soil and bring up nutrients, and told the story of a farmer who owned an orchard in California. He used chemical fertilisers to assist in the production of large and abundant fruits and in weed control, and eventually after he used more and more, the trees deteriorated and some actually died. So he abandoned the orchard and only occasionally watered it, and the weeds took over. After a couple of years the orchard started to re-grow magnificently, and bear fruit particularly well where the weeds were thickest! So the farmer abandoned his chemical fertilisers and sprays and went back to farming the way he had when he was younger, and the orchard survived healthily!

So, think differently about weeds and how they clothe disturbed ground, saving the soil from erosion and returning nutrients to the soil! My greatest favourites do just this – Amaranth (page 19), Dandelion (page 107) and Khakibos (page 106) – so I actually plant these!

I can extol the virtues of certain other weeds too, at length, and have at times planted up a whole area devoted to these stalwarts! I can also cook up a truly delicious soup using weeds, and I can also sing their praises, often loudly, for what they can do if turned into compost, dug back into the soil, and how deep-rooted weeds literally mine up nutrients which can be returned to the plants like a tonic, by merely using them as a decomposing mulch or by adding them to the compost heap!

Let me introduce you to my favourite weeds, let me assure you of their usefulness and in the greater scheme of things let me assure you of their place in the environment. Long ago Emerson wrote "A weed is a plant whose virtues have not yet been discovered". Well, I have discovered some simply marvellous virtues of these weeds, my particular favourites!

Purslane (*Portulaca oleracea*)

Sometimes known as pig weed – as it is much loved by pigs – this flat spreading succulent small-leafed weed, often with reddish stems, is an international weed, and has been used as a vegetable for thousands of years. The leaves are delicious in salads and it can be added to soups, sauces and pickles and is much loved stir-fried with onions and slivers of potato and mushrooms in a mustard sauce in France.

Research shows it is rich in omega-3 fatty acids and it was first described in Chinese medicine in AD 500 where it is used to this day to treat sore eyes, skin inflammations, swellings, bacterial infections, dysentery, enteritis, mastitis, haemorrhoids and to clear toxins, and used externally for boils, bee stings, eczema, rashes and grazes.

On the compost heap it breaks down quickly and with comfrey and nettles makes a fabulous foliar feed – they are all so rich in minerals.

Chickweed (*Stellaria media*)

This precious little tender ground hugging annual with its tiny leaves and minute little white star flowers has been used through the centuries to treat skin rashes, grazes, burns, eczemas and psoriasis. It is a soothing, cooling, gentle, slightly saline little herb that promotes healing, and it is eaten to soothe rheumatic pains, chest infections, ulcers, boils and abscesses.

Contraindicated during pregnancy, it has been used in salves and creams and ointments, and in many countries it is valued as a feed for domestic fowls, pigeons and caged birds – hence its name chickweed.

Eat it in salads and stir-fries – it is rich in vitamins and minerals and so valuable across the world that it has become an international weed. It often appears in the cooler months as it thrives in shady moist cool places (do not confuse it with the poisonous small-leafed spurge which has a milky sap).

Dig it back into the ground while it is green and vigorous for a mineral boost. It acts like a tonic to plants near it.

Fat Hen (*Chenopodium album*)

Also known as goosefoot, this is another cosmopolitan weed that is so rich in minerals, it is extremely valuable as a food, and it belongs to the great Chenopodiaceae family that has about 150 species in it!

The leaves are rich in iron, calcium, phosphorus and vitamins B1 and C, and it contains protein in both leaves and seeds and was one of the Aztecs' favourite "grains". The tiny seeds in the tight little bunches of calyxes, even the green immature seed sprays on this tall weed – it can reach 1,5 metres in height – are delicious in stir-fries and the leaves make the most divine spinach you have ever eaten. Literally cook for a minute in boiling water, strain, serve with salt, butter and lemon juice, or mash into potatoes or brinjals and tomatoes.

The leaf is shaped like a goose's foot and ducks, geese and chickens love it – and it has been a valuable food crop through the centuries throughout Europe and the Mediterranean area not only for poultry and pigs, but for humans too, and as a medicine it has been used to treat skin problems like eczema, circulatory and blood disorders, to give energy and strength, and to treat fatigue, depression and anxiety.

Dig it into the compost heap to put iron into the soil.

Asthma Weed
(Euphorbia hirta)

This low-spreading annual comes up everywhere, especially between paving stones. Its insignificant clusters of "flowers" seed rapidly, spreading it far and wide. Coarse, almost bronzy, leaves distinguish it, and it has to be one of the toughest survivor weeds around!

Sometimes known as "pill-bearing spurge", this international weed has a long history of well used, well respected treatments, specifically for asthma, bronchitis, emphysema, nervous coughs that never seems to clear up, hay fever, sneezing, catarrh, and in Spain and Portugal, it is used to treat amoebic dysentery.

This prolific weed is a wonder plant. It is an acrid and very bitter, strongly antiseptic herb that has been used through the centuries to treat spasms, especially digestive and coughing spasms, and to expel phlegm. To make a tea, pour 1 cup of boiling water over ¼ cup fresh leaves and sprigs, stand 5 minutes, strain. Take no more than 2 cups of the tea daily, a little at a time. The milky sap, if dabbed onto warts frequently, will dry them up.

Thrown onto the compost heap the high silica and magnesium and calcium content in the leaves and stems is invaluable, and there is no herb that is as effective in treating asthma as this one!

Sow Thistle *(Sonchus oleraceus)*

I remember always being very careful not to weed this milky weed out with its succulent buds and little yellow thistle flowers and serrated, often prickly leaves, as my sister kept canaries and sow thistle is their favourite food! It's also the pigs' most luscious mouthful, and its strong taproot is quite tough. So the pigs would just munch off the tops so that next week a tasty little cluster of new leaves would emerge.

Rich in calcium, phosphorus, magnesium and silica, sow thistle has been a favourite cosmopolitan weed for centuries, and was eaten as a spinach for rheumatism and fatigue, added to other wild spinach like amaranth and dandelion, and its milky sap was used for warts, dabbed on frequently.

For farmers it is a great green manure and can be slashed and immediately dug in to enrich the soil. Be sure to dig it in before it scatters its little puffballs of wind-dispersed weeds!

Natural pest control

This does not have to be complicated! Many years ago I developed my own natural sprays, and I set out to find the most pungent plant bases. There was no one to ask and I experimented constantly. My mother's love of roses prompted my experiments on roses, and my winter cabbages brought my sprays to the vegetable gardens. To this day my early khakibos experiments still hold good and I never stop trying new plants in my basic mixture, which as a rule I've never changed:

Basic spray mixture

Use 1 bucket of fresh roughly chopped khakibos or basil or tansy or wormwood or southernwood or any pungent strong herb or combination. Pour over this 1 to 2 buckets of boiling water and leave to draw and cool overnight. Next morning strain, add ½ cup of soap powder (I usually use Sunlight soap powder as I find this marvellous soap has stood the test of time and is as pure as one can get). Mix well, then splash onto plants by dipping a bunch of leaves into the mixture and shake all over infected plants or water around plants, down ant holes and between paving stones, or spray in a spritz bottle.

Remember only spray if necessary and not as a preventative measure, and never spray where the bees are busy or where you see ladybirds. Evenings are usually the best time – just to be safe – when the ladybirds and the bees "all fly away home". Even though you use safe natural sprays always wash the vegetables well and don't inhale the sprays. Protect your eyes and wash your hands well after spraying.

My grandmother made strong soapy splashes for aphids just with grated green Sunlight soap bars – in those days soap powders were not known – and this soapy spray made with hot (not boiling) water was amazingly effective. The reason why soap is added to the sprays is because it has a stickiness that keeps the spray from running off completely.

Pyrethrum flowers are used commercially in sprays, but can also harm beneficial insects, so use with care. Onions, garlic, rape seed oil, sulphur, mustard and chillies can all be added to sprays, but always treat them with respect and spray away from the eyes and avoid skin contact.

I still tend to use strong warm jets of water from the hose to dislodge aphids. This can be very effective if done daily. My garlic and canola oil (rape seed oil – and *not* genetically modified) spray is beautifully effective as is the natural fungicide spray for powdery mildew.

Avoid tobacco dust – I have found this toxic and disturbingly irritating to the nose and skin.

Derris is often written about in overseas books. This is a root and bark natural insecticide. *Derris elliptica* can be ground and powdered and added to sprays. As yet it has not been successfully grown in South Africa that I know of.

Hint

Keep a notebook of plants you use for sprays, and your own recipes based on these. Be careful which plants you use – don't just use anything. Stay safe with the list of plants in this book.

Chilli and Garlic Spray

Finely chop and grind enough garlic bulbs to make 1 cup of garlic mush. Add ½ to ¾ cup of cayenne pepper powder (very carefully and avoid contact with the skin and eyes!). Very gently, pour over this 4 litres of hot (not boiling) water, stir well and cool. Strain and add 2 tablespoons of soap powder. Mix well. Pour into a spritz bottle and shake up. Spray caterpillars, aphids, whitefly and red spider mite.

Chilli, Khakibos and Onion Spray

In a blender whirl 10 chillies, seeds and all, with 4 large onions. Pour 1 bucket of boiling water over ½ a bucket of fresh khakibos and add the onions and chillies. Cool. Add ½ cup soap powder and mix well. Spray aphids, red spider mite, whitefly and mealie bug.

Basil, Khakibos and Lemon Verbena Mosquito Spray

4 cups fresh basil sprigs
4 cups fresh khakibos sprigs and leaves
4 cups fresh lemon verbena leaves

In a large pot boil everything up in 4 litres of water. Keep covered and simmer gently for 30 minutes. Cool and strain. Pour into a spritz bottle and spray into the air for mosquitoes. Avoid the eyes. This spray is safe to spray onto the skin, but *always test for skin sensitivity first* by dabbing a little on the inside of the wrist and elbow. Should there be a red itchy reaction, wash off immediately and apply fresh aloe vera juice. Dilute the spray with warm water and test again.

khakibos

Cutworm Spray

Add 6 cups of shredded pawpaw leaves and seeds that have been well crushed to 3 litres of boiling water. Add 10 crushed and finely cut chillies. Stand and cool, then add 2 tablespoons paraffin and 2 tablespoons soap powder and mix well. Pour around newly planted lettuces, spinach, and other leafy vegetables.

Note: I have not used syringa (*Melia azedarach*), thorn apple (*Datura stramonium*), stinkblaar or castor oil plant (*Ricinus communis*) or rhubarb (*Rheum rhabarbarum*), whose leaves are extremely poisonous. All of these are too dangerous to use.

Natural pest control for seed and grain storage

This is the old-fashioned way of safeguarding the reaped crop, to keep weevils, borers, moths, fungi, bacteria and viral disease away. Seed can be disinfected, preserved and safely stored by these inexpensive and safe methods:

- **Sieved wood ash**, fine sand and salt – Seeds can be stored indefinitely in any of these mediums.
- **Oil** – Toss the seeds in a little sunflower oil and spread in large tins that can be kept closed and sealed. This helps stored beans and peas particularly.
- **Heat** – Spread trays of seeds infected with weevils, fungi and bacteria and heat in the oven to no more than 50 °C (anything higher than this will destroy the germination of the seeds).
- **Cold** – Put the seed in a container in the fridge overnight. Weevils will perish.
- **Citrus peels** – Lemon, lime, orange and naartjie peels added into stored grains repel pests effectively. Dry the peels in the sun and add 1 cup of peels to every 10 cups of grains.
- Solar energy – Spread the seed on shiny metal trays in the sun in a thin layer. Stir frequently. A temperature of 45 °C maintained for 10 minutes will kill weevils, bacteria and fungi.
- Don't forget to push in fresh **fig twigs**, without leaves, and **bay sprigs**, with leaves, into flour and meal and grains.
- Lay thick nests of fresh **khakibos**, **rue** or **tansy** under bags of grain and tuck in between.
- Line the floor of the storeroom with heaps of pungent strewing herbs: any with a strong smell, for example the **basils**, **wormwood**, **rue**, **tansy**, **southernwood**, **lemon verbena**, and so on.

a fig twig

Soil Improvers

WITH SIMPLE, PRACTICAL KNOWLEDGE, SINGLE HANDED, ONE CAN SET ABOUT MAKING THE SOIL RICHER, MORE FRIABLE, AND MORE VIABLE. THE SOIL IS EVERYTHING AND PLAYS SO VITAL A ROLE AS THE MEDIUM ON WHICH THE CROP, HOWEVER SMALL, HOWEVER BIG, DEPENDS, THAT WE NEED TO BRING AS MUCH AS POSSIBLE INTO PLAY.

Compost

There are a number of organic soil improvers that can be safely added yearly, or twice yearly, to supply plant foods, to assist light sandy soils hold onto nourishment and moisture, and to lighten and drain heavy clay soils.

Top of the list are usually the composts – these can come from kitchen peelings and vegetable and fruit waste, as well as from garden sweepings and weeds, and will supply a mass of nourishing nutrients. I am never without a few compost heaps, and through the years I have made every kind of compost heap imaginable – some complicated and time consuming and some quick, easy and light on the digging and the back!

This is the simplest, most effective and the easiest method of composting, and is an absolute must for every organic gardener:

Easy composting

Start off by clearing an area – as big as you can. Scrape off weeds, dig out roots of grasses, and chop out stumps. Plant an elder tree or two near it, and set down the first layer of twigs, coarse prunings, small branches and shrub prunings – this layer will bring air into the bottom of the heap and help with the heat build-up. Now pile on raked leaves, weedings, vegetable peelings from the kitchen, lawn mowings – all layered and mixed in. Top this now interesting looking heap with a 10 to 15 cm deep covering of manure, and finally cover the manure with more weeds, cut grass or hay from stables. Trample it down and set a gentle sprinkler on top of the heap to thoroughly soak it. Later, keep on piling on the garden prunings, raked leaves, grass mowings mixed with weed and leaves, and every now and then a layer of comfrey leaves, and a bucket of yarrow leaves. These two remarkable herbs will help to break down and heat up the heap.

Keep going with layers and occasionally add a sack of manure, water well weekly in dry periods and, when it starts to break down, turn it lightly to aerate and to keep it friable, hot and steamy. Within 6 to 10 weeks you'll have sweet smelling, dark, friable and nourishing "soil", light and crumbly, moist and beautiful, "black gold", as my father called it.

Once you've seen how easy it is to make a compost heap (watch the earth worms thrive) you'll never be without one, and a mere bucket of this mature "black gold" dug in around an ailing plant, will give it new life and vigour within a day or two, which will so impress you, you'll start allocating more space for compost!

Other soil improvers are shredded bark, leaf mould, which can be raked up once the deciduous leaves have rotted down, hay from stables and chicken coops, prunings and weeds and green manure crops.

A shredder is a most marvellous contraption, and you can buy gardener-sized shredders from most hardware shops and some nurseries. All you do is shred tough weeds, prunings, clippings and woody annuals through it. This shredded mass of organic matter can be used as both a mulch or dug into the soil where it will quickly break down, or it can be added as a "blanket" to top your compost heap.

Note

Be careful not to "smother" your compost heap with thick layers of packed lawn mowings – this will stop it "breathing"! Mix it with leaves and shredded clippings.

You can compost:
- Egg shells
- Newspaper opened up and crumpled
- Wood ash only
- Cardboard boxes torn into small pieces, egg boxes torn up
- Hamster bedding (if it's sawdust)
- Rhubarb leaves

What not to compost:
- Meat and fish scraps
- Disposable nappies
- Cat litter – not even in sawdust
- Dog faeces
- Glass and tins and plastics
- Any synthetic fibres
- Coal ash and lumps of coal

Organic fertilisers

My most informative source of natural organic fertilisers came from Ryton Gardens, the Henry Doubleday Research Centre near Coventry in England. I took many tours to the herb gardens of England and we always spent a full day at Ryton Gardens. There is a feast of organic practices for gardeners to inspect, the entire public garden is dedicated to organic research and promotion of organic gardening, food production and farming. I had the privilege of meeting Lawrence Hills who developed the project further and included his exciting work on comfrey and organic sprays – he had devoted his life to it and was very old when I met him.

I have always longed to have just such a learning garden in South Africa – maybe it will happen one day. It was there that I learned there are certain natural "fertilisers" that can be happily included in the organic garden.

Bonemeal tops the list – it promotes strong root growth. Sprinkle it lightly over well-dug soil that already has a good supply of compost in it, and the new shrubs and trees and perennials will thrive planted in this medium.

Blood, bone and fish meal is another very nutritious fertiliser for trees particularly as it boosts root and leaf growth and can be applied and quickly dug in as a booster in early spring before the summer heat releases too much of the strong smell.

Chicken manure, but only free-range chickens, is high in nitrogen and it is the richest of the natural fertilisers that will quickly rebuild poor depleted soils. Always use it carefully and sparingly – it is powerful and can burn plants very easily.

Ground down limestone – this puts calcium into the soil and raises the pH levels, as does dolomite, which contains both calcium and magnesium. Both lime and dolomite are beneficial every now and then, and some soil experts believe that if gypsum is mixed into the lime – three parts lime to one part gypsum –

the soil will be lighter and more friable and beneficial to the plants, especially in the case of heavy clay soils.

One farmer in the valley near me spreads equal parts calcium carbonate (lime), calcium magnesium carbonate (dolomite) and calcium sulphate (gypsum), carefully mixed, onto his cabbage fields every second autumn for his winter cabbage crop, and with a huge amount of aged chicken manure every year, twice a year, he has the best cabbages and never rotates the crop. He says it's because of the limestone mix.

In order to make the soil more acidic, pine needles are the best natural additive. Use decomposed pine needles gathered under the trees in autumn.

A note on animal manures

As we know old, well-dug, well-rotted manures are nitrogen rich and keep the compost soft and moist and friable – and the more that is added, the better – usually a wheelbarrow load to every 5 square metres of soil. But some gardeners may prefer not to use animal manures – here is where green manure crops with comfrey and yarrow and a good crop of borage and even stinging nettles, can replace the animal manures and improve the soil.

For several years when I was a full vegetarian, I actually practised "vegetarian gardening" – much to the derision and amazement of the traditional manure-using farmers nearby! My basic compost heaps were made with comfrey and buckwheat and they shook their heads in disbelief when my vegetables turned out so well!

Seaweed, dried and coarsely chopped and sent up in trucks from the West coast, was my answer. I sprinkled light layers in between my compost mixes and it really has been a remarkable additive – but living so far from the sea and with new laws in controlling seaweed gathering in place, it is no longer really economical. Dried chopped kelp may still be offered in certain areas with permits – so investigate this first.

Green manure

This is one of the quickest, easiest and best ways to improve the soil. These "crops" or plantings improve nitrogen fixing in the soil, they smother out the weeds and their intense rooting systems aerate and open up the soil, making it friable and easy to dig, and the plants themselves make a rich food for whatever crop follows.

The green manure crop protects depleted soils from compaction and wash away during heavy rain, wind and storms, and, in case of severe and constant cultivation, a season-long green manure crop will help the soil structure recover and improve as nothing else can.

Here are some ideas:

Buckwheat – Can be grown at any time of the year except midwinter. It has a growing period of 3 months and it thrives in poor soils.

Broad beans – A winter crop. Plant 50 cm apart in rows in late summer. Does well in heavy clay soils and is an excellent nitrogen fixer.

Clover, especially red clover – Takes from 3 to 18 months, sow in spring through to late summer. An excellent nitrogen fixer, it thrives in most soils.

Lupin – Plant 50 cm apart in rows in spring. It is ready in 4 months to dig in and does well in light acid soil. An excellent nitrogen fixer and aerator.

Mustard – Any time of the year, except midwinter. Ready in 2 to 3 months and does well in any soil. Breaks down quickly and easily, very rich and beneficial to the soil.

Lucerne – Spring sowing ensures an almost 100 per cent germination – scatter the seed. This is a perennial crop and it does not like acid clay soils. A superb nitrogen fixer, the plant can be mowed and the mowings spread thickly over bare patches of ground and dug in. Because of its deep and wide root system, it literally needs to be ploughed in and it takes a full year to reach maturity. I have found the field of lucerne so useful for cutting and mulching and digging in that I have let it grow for 2 or 3 years before ploughing it in. As a long-lasting green manure, lucerne is a hugely valuable investment if you have the space. In the home vegetable garden grow a row at the edge of the garden and cut it frequently for a mulch and dig it in.

Phacelia – A pretty blue-mauve flowered quick annual. *Phacelia tanacetifolia* is an easy-to-grow crop used constantly in Britain and Europe as a between crop green manure. If it is allowed to flower – which I do for the amazing show it puts on – it acts as a magnet for a host of beneficial insects. It is quite stunning and the bees and butterflies and ladybirds are dizzy with delight at it. So look out for seeds and scatter them in spring through to midsummer. They thrive in most soils and are rich in soil improving nutrients. One year I grew mustard and *Phacelia* together to improve my sandy, rocky, mountainside small meadow and I let it mature and set seed, and at the end of autumn I ploughed it in. Next spring seeds came up in their thousands, which could literally be ploughed back giving a double dose of vitality to the soil, and the crop of vegetables that followed was superb. Both mustard and *Phacelia* are worth experimenting with. Seed merchants will import the seed for you.

Rye, barley and winter wheat – are also worth growing over winter as a green manure crop and ploughed in while they are still green, before the ears ripen. Allow the soil to rest for 1 month before re-ploughing and planting the next crop.

Green manure crops are more beneficial than one could imagine, and even done on a small scale in the vegetable garden, will surprise you! Keep a diary and make notes – this could become a habit!

lupin

Mulches

I love the word MULCH! It sounds and feels heavy, and safe, and rich, and sustaining – which is exactly what mulches are about!

I learned to mulch under my father's watchful eye as an eight-year-old gardener in the heat of Pretoria's summers. Our huge and beautiful family garden was filled with vegetables, fruit trees, and in front, surrounding the big lush lawn, cut flowers of breathless variety and hue, for my mother's flower arranging for the church and official dinners. Without the mulches there would not have been the bounty or the quality, and tender annuals could never have survived the relentless heat.

Living mulches

Often my father planted "living mulches", as he called them, like the prolific alyssum, and the old fashioned mignonette, which covered the ground between the dahlias and the larkspurs and the spinach and the Sweet Williams. Later, on the farm where I gardened for my own family, I grew thyme, specially creeping thyme (*Thymus serpyllum*), ground ivy (*Glechoma hederacea*), clover, spring onions, parsley and strawberries in between sweetcorn and cabbages and my cut flower carnations. These are good ground cover plants, which are edible, and they successfully smother weeds as well as keeping the soil cool and moist. The green manures, especially buckwheat, grazing rye, phacelia, lucerne, pennyroyal and coriander, make excellent living mulches for ground that lies fallow – these "smother crops" keep the weeds from invading and all can be used.

In the Herbal Centre Gardens six decades on, I still use these living mulches, and in the shade the ground ivy, and the precious pennywort (*Centella asiatica*), and the pungent pennyroyal (*Mentha pulegium*) – these are true smother crops and look attractive, lush and neat all year round, and keep the weeds down and the soil cool and protected.

Loose mulches

These can be a variety of materials, on their own or mixed, but in order to protect against the heat, the loss of moisture and the weeds, need to be no less than 10 to 12 cm deep. Should any tough survivor weed push through, it can be easily removed.

But there is a new product available from hardware stores and nurseries that can be effectively spread over the soil as a protective membrane and on top of which a far lighter spread of mulch can be placed – even a 4 cm deep mulch, enough to hold the membrane in place, works well. This mulch fabric, or membrane, breathes, is water permeable and it is a light and tough protection.

For show gardens, the membrane is spread over newly dug, neatly raked, moist soil. Holes can be cut into it for planting, cut in a cross, not a circle, so that it can be used again and again. The membrane is then covered with a loose mulch to hold it in place. This extends its lifespan and improves the appearance, and it looks good all the time.

Loose mulches can be leaves, straw, bark, composted bark and wood chips that have gone through a hammer mill or shredded – all these can be dug in later. Leaf mould is my favourite mulch as it can be used in the shade as well, and will nourish the soil. Shredded newspaper and cardboard can be added, or sheets of newspaper and flattened cardboard boxes can be spread and covered with hay or swept up leaves.

Eventually all these organic mulches will disintegrate and become compost and can be dug back into the soil next season.

As a child I remember we were able to buy coir cheaply from mattress factories, and sometimes coir mats or loose fibres are still available – usually for hanging baskets. Coir is an excellent mulch and as it comes from coconuts is a long lasting organic fibre which is simply wonderful mixed with shredded prunings. Macadamia, pecan, peanut and walnut shells, and peach and apricot pips are long-lasting organic mulches that can be spread to keep the soil moist and cool. A farmer nearby who produces oranges for juicing and shelled pecan nuts for the sweet industry, combines the shells and the shredded orange peel waste as a mulch in his orchards. He has literally no weeds and no insect problem! He reckons the strong citrus oils present even in the dried peel keep thrips, aphids and whitefly in control!

Don't use lawn mowings alone as a mulch! They tend to pack down, become mouldy and sour, block out water, an even smell! Ants love building under a blanket of grass mowings, and for termites it's paradise. So use the mowings only mixed with other things like leaves, kitchen peels, or chopped and shredded weeds. Mix well, and rather layer onto the compost heap and not as a mulch.

Also don't use polythene or plastic sheeting as a mulch. Tremendous heat and lack of air build up under plastic, and no moisture can penetrate. So this just causes a heat problem, unless it has many holes cut in it. Even then it is not an ideal mulch.

Gravel, especially the beautiful coloured or white gravels, can be effectively used as a permanent mulch in difficult to manage areas, *but* always use a mulch membrane underneath the gravel first. Start by clearing the ground completely of roots and weeds and any perennial grasses and plants. Rake and level. Lay the membrane down, overlapping where necessary. Secure with a few stones here and there, and then gently spade on the gravel and smooth it bit by bit as you proceed. If you dump barrow loads of gravel you will have difficulty levelling it and the membrane will shift and ruffle up. So take the time – spade by spade – and wear heavy-duty gloves to push it very gently into place. Complete one small area before moving on to the next. The gravel should completely cover the membrane, and layer it as deep as you can – never less than 10 cm.

You can also pack smooth river pebbles over the membrane. Again the secret is to prepare, level and rake the soil well before laying the membrane. This is a very effective method on slopes where nothing grows and if the pebbles are retained by support walls built of stone or brick, cemented into neat retaining areas, even the worst storms will not wash it away, and what soil there is on the slope will not be eroded out.

Rich compost added to a city garden soil, assures a year-round harvest

The Herbal Centre potager garden with its mulching and composting programme

Always remember mulches help to retain moisture, and water is our most precious and vital possession. We need to save every drop and use it wisely and well.

Disease and mineral deficiencies, yellowing and leaf curl, blossom end rot, and splitting and bolting and so on can be prevented with soil care. Composting, mulching and careful watering keep the organic garden prolific.

I have lived through the worst storms and droughts where all would have been lost were it not for my mulching and composting. The heat is intensifying, global warming is here now upon us, with us, making gardening, farming and food production a tremendous battle. The only way forward is the organic way, and mulching will become a living necessity in the years ahead.

Become familiar with it, become efficient in covering all the bare spaces. Keep a light band, fork it occasionally to loosen it, and if you use the marvellous plant membranes plan them in such a way that you can sweep off the mulch, lift them, add compost to the soil, water it, rake and level it, and replace.

Every year in spring, I dig in my old mulches and add extra compost, and I replace with new mulches. It is worth every bit of that yearly effort. I push stable straw through my shredder to make it look more attractive,

and in winter I grow rows of oats, rye and wheat to shred once they have ripened. I farm and garden, against all odds, against the side of the mountain, with rocky, sandy, nutrient-starved soil, with erratic and sparse rainfall, searing heat and endless drought, and with very small water supply from one borehole, and sometimes we can only pump 2 hours a day! But the public gardens we create are nothing short of miraculous! We would not survive were it not for mulches, our rainwater tanks behind every building, our compost heaps, and our absolute and complete dedication to all things natural and organic!

It is tough going, but worth every bit of the tremendous effort, and visitors gape in awe at our huge areas of compost heaps – the making of the black gold that keeps these mountain side gardens going!

One last thought on mulching has served us well through the worst drought: We have experimented with the array of true organically certified natural "fertilisers" available on the nursery shelves today. Our most effective way to keep the soil nourished and protected has been to mix together 1 part organic fertiliser to 5 parts mulch of shredded prunings, weeds and kitchen peelings and to spread this around the vegetables particularly. Try it – it's worth experimenting with.

Our changing world – global warming

This chapter seems to find its way into this book and although throughout its writing I have found my pen pausing at the words "plant in full sun", now at the time of finally completing my writing during the last months of the year 2005, a fearful summer of such intense heat and drought has so shaken our country that I clearly need to rethink my farming activities.

Thirty-five years ago my children were still small and I walked with my father in my two-acre-sized vegetable gardens. It was hot and the Christmas holidays were nearly over. He pointed to the distant border of the garden edged with ripening prickly pears and said, "In the not too distant future maybe those prickly pears will be the only survivors in full sun."

I remembered being startled, as my vegetable gardens were my family's lifeline – I grew so huge a variety of fruit and vegetables, it sustained us all throughout the seasons, and economically it was vital. He then said (35 years ago!), "Here are two words I want you to think about – for it will come faster than you realise – *global warming*!"

Create a micro-climate by enclosing a space – here with 20 per cent shade cloth over the chicken wire netting to keep the squirrels, birds and specially the monkeys out. Never have I grown such luscious lettuces, spinach, onions and broccoli! Shade net manufacturers have field officers who will advise you

I felt my stomach turn, and the sun felt even hotter on my bare arms as I looked at the rows of wilting lettuces and spinach. He went on to talk of the changes in the weather patterns, the environmental damage, the ozone layer, pollution and the melting glaciers, and I felt quite sick. That was thirty-five years ago.

I was already growing everything organically then. He took a keen interest in everything I did, and said it was the only way. He suggested I look into 40 to 50 per cent shade for my more tender vegetables – there was no shade cloth in those days – and with his walking stick he pointed down the valley to the poplar trees growing closely together in a wood, and turned to indicate the giant reeds growing along the banks of the river a hundred metres away.

"Make frames of strong poplars," he suggested, "high enough for you to work under and then secure the reeds to the frames with spaces between them so that you can get 40 to 50 per cent shade. Think about it, plan it, as the summers will get increasingly hot, and the rain sparser and more unpredictable."

This is exactly what has happened, and my vegetables have had a worse struggle every year in the midsummer heat, so much so that I now cannot grow lettuces in summer, and my squashes and cucumbers and lavenders struggle with poorer results every summer.

I have never forgotten his words, and this summer, thirty-five years on, I have been forced into taking a stand, just as my father predicted. I am erecting frames and covering areas with 40 per cent shade cloth over the trial lavender plantings, over the vegetables, which are now caged due to birds, squirrels, monkeys, and the endless and thorough destruction they inflict on my vegetables and fruit. Never have I gardened with such poor results, and in such stifling heat – and to have had nine, almost ten months of a year without even a shower of rain, has literally brought us to our knees. Global warming is happening, which my father all those decades ago predicted.

In the last 15 years I have placed rainwater tanks under every gutter, 5 000-litre tanks, to take whatever rain or dew falls. It is surprising to actually measure roof run-off, and the numerous buildings at the Herbal Centre, with careful guttering and down pipes, have a massive run-off that is now stored, drop for precious drop, in cool tanks, awaiting the moment when the borehole drops too low. These rainwater tanks have saved us this year.

The shade nets cut down on watering by almost half, and today we use steel poles and strong crossbars to take the weight of the monkeys who use the nets as trampolines!

We need to be aware that this is a dry country, and we need to watch and record our plantings with protective companions and to cover dry, open places with light mulches and quick green manure crops and to give our precious water, whether municipal city water or our fragile boreholes and rivers, our constant care and attention.

We need to guard and nurture every drop to save this, the most precious thing on earth, and instil it into our helpers in the garden and into our children and their children.

Without water there is no life!

Companion Plants
at a glance

Good companions

African marigold	apple trees, beans, beetroot, celery, potatoes, tomatoes
Amaranth	beetroot, mealies, onions, potatoes, sorghum
Anise	brinjals, cabbages, coriander, courgettes, green peppers, kale, lettuce
Apple trees	African marigolds, blackberries, flax, chives, clover, foxgloves, nasturtiums, wallflowers
Apricot trees	basil, flax, buckwheat, nasturtiums, rosemary, southernwood, tansy
Artemisias	beans, beetroot, brinjals, cabbages, carrots, fruit trees, gooseberries, green peppers, hollyhocks, nasturtiums, raspberries, roses, strawberries
Asparagus	beans, cabbages, carrots, chervil, parsley, radishes, tomatoes
Barley	buckwheat, cornflowers
Basil	apricot trees, carrots, grape vines, queen Anne's lace, tomatoes, but all plants will benefit from its insect-repelling properties
Beans	African marigolds, artemisias, asparagus, beetroot, cabbages, carrots, cauliflower, celeriac, celery, chives, costmary, cucumbers, fenugreek, feverfew, goldenrod, kale, kohlrabi, leeks, lovage, mealies, nasturtiums, parsley, peppers, potatoes, pumpkins, queen Anne's lace, radishes, rosemary, salad burnet, strawberries, summer savory, winter savory
Beetroot	African marigolds, amaranth, artemisias, beans, bush beans, cabbages, calendulas, caraway, cauliflower, chives, garlic, kohlrabi, larkspur, leeks, lettuces, onions, parsley, peppers, radishes, Swiss chard
Blackberries	apple trees, elderberries, stinging nettle, sunflowers, tansy
Borage	brinjals, cucumbers, peach trees, pear trees, pumpkins, strawberries, tomatoes
Brinjals	anise, artemisias, borage, calamint, carnations, cumin, lovage, marjoram, oats, oregano, pigeon pea, summer savory, thyme, winter savory
Broccoli	celery, chamomile, clover, dill, mustard, nasturtiums, parsley, petunias, sage, santolina
Brussels sprouts	chamomile
Buckwheat	apricot trees, barley, globe artichokes, flax (linseed), oats, pigeon pea, roses, rye
Cabbages	anise, artemisias, asparagus, beans, beetroot, catmint, celery, chamomile, chives, clover, dill, feverfew, leeks, lettuces, mustard, nasturtiums, oak tree, onions, pennyroyal, radishes, rosemary, sage, santolina, scented geraniums, Swiss chard, thyme, violets

Calabashes	marjoram, calabashes, oregano, Russian sage, yarrow
Calamint	brinjals, fennel, green peppers, lettuces, onions, roses, strawberries, tomatoes
Calendula	beetroot, celery, turnip
Californian poppy	turnips
Caraway	beetroot, leeks, peas, radishes, sweet peas
Carnation	brinjals, garlic, green peppers, mustard, potatoes, soya beans, strawberries
Carrots	artemisias, asparagus, basil, beans, chives, flax, leeks, lettuces, marjoram, mint, onions, oregano, parsley, peas, peppers, radishes, rosemary, sage, tomatoes
Catmint	cabbages, cauliflower, kale, roses, tomatoes, but all plants will benefit from its insect-repelling properties
Cauliflower	beans, beetroot, catmint, chamomile, clover, dill, mustard, petunia, sage, santolina
Celeriac	beans, leeks
Celery	African marigolds, beans, broccoli, cabbages, calendulas, kohlrabi, land cress, leeks, pansies, parsley, peppers, spring onions, Swiss chard, tomatoes, violets
Chamomile	broccoli, Brussels sprouts, cabbages, grape vines, kale, mint, onions, turnips, wheat
Chervil	asparagus
Chickpeas	radishes
Chillies	cumin, lovage
Chives	apple trees, beans, beetroot, cabbages, carrots, cucumbers, fruit trees, grape vines, green peppers, lettuces, marrows, melons, pumpkins, roses, spinach, squashes, tomatoes
Citrus trees	comfrey, lavender, oak
Clover	apple trees, broccoli, cabbages, cauliflower, fruit trees, grape vines
Comfrey	citrus trees, roses, but as a soil tonic it will benefit most plants
Coriander	anise, dill, mealies, nasturtiums, roses, spinach, summer squash, sweetcorn, tomatoes
Cornflower	barley, oats, rye, wheat
Costmary	beans, nasturtiums, pumpkins, radishes, roses
Cucumbers	beans, borage, chives, dill, fenugreek, green peppers, lemon balm, lettuces, marjoram, nasturtiums, oregano, queen Anne's lace, radishes, yarrow
Cumin	brinjals, chillies, green peppers, paprika, radishes
Dandelion	fruit trees
Dill	broccoli, cabbages, cauliflower, coriander, cucumbers, kale, mealies, tomatoes
Echinacea	benefits most plants grown near it
Elder	blackberries, but most plants will benefit from its insect-repelling properties
Fennel	calamint

Fenugreek	beans, cucumbers, kohlrabi, lettuces, peppers, squash, tomatoes
Feverfew	beans, cabbages, lettuces, peas, radishes, spinach, squash
Flax	apple trees, apricot trees, buckwheat, carrots, potatoes
Fruit trees	artemisias, chives, clover, dandelion, horseradish, lemon balm, lucerne, mustard, oak, onions, rue, scented geraniums, tansy
Garlic	beetroot, carnations, grape vines, lemon trees, lettuces, Malawian spinach, orange trees, peach trees, pear trees, raspberries, roses, Swiss chard, tomatoes
Garlic chives	melons, pumpkins
Gem squash	queen Anne's lace
Ginger	lilies, taro (madumbi)
Globe artichokes	buckwheat
Goldenrod	beans, mealies, pumpkins and squashes
Gooseberries	artemisias
Grape vines	chamomile, chives, clover, garlic, lucerne, mustard, onions, perennial basil, sage
Green peppers	anise, artemisias, calamint, carnations, chives, cucumbers, cumin, lovage, marjoram, mint, oats, oregano, pigeon pea, potatoes, Swiss chard, thyme
Hollyhock	artemisias
Horseradish	fruit trees, potatoes, stinging nettle
Jugo beans	moringa
Kale	anise, beans, catmint, chamomile, dill, kohlrabi, onions, parsley, sage, santolina, violets
Kohlrabi	beans, beetroot, celery, fenugreek, kale, lettuces, mustard, onions, parsley, radishes, spring onions, thyme
Land cress	celery
Larkspur	beetroot
Lavender	citrus trees, petunia, roses, Russian sage, but lavender benefits all plants growing near it
Leeks	beans, beetroot, cabbages, caraway, carrots, celeriac, celery, lettuces, radishes
Lemon balm	cucumbers, fruit trees, tomatoes
Lemon trees	garlic, Russian sage
Lemon verbena	yarrow, but all plants will benefit from its insect-repelling qualities
Lettuces	anise, beetroot, cabbages, calamint, carrots, chives, cucumbers, fenugreek, feverfew, garlic, kohlrabi, leeks, moringa, mustard, oak, onions, parsley, peppers, radishes, salad burnet, strawberries, turnips, violets
Loofah	marjoram, oregano
Lovage	beans, lovage, brinjals, chillies, green peppers, peas, St Joseph's lilies

Lucerne	fruit trees, grape vines, but all plants will benefit from its ability to enrich the soil
Marjoram	brinjals, calabashes, carrots, cucumbers, green peppers, loofahs, pumpkins, radishes, roses, stinging nettle, strawberries, summer annuals, tomatoes, yarrow
Marrows	borage, chives
Mealies	amaranth, beans, coriander, dill, goldenrod, mustard, nasturtiums, peppers, potatoes, pumpkins, sesame, soya beans, sunflowers, yarrow
Melons	chives, garlic chives, mint, morning glory, pennyroyal, radishes, Russian sage, thyme, yarrow
Mint	carrots, chamomile, green peppers, melons, roses, salad burnet, strawberries, tomatoes
Moringa	jugo beans, lettuces, spinach, tomatoes
Mustard	broccoli, cabbages, carnations, cauliflower, fruit trees, grape vines, kohlrabi, lettuces, mealies, potatoes, tomatoes, tree tomatoes
Myrtle	all plants will benefit from its insect-repelling properties
Nasturtium	apple trees, apricot trees, artemisias, broad beans, broccoli, cabbages, coriander, costmary, cucumbers, mealies, pomegranates, quince trees, radishes, tomatoes
Oak	cabbages, citrus trees, fruit trees, lettuces
Oats	brinjals, buckwheat, cornflowers, fruit salad plant, green peppers, raspberries, strawberries, tomatoes
Onions	amaranth, beetroot, cabbages, calamint, carrots, chamomile, fruit trees, grape vines, kale, kohlrabi, lettuces, peas, peppers, petunias, raspberries, roses, spinach, strawberries, summer savory, Swiss chard, tomatoes, winter savory
Orange trees	garlic
Oregano	brinjals, calabashes, carrots, cucumbers, green peppers, loofahs, pumpkins, radishes, roses, strawberries, summer annuals, tomatoes, yarrow
Pansies	celery
Paprika	cumin
Parsley	asparagus, beans, beetroot, broccoli, carrots, celery, kale, kohlrabi, lettuces, peppers, roses, spinach, strawberries, tomatoes
Peach trees	borage, garlic, onions, tansy
Pear trees	borage, garlic, onions, tansy
Peas	caraway, carrots, feverfew, lovage, onions, potatoes, radishes, salad burnet, santolina, Swiss chard
Pennyroyal	cabbages, melons
Peppermint	stinging nettle
Peppers	beans, beetroot, carrots, celery, fenugreek, lettuces, mealies, onions, parsley, pumpkins, radishes, stinging nettle
Petunia	broccoli, cauliflower, lavender, onions

Pigeon pea	brinjals, buckwheat, green peppers, summer rocket
Pine trees	potatoes, strawberries, tomatoes, any acid-loving plant
Pomegranate	nasturtiums
Potatoes	amaranth, beans, carnations, flax, green peppers, horseradish, marigolds, mealies, mustard, peas, pine trees, Russian sage, stinging nettle, strawberries
Pumpkins	beans, borage, chives, costmary, garlic chives, goldenrod, marjoram, mealies, oregano, peppers, radishes
Queen Anne's lace	basil, beans, cucumbers, gem squash, strawberries, tomatoes
Quince trees	nasturtiums
Radishes	asparagus, beans, beetroot, cabbages, caraway, carrots, chickpeas, costmary, cucumbers, cumin, feverfew, kohlrabi, leeks, lettuces, marjoram, melons, nasturtiums, oregano, peas, peppers, pumpkins, salad burnet, santolina, squashes, stinging nettle, strawberries, tomatoes, turnips
Raspberries	artemisias, garlic, oats, onions, spring onions, tansy, wormwood, yarrow
Rocket	summer savory, winter savory
Rosemary	apricot trees, beans, cabbages, carrots, roses
Roses	artemisias, buckwheat, calamint, catmint, chives, comfrey, coriander, costmary, garlic, lavender, marjoram, mint, onions, oregano, parsley, petrea, rosemary, sage, santolina, strawberries, summer savory, tansy, tarragon, thyme, winter savory, yarrow
Rue	fruit trees, strawberries, tansy, tomatoes, but most vegetables will benefit from its insect-repelling properties
Russian sage	calabashes, lavender, lemon trees, melons, potatoes, sorghum, sousou squash
Rye	buckwheat, cornflower
Sage	broccoli, cabbages, carrots, cauliflower, grape vines, kale, roses, stinging nettle, tomatoes
Salad burnet	beans, lettuces, mint, peas, radishes, sunflowers, thyme, tomatoes
Santolina	broccoli, cabbages, cauliflower, kale, peas, radishes, roses, spinach
Scented geraniums	cabbages and other vegetables, fruit trees
Sesame	mealies, sunflowers
Sorghum	amaranth, Russian sage
Southernwood	apricot trees, cabbages
Soya bean	carnations, mealies, but will benefit any plant growing nearby
Spinach	chives, coriander, feverfew, moringa, onions, parsley, santolina, strawberries, turnips, violets
Spring onions	celery, kohlrabi, raspberries, strawberries
Squashes	chives, fenugreek, feverfew, goldenrod, radishes, thyme

Stinging nettle	blackberries, horseradish, marjoram, peppermint, peppers, potatoes, radishes, sage, tomatoes
Strawberries	artemisias, beans, borage, calamint, carnations, lettuces, marjoram, mint, oats, onions, oregano, parsley, pine, potatoes, queen Anne's lace, radishes, roses, rue, spinach, spring onions, Swiss chard
Summer savory	beans, brinjals, onions, rocket, roses, tomatoes, coriander
Sunflowers	blackberries, mealies, salad burnet, sesame
Sweet peas	caraway
Sweetcorn	coriander
Swiss chard	beetroot, cabbages, celery, garlic, green peppers, onions, peas, strawberries
Tansy	apricots, blackberries, fruit trees, raspberries, roses, rue
Tarragon	roses
Thyme	brinjals, cabbages, green peppers, kohlrabi, melons, roses, salad burnet, squashes, tomatoes
Tomatoes	African marigolds, asparagus, basil, borage, calamint, carrots, catmint, celery, chives, coriander, dill, fenugreek, garlic, lemon balm, marjoram, mint, moringa, mustard, nasturtiums, oats, onions, oregano, parsley, pines, queen Anne's lace, radishes, rue, sage, salad burnet, stinging nettle, summer savory, thyme, winter savory, yarrow
Tree tomatoes	mustard
Turnips	calendulas, Californian poppies, chamomile, lettuces, radishes, red field poppies, snapdragons, spinach
Violets	cabbages, celery, kale, lettuces, spinach
Wheat	chamomile, cornflowers
Winter savory	beans, brinjals, onions, rocket, roses, tomatoes, yarrow
Wormwood	raspberries
Yarrow	calabashes, cucumbers, lemon verbena, marjoram, mealies, melons, oregano, raspberries, roses, tomatoes, winter savory

Poor companions

These plants dislike one another and should not be planted close together.

Apple trees	brinjals, carrots, potatoes, sweet peppers, tomatoes
Apricot trees	barley, brinjals, fruit salad plant, oats, potatoes, tomatoes, wheat
Barley	apricot trees
Basil	rue
Beans	dill, fennel, garlic, sunflowers, all members of the onion family
Brinjals	apple trees, apricot trees, walnut trees
Broccoli	carrots, garlic
Buckwheat	wheat
Cabbages	carrots, garlic
Caraway	dill, fennel
Carrots	apple trees, broccoli, cabbages, cauliflower, dill, fennel, potatoes
Cauliflower	carrots
Citrus trees	melons
Coriander	fennel
Cucumbers	sage
Dill	beans, caraway, fennel
Fennel	beans, caraway, carrots, coriander, dill, kohlrabi, tomatoes
Garlic	beans, broccoli, cabbages, peas, strawberries
Gladioli	strawberries
Grape vines	Swiss chard
Green peppers	kohlrabi
Kohlrabi	fennel, green peppers, strawberries, tomatoes
Melons	citrus trees, potatoes, radishes, sweet potatoes
Mint	strawberries
Mustard	acid-loving plants
Oats	apricot trees
Onions	beans, peas
Peas	garlic, onions
Potatoes	apple trees, apricot trees, carrots, melons, pumpkins, raspberries, sunflowers, tomatoes, walnut trees

Pumpkins	potatoes
Radishes	melons
Raspberries	potatoes, youngberries
Rosemary	strawberries
Rue	basil
Sage	cucumbers, Swiss chard
Sesame	sorghum
Sorghum	sesame
Strawberries	garlic, gladioli, kohlrabi, mint, rosemary, thyme
Sunflowers	beans, potatoes
Sweet peppers	apple trees, melons
Swiss chard	grape vines, sage
Thyme	strawberries
Tomatoes	apple trees, apricots, fennel, kohlrabi, potatoes, walnut trees
Walnut trees	brinjals, potatoes, tomatoes
Wheat	apricot trees, buckwheat
Youngberries	raspberries

Soil improvers

These plants add nutrients and help to improve the structure of the soil, or are excellent additions to the compost heap. Refer to the individual entries and the sections on pages 117 and 123 for more on how to use them.

Amaranth, asthma weed, barley, beans, blackberries, borage, broad beans, buckwheat, chamomile, chickweed, clover, comfrey, dandelion, elder, fat hen, fenugreek, goldenrod, lucerne, lupin, moringa, mustard, oak, oats, peas, phacelia, pigeon pea, purslane, queen Anne's lace, rye, salad burnet, silver birch, sow thistle, soya bean, stinging nettle, sunflower, Swiss chard, tomato, winter wheat, yarrow

Insect-repelling plants

These strongly scented plants chase insects and pests in the garden, or can be used in insect sprays and splashes. Refer to the individual entries and the section on page 120 for more on how to use them.

African marigold, basil, bay, carnation, catmint, chives, citrus species, coriander, costmary, elder, feverfew, garlic, khakibos, lavender, lemon verbena, marjoram, mint, mugwort, myrtle, neem, onions, oregano, pennyroyal, peppers, petunia, pyrethrum, rosemary, rue, Russian sage, sage, santolina, scented geraniums, sesame, soapwort, southernwood, tansy, tea tree, thyme, turnip, vetiver grass, walnut, wildeals, wormwood, yarrow

Trap crops

These often pretty plants act as a trap crop for insects, luring them away from other plants.

Chives, garlic chives, giant spring onion, morning glory, mustard, nasturtiums, pigeon pea, queen Anne's lace, sunflowers, violets.

Index